Adventures of the Famine Diver,

William Campbell

Roy Stokes

First Published in 2021 by The Manuscript Publisher
ISBN: 978-1-911442-30-1
A CIP Catalogue record for this book is available from the National
Library

Typesetting, page design and layout, cover design by
DocumentsandManuscripts.com

Published, printed and bound in Ireland

Adventures of the Famine Diver, William Campbell

Copyright © Roy Stokes, 2021

Acknowledgements

Despite having a large extended family, piecing together the life of William Campbell has taken several years. And notwithstanding all the research that has been carried out, the story would not have come this far without the help of a number of people and official bodies.

Particular words of appreciation are reserved for Trevor Dowling, who is the great-great-grandson of William James Campbell. He and I have been in contact by mail for several years, answering questions, sorting out many different aspects of the Campbell family after they landed on the shores of South Australia in 1864. I would also like to thank his wife Marion, who must also have had a serious input into the story as it unfolded. To my regret, I have not yet met either.

Notwithstanding the assistance from a number of archives, my appreciation is also extended to other relatives and members of the Campbell Clan: John Campbell, Bevan Campbell RIP with Len Fosdike. The Council members of Streaky Bay, the staff at Streaky Bay National Trust Museum and the Australian State Library were also very helpful. I wish the town of Streaky Bay long prosperity and hope the Campbells will always occupy a special place in its memory.

This book is dedicated to all of my own family, who have supported me for so long in my endeavours, involving lots of precious time spent at computers or travelling hither and dither, chasing down people and leads. I wish the best for my not so young children, Gavin, Graham and Jennifer, and their children and, I hope they get the same enjoyment telling and listening to stories of life as I have.

Foreword

This is the story of a man who lived two lives. From his birth, in 1813, he spent the first fifty years of his life in Scotland and Ireland. To this day, none of his descendants have ever understood why he travelled to and spent the second half of his life on the other side of the world – down under. However, the second half of the 19th century was also a period when millions were on the move, criss-crossing the globe in emigrant ships in search of fortune, which for many simply meant a job and a life.

William Campbell would remain an obscure contractor until the press began to flatteringly describe him as an 'Accomplished Diver' or 'The Talented Diver' and even as 'The Celebrated Diver'. A salute to his abilities and profession, they were glowing compliments afforded to few divers of the period but, Campbell was more than just a diver.

Crossing paths with historical and well-known public figures of the time and working firsthand with technological innovations of the Victorian period, William Campbell experienced more than a fair share of danger and adventure. Travelling throughout Ireland during one of the darkest periods of its history (the Great Famine) and eventually becoming the Superintendent of Works at one of the biggest harbours in Europe, Kingstown Harbour, is Mr Campbell's story – the first half of it at least.

The second half of Mr Campbell's life began after the whole family, quite suddenly, upped stakes in Ireland and travelled, by various adventures, to the other side of the world. Although they were amongst the founding fathers, little personal history of this Campbell Clan and Streaky Bay, Adelaide, South Australia survive. Nevertheless, Campbell's latter life is now well known, having been documented by his family, friends and by the communities in which he and his family lived.

Contents

Photos & Illustrations

Prologue

Despite poor records, it is believed that William Campbell was born to James and Margaret Campbell (née Thompson) in 1813, on their farm in Ayr, Scotland. Not poor, the family was by no means wealthy either. William grew to take his place in the social order just above the working class. Despite his abilities and, for one reason or another, he never migrated to an upper or more prosperous class. By the nature of his employment, civil engineering and diving, he and his family remained awkwardly and sometimes uncomfortably straddled between the two.

We would not attempt to describe William Campbell today as just an ordinary skilled worker, as his particular skills as an artisan and a diver, at the cutting edge of rapidly advancing industrial technologies in the 19th century, would eventually set him apart. His profession meant that he was almost constantly employed throughout Britain and Ireland – at a time when it is estimated that millions were dying as a result of the Famine.

The first half of the 19th century was also a period during which significant milestones in historical and social development were established. Millions were on the move, criss-crossing the globe in emigrant ships in search of fortune, which for many simply meant a job and a life.

William Campbell would remain an obscure contractor until the press began to flatteringly describe him as an 'Accomplished Diver' or 'The Talented Diver' and even as 'The Celebrated Diver'. A salute to his abilities and profession, they were glowing compliments afforded to few divers of the period but Campbell was more than just a diver.

William Campbell's celebrated career was referred to earlier in the story, "Dreadful Shipwreck at Howth", which was included in the book, *Between the Tides*. This carried a description of his work as a salvage diver on the wreck of the paddle steamer, *Queen Victoria*, in 1854, which was lost at the entrance to Dublin Bay and rediscovered in 1985. I signed off this story with the remark, "sin scéal eile" (*that's another story*). It was only a hunch then but, I had strongly suspected, at the time, that there was a lot more to the man.

Not long after that book was published, a complete stranger, Trevor Dowling who lives in Australia, made contact with me in 2017. He explained that, while researching his ancestry during a Google search, he was confronted with excerpts of a man's life portrayed in the book mentioned that sounded familiar. Although having a familiar ring, these events were totally unknown to him and the wider family. My suggestion, that there was more to Mr Campbell's story, prompted him to wonder, if 'Mr Stokes knew more...'?

After a brief exchange of e-mails, it was confirmed that the man described was Trevor's great-great-grandfather, William Campbell. Not to give too much of the story away, Trevor explained that very little was known about William or, you might say, about his previous life other than that he had worked as a harbour master in Dublin. One could say that this job description was almost correct but technically misleading.

Trevor also admitted that the surviving members of their clan never understood why William emigrated from such a lively, fashionable and sometimes described as progressive metropolis such as Dublin, as it was believed at first. When it was discovered that it was actually from Kingstown that he departed, a very fashionable and proudly autonomous suburb of south of Dublin, comprehension and confusion grew. They wondered, how on earth could he have left such a fine place and settled his family in an out-of-the-way, god-forsaken, arid region on the other side of the world? Equally, they were never aware just how unusual William Campbell's sudden departure from Ireland had been.

Crossing paths with historical and well-known public figures of the time and, working firsthand with technological innovations of the Victorian period, William Campbell experienced more than a fair share of danger and adventure. Travelling throughout Ireland during one of the darkest periods of its history, the Great Famine, and eventually becoming the Superintendent of Works at one of the biggest harbours in Europe, Kingstown Harbour, is Mr Campbell's story – the first half of it at least – almost nothing of which has passed to the memory of his wider family and their descendants before now. The second half of Mr Campbell's life began after the whole family, quite suddenly, upped stakes in Ireland and travelled, by various adventures, to the other side of the world.

Language frowned upon before the eloquence of the United States' Secretary of State, Mr Donald Rumsfeld (RIP) popularised it, we have to admit that many details of Campbell's formative years, education, and very early working life are unknown to us. Notwithstanding such disappointment, a rich source of material about William Campbell was discovered in the archives of the Office of Public Works in Scotland and Ireland, which paints a picture of William Campbell's earlier life that was totally unknown to his descendants and, has laid much of the foundation for this book.

Campbell's latter life is now well known, having been documented by his family, friends and by the communities in which he and his family have lived. The story of he and his family's lives has thus remained in two halves: the latter family record and social commentaries until the present day and his former, an unknown life that has remained disconnected from the latter, until now.

Despite unearthing a hoard of newspaper and archival gems about William Campbell, some significant unknowns remain.

William Campbell lived through two notable careers, two marriages, had a very large extended family, many of them still alive at the time of writing but despite this, no intimate details of his parents or siblings could be found. His own birth details were only unearthed to a minimum extent and other than some additional, significant, personal details of his youth and early manhood, further details remain elusive.

After *Between the Tides* was published, it was discovered that despite the common description of Campbell as a 'diver', William was also a man of many talents. Described as a marine diver and also as a ship's carpenter, these skills complimented his engineering talents as a professional civil works contractor and would broaden in later life. The term carpenter, as it was applied in Campbell's case, was confusing and relates to his work and trade description as a diver. In the latter part of his life, he would be described differently: as a well-respected artisan, architect and builder.

He not only became a well-respected and formidable wreck and civil works diver but, he was also an engineering contractor of considerable abilities, employed on a number of government contracts. These included the latter stages of the enormous construction project completed in the first half of the 19th century, in south County Dublin – the Great or Royal Harbour at Kingstown in Ireland. Campbell was employed on and part supervised one of the final projects within the harbour itself, the Carlisle Pier, a pier developed primarily for mail steamers and packet boats. It remains a preserved construction of some historical interest. It is unclear how the pier was named after Lord Carlisle but was, at first, affectionately known as the Gibbons' Pier, after the engineer who designed and built it.[1]

---

1 Except for the occasional benevolence bestowed on some of Kingstown's citizens, there is scant evidence that Lord Carlisle took any particular interest in the development of the new pier. Despite a trawl of OPW archival material, *Series 1 & 8*, the archives of the *Kingstown Town Commissioner Minutes*, *Chief Secretary's Office Registered Papers* and extensive search of newspaper and literary databases, no record could be found of a proposal to name the pier after Lord Carlisle. So it may have been that the "New Pier" (as it was also known as)

It has been nigh on impossible to piece together all aspects of William Campbell's earlier life. Despite this and with the generous cooperation of his great-great grandson, Trevor Dowling, living in Southern Australia, as well as relying heavily on press articles, testimonials, the archival records of the Office of Public Works (Ireland) at the National Archives in Dublin, a fascinating story of a man's life and his times has emerged.

Bearing the name Campbell during the middle of the 19th century in Ireland, particularly in Dublin, didn't help matters of research – the place seems to have been almost overrun with Campbells at the time. If he had remained in Scotland, I guess this book may never have been written. However, as luck (and it was luck) would have it, William's professional career first came to our attention when he was reported to be working in a diving bell, on the west coast of Scotland, in 1838.

Although they were amongst the founding fathers, little early, personal history of this Campbell Clan and Streaky Bay, Adelaide, South Australia survives. No longer fitting the description of a 'one horse town' (Trevor would rush to correct) it has been added to the collection of tourist slogans – a 'must visit' region of Australia. Family lore and verbal history nevertheless remains strong there and is supported by a broad history of the people and the area, contained in the book, *The Streaky Bay*. This publication is a compilation of contributions and recollections by a number of its early inhabitants and, to their great credit, its committee had it published in 1988.

Campbell's elevation to 'Celebrated' status in 1854 and why such compliments continued can also be revealed with the help of the vast records of the digitised press archives that are available online today. These reports of his life are also in two halves: two very different lives in two very different parts of the world.

Trevor Dowling's correspondence triggered a chain of discoveries and after several years of research, correspondence and the generous cooperation of his descendants, William Campbell's life and times (for its first half anyway) can be revealed.

This is that other story – *Scéal Eile*.

---

could have been called "Carlisle" after 'His Lordship' purely by default – being the result of patriotic favour by some officials.

Chapter 1

William Campbell's Early Career, 1813-1847

William Campbell was born in Ayr, Scotland on 13 October 1813. His descendants believe that his father's name was James and that of his mother was Margaret (Thompson). Another branch of research suggests that William could also have been born to the couple in February of the same year, at New Monkland in Airdrie. From later documents, we learn that William's father, James was described as a farmer (He was also described in William's birth document as a "weaver".) and that William studied as an engineer at an unknown school. Genealogists also suggest that William had a brother, James born in 1808 and a sister, Margaret born in 1815, both at the adjoining parish of Old Monkland, Coatbridge.

With some certainty, surviving clan members believe that William married Mary Simpson, on 15 October 1837, at the parish of Old Monkland, Lanarkshire. According to surviving Campbells, a son, James John Campbell was born to William and Mary on 24 July 1838. Despite James and his father living until ripe old ages amongst their kin, no place or details of the birth have been traced. William's first wife, Mary, may have died during or not long after this childbirth, as William was later described as a widower. Rather unusually in this case, no further details of William's first marriage to Mary, or details of her past, have been passed down or discovered.

Although details for the following piece of research are not a complete match, with the forgoing marriage details, I nevertheless believe that young James may have been baptised as follows.

Once included in the small ancient parish of Saint Mary's, situated on the northern bank of the River Liffey, the remains of the ancient parish and Abbey of Saint Marys is divided by Capel Street from its later Anglican Church of the same in Jervis Street. Once known as the "Scot's Parish", it is now demolished. Part of the nearby hospital that became known as Jervis Street hospital was once called Simpson's Hospital, after the merchant, George Simpson, who lived in that street. Simpson's Hospital has survived and is operating at Ballinteer, Dundrum, in the southern suburbs of Dublin.

Evolving from around Essex Bridge (Capel Street Bridge) and the old Custom House opposite on the southern bank of the river, this area spread outwards and became the heart of Dublin's commercial centre.

St Mary's Church recorded that, on 26 June 1837, James John Campbell was baptised to mother and father, William and Mary Campbell. The father's profession was listed as a "carpenter".[1]

The couple are recorded in residence almost beside the church mentioned, at 12 Abbey Street. The suggestion is that James was born out of wedlock, in Dublin, but that the couple might have had their marriage ceremony performed later, in Old Monkland and eventually returned to Ireland, after working for a time on the harbour construction, which was ongoing at Portpatrick. After all, Portpatrick was seen as 'Ireland's Gretna Green' – a place where you could be married for £10 with less formal requirements. The practice is reported to have ended in 1826 but 'light touch' unions continued across parts of Scotland for many years.

Not so obvious but compounding any validity of this theory is that this Saint Mary's was Church of Ireland.

Later, when young James was married, his first child was christened Hanna Mary Simpson Campbell, clearly in memory of his mother. A Mary Simpson was born to Hannah and William Simpson in Bride Street, Dublin in 1821 and was baptised at Saint Mary's but this was the nearby, Roman Catholic Saint Marys, probably at 'Liffey Street mass house' and it too was also around another corner from 12 Abbey Street. This Saint Mary's would later be established as the Pro-Cathedral in Marlborough Street, Dublin, which was only being constructed at the time.

If the conjecture is correct, it suggests that the couple may have had to elope to Scotland in order to be married across the Faiths or/and that Mary became Church of Ireland.

The names and profession are an unusually good fit but young James' date of birth does not correspond. There are also other factors that indicate a strong association between the couple and this area of Dublin, which will emerge as the story unfolds.

Portpatrick

The earliest mention of William Campbell, in any professional capacity, occurs when he is reported, in the Scottish press, working as an assistant bell diver at the harbour works in Portpatrick, in 1838. A picture postcard

---

1 William Campbell's profession was initially described as "bell diver" and later as a "marine diver". The term bell diver, although in popular usage at the time, for payment purposes the terms "bell diver mason", a "bell diver labourer", a "bell diver carpenter", etc were in use to describe a diver's trade. Just like today, a working diver has to have skills other than just being able to hop into a diving bell and descend beneath the water. We believe that a later description of William as a "diver and a carpenter" is also accurate.

harbour now, Portpatrick is situated on the south-west coast of Scotland, just a little south of the ferry port at Stranraer. Campbell's name was only spotted after a fatal accident occurred in Portpatrick in 1838 and charges were brought to court in 1839. The incident involved the Public Works diving bell he was working in at the time and he had witnessed the event.

William was aged twenty-five at the time. He had completed his studies and may have been only 'serving his time' or, understudy to a senior harbour engineer at the time. Or, he may have already begun a career as a transient contract diver. It is perhaps fortunate then for those who have been attempting to pick the threads of Campbell's life, that he was almost killed at Portpatrick on 27 July 1838.

Construction of the older pier at Portpatrick had been consulted and construction directed by the well-known engineer, Sir John Rennie. The work began in 1821 and the Campbells (William only an eight-year-old boy at the time) would possibly have visited the harbour, like many others, as work on the new piers progressed. The development represented the future and progress, and a path was worn to the area by writers and budding engineers, in order to view civil construction employing a diving bell. The diving bell was described in various reports, as a "square cast metal frame about 8 feet high and 22 feet in circumference and weighing upwards of 4 tons."[2]

It had 12 small windows of very thick glass and let in sufficient light to make the lighting of candles unnecessary a lot of the time. It was attached to a double leather hose connected to an air pump on the surface.

The later designs of improvements and extension to the piers were completed by the renowned engineer, John Smeaton. The Resident Engineer during Campbell's work on the pier was John Linn. The work had been instigated by the Board of Public Works in England, and construction of the south pier was in progress during 1838.

William Campbell was assistant diver to chief diver, James McClymont, who was employed on the project and both men were involved in the fatal accident that took place when the diving bell, with supporting crane and trolley, toppled off its travelling gantry on the top of the pier. The diving operations differed in this latter phase of the work from the earlier diving bell, which had been lowered from a floating barge, to the diving bell being lowered from a gantry that was erected and extended over the walls as they progressed into the sea.

Although the divers normally entered the bell from a boat, when it was raised and suspended in mid-air, the operation of the mobile crane was

---

2   See diagram on front page of *Mechanics' Magazine* (1825) on page 43

from above, on the pier, which is where the crane was situated at the time of the accident. Also assisting were a number of topside labourers and winch men, and John Maltman, who was also working in the bell with the divers.

The three men were rowed to the mouth of the bell and were getting inside when the accident occurred. Due to a miscalculation, inattention or misunderstanding as to the proper position that the counterweight on the apparatus used for raising and lowering the diving bell should have been, it and the whole gantry tipped over and fell twenty-five feet onto the tender and into the sea. The boat was broken into bits and two men were killed, two had broken legs, and four suffered concussion. The bell plunged to the seabed and the principal diver, McClymont, Campbell and Maltman were trapped inside. Due to some quick-thinking topside, when it was noticed that the hose from the air pump to the bell had been severed, a workman quickly sealed the open hose and reconnected it to the air pump. After some frantic signalling with the men inside the bell, a derrick was contrived and the bell was lifted. The three men inside escaped, apparently uninjured.

Negligence was suspected, and a prosecution of culpable manslaughter – 'a crime of a heinous nature' – proceeded against the chief diving director, Robert Young. The charge was 'not proved', and after being admonished by the judge, Young was finally acquitted in October 1839.

The above is more than what was disseminated by the press but archival records contain further uncomplimentary details of the incident.

After all of the men, divers, winchmen, directors and labourers had turned up for work at first light, work continued as before. By 10 o'clock, the men cried out for their 'breakfast' and proceeded to Rankine's pub on the quay. The chief diver's wife, Mrs McClymont came down to the quay in search of her husband, who hadn't shown up for his breakfast and joined the gang in the pub. Adding to the two bottles already delivered to the work site, a few more whiskeys were consumed by the chief diver, McClymont and the crew before returning to the pier. Obviously worst for wear, the men shifted the bell to a new position without adjusting the counterweight and, when it took the strain of the diving bell, the whole lot fell into the drink.

Charges were levelled, and the case proceeded through the normal legal channels. Prosecuted by the Lord Justice General, a plethora of witnesses present on the day were noticed to appear in court. Scattered from Scotland and Ireland to New York, little effort was spared contacting witnesses and their depositions recorded. The only exceptions seemed to have been the harbour cat and William Campbell, who doesn't appear to have partaken of 'breakfast' on the morning in question.

Campbell's work involved the positioning of huge stone blocks on the footings at the base of the construction of the pier wall. The footings had been levelled and prepared over existing rock in places, by lowering a diving bell, boring the rock and then placing explosives. The means of detonating explosives underwater had been a fairly basic and tricky operation when William Campbell first began his trade. The earlier method consisted of making one or more holes, large enough for what we would now describe as a pipe bomb, which was sandbagged and detonated by a fuse that extended from the surface. When required and practical, a sealed container, canister or even a 'tight' barrel was filled with blasting powder, stuffed with a primer and connected by a water-sealed joint to a lead pipe that reached to the surface. The lead pipe contained the fuse powder, which was lit on the surface with a hot coal or iron. If the flame successfully travelled through the narrow pipe and reached dry powder in the container, it exploded the charge.

The method was improved during the latter stages of Campbell's work on the pier, when the charges were detonated with a battery that was connected to electrical wires from the surface to the charge below. A far safer and more efficient operation, it was a skill William became very proficient at.

Simultaneously, Colonel Pasley had been working on the wreck of *HMS Royal George* and performing similar operations with sappers on the wreck in the south of England. After a series of experimental detonations by electrical means, he finally advanced and perfected a method of detonating explosives underwater with an electrical charge in the 1840s.

The innovation of underwater detonation remotely by electricity was highly sophisticated for the time. The charge was connected by insulated wires to a remote wet battery and was detonated when an electrical circuit was completed. This was a revolutionary step and was the method used to finally disperse the stubborn remains of the *George*, that had sunk at Spithead in 1782.

Around the same time, the familiar canvas and rubber diving suit and helmet, supplied by an air pump from the surface, had also reached a much higher degree of sophistication. Despite being unable to discover whom he had trained under, Campbell became proficient in both disciplines during the next few years.

Already damaged from an earlier storm, another severe storm at Portpatrick, in 1839, damaged the pier even further and construction was suspended. It is unclear if Campbell was laid off as result or if he moved on to another construction project. A number of projects at Port William, Stranraer and Donaghadee were in progress around that time.

A phenomenal growth in civil works was undertaken in the British Isles during the following decades. Huge sums of money were voted through the British parliament in order to facilitate the development of steamships, harbours, railways, roads, civic buildings, reservoirs and so on, in order to pave the way for commerce and the march of civilisation. The earlier revolution of water moving wheels and powering machines was then heated and pressurised. Converted to steam, it drove new engines for transport and industry. The result of that invention led to the 'industrial revolution' and was responsible for the rapid advance of civilisation – and also established multiple new layers of civil bureaucracy.

In some respects, it is mere coincidence that the explosion of public and private civil works began at the very time that the plague of famine spread across Ireland. It was recognised however, by a number of public bodies and well-meaning societies, that relief work should and could be provided amongst the communities that were suffering most and being laid waste by famine or starvation. Whether or not this was purely from the effects of rotten crops of potatoes or, starvation by conspiracy is a distinction many historians have continued to grapple with.

There is no end to the criticism that has been levelled at the subsequent distribution of these funds and the employment opportunities that were created by Public Works during this dark period. And although finance was disbursed with tight fists and sometimes with preference that seemed unwarranted, much good was accomplished.

The Missing Years: 1839-1846

William Campbell does not appear in newsprint or in any official documents until 1846. Notwithstanding the lack of record, it would be safe to assume that William could not have progressed to the stage his career had reached in the late 1840s, unless he had continued as a professional contract diver, in or out of Public Works, to some degree.

When we rediscover Campbell, it is clear that he is familiar with the latest underwater engineering developments, which were advancing at a pace. He had also become a skilled 'marine diver' – an important distinction from a 'bell diver', his new employers were keen to emphasise. This meant that he had moved from, not only working in, with, and out of a diving bell but, had become proficient with the new suit, helmet and air-pumping apparatus, which could deliver limitless air from the surface to a mobile diver underwater.

He appears to have been working as a lone contractor at first and was often contracted with an allowance for an assistant – a position occupied at times by his son, James.

While contracting for Public Works, there is no indication that he operated his own service vessel. It was quite often the case that a tender for the main contract on harbour or pier construction included the transportation of all the necessary diving equipment to the site and a service vessel by the Commissioners for Public Works. And in later years, it also included the provision of the diving gear itself. In the case of pier maintenance, Public Works again arranged for the transportation of the same equipment. It is nevertheless suggested that Campbell may have, at one time, acquired a sailing vessel of his own and that this could have been the sloop, *Pride* or *Prude*, mentioned further on.

Being a contract diver during the early Victorian period did not mean that one just turned up for work, got into a bell or put on a diving suit and helmet and just descended into the water. A successful contract diver had to be skilled in other disciplines, such as laying and cutting stone, competent in the use of underwater cement (Roman concrete), ironwork, pipe work, carpentry and shipwright skills. A successful contractor had to have a complete understanding of hydrostatics, all of his equipment and its maintenance. Limited as it was, he also had to have an understanding of the dangers associated with prolonged periods of work underwater.

The work was tough, physically demanding and to an ever-greater extent, meant travelling and working in the arduous conditions that prevailed in remote places of Ireland during the middle of the 19th century.

Campbell's proven ability with blasting powder and its detonation underwater with a remote battery was a bonus and earned him additional contracts for dispersal and clearance work. Taken all his skills together, he amounted to a 'one-stop-shop' diving contactor.

The science of detonating explosives with a charge from a battery was new, thanks to the Irish priest, Dr Callan, who had been beavering away in the science of electricity at Maynooth Seminary, County Kildare, ensuring that with God's help, the process might progress at an even greater speed. Campbell's abilities with explosives also enabled him to split and clear rocks and obstructions from the seabed, and to disperse sunken wrecks.

Being able to place an explosive charge beneath an enemy ship, and detonate it remotely, would very soon prove to be an important weapon. The American Civil War was just twenty years away and would see the use of mines (called torpedoes) that would explode under enemy vessels. Within forty years, a boat would be able to travel underwater and sink a ship with an underwater bomb. Such a vessel quickly advanced in design and in just a further thirty years, self-propelled, high-explosive torpedoes could be launched underwater from highly advanced submarines. Such innovation in weaponry eventually changed the course of civilisation and continues to do so.

Apart from becoming proficient at the day-to-day skills of a diving contractor, one had to be able to gauge costs, price work accurately and to show a profit. This was probably where Campbell was weakest and eventually found himself the subject of a writ for bankruptcy – a not uncommon predicament at the time. It was noticed in the papers of 29 July 1846 that William Campbell was summonsed to court as an insolvent debtor. Seemingly only marking a temporary halt to his contracting career, he began to work as a ship's carpenter for the Dublin-based shipbuilder, Teall.

Bankruptcy proceedings against William Campbell were eventually dismissed but the encounter with the financial authorities left its mark. For some time afterwards, Campbell was careful not to show any signs of well-offishness, for fear his debtors might take up the chase once more. The reasons for dismissal of the bankruptcy charges against William, in 1846, were not made clear and it wasn't until research uncovered correspondence relating to his contracting operations at the new pier at Bunowen, County Galway in 1849, that a possible explanation was discovered.

As it appears that William Campbell's first wife may have been deceased by this time, and that he was rearing his son James alone, this may have contributed to the mismanagement or his lack of sufficient finance.

After William's threatened insolvency, mentioned several times in the newspapers, the trade directories listed him as a ship's carpenter and a diver, living at Sir John Rogerson Quay, Dublin and in the employ of shipbuilder, Mr Henry Teall. Mr Teall was contracted to raise and repair a number of vessels at the time, and Campbell's skills were obviously a distinct advantage.

Mr Teall's shipyard, the Brunswick Shipbuilding Yard, had been situated on the south-east side of the Grand Canal Basin, on the banks of Dublin's River Liffey, in the place of its previous occupier, Mr Robert Morton, also a shipbuilder who constructed a large bell boat, *The Bell*, for diving operations during the construction of the harbour at Howth. The yard later became the site of Boland flour merchants' huge grains silos and was adjacent to that well-known landmark, the lifting bridge that joined Great Brunswick Street to Ringsend Road.

Both shipbuilders were moderately successful – Teall, from a large family of timber merchants and shipbuilders in England, even more so. Carrying pistols with him from time to time, he was also a man with a flair for the dramatic and well warranted on occasions. It was a period during the development of Dublin's dockland, when those entering the shipwright trade were carefully vetted by the incumbent workers – heavily unionised, might be a modern description. Although Teall found himself in repeated conflicts with local shipwrights, he nevertheless and with his less restrictive hiring practices (not quite 'cheap labour') became a very successful shipbuilder.[3]

In a rather fashionable area of Dublin, events in the life of a very different class of family were also unfolding. Haddington Road ('D4', as it is known today) was where the Saunders family resided and on 28 April 1842, Lucy Elizabeth was born to her father, John Robert and mother, Sarah (née Lister) Saunders, their second daughter.

A name suggesting some importance, John Saunders was a retired Captain of the Royal Artillery, seemingly suffering ill health from the effects of his service abroad. The couple's first child, Ann or Anna, was born in 1840. A son, John Richard, was later born to the couple on 12 December 1843 and a second son, Henry, was born on 8 August 1845. Prior to their home at Haddington Road, the family lived at Upper Baggot Street, both addresses being quite close to the large army barracks at Beggars Bush.

Turning the family's lives upside down, Captain Saunders was declared deranged and incapable of managing his affairs in 1846 and died in 1855. It appears that before his death, he was committed. A financial dispute over legacy issues ensued and the family became somewhat dispersed. Some of the children were taken into care and others were filtered out through life in ways one might expect.

With fate holding a hand in the game of their lives, Lucy and her brother, John Richard would eventually cross paths with those of the Campbell family and would alter the course of both families' lives, with a most unexpected outcome.

---

3   It is unlikely that Campbell was employed by Teall as a ship's carpenter in the ordinary understanding of that trade – a shipwright. Given his other capabilities and the events that were to follow, it is more likely that he was involved in the development of Teall's shipyard slips, either at Grand Canal Basin or his subsequent yard on the River Dodder, at the northern end of Thorncastle Street, Ringsend. As well as raising shipwrecks for him.

Chapter 2

Famine Harbours and Piers, 1848-1850

Given the close trading relationship between Ireland and England – effectively the same political entity – and the nature of the harbour work that was developing in Ireland at the time, Campbell may have travelled from Portpatrick during the early 1840s, to one of its opposite numbers on the other side of the North Channel: Larne or Belfast or even Donaghadee. Certainly, he and his son James were recorded as working together there, ten years later. Their boss, at the time, was Barry Gibbons, Resident Engineer with the Board of Public Works, based at Kingstown Harbour, just a few miles south of Dublin.[1]

All the major centres of railway and sea travel that exist today were being developed and improved by Public Works, and might explain why, when William next came to notice, it was as a serious contractor vying for these works. Steering shy of the press, he was hired by the Board of Public Works in 1848, to improve the rather puny harbour in Ballycotton, adjacent to the entrance of Cork Harbour on the south coast of Ireland.

At this time, vision of the commercial expansion of Ireland's fishing industry lacked any real adventure of foresight. Given the ravages suffered by the population at the time, this is understandable and no vision as to just how a national fleet of fishing vessels might eventually evolve was present. With some exceptions during the Victorian period, marine structures that were 'harbours' seemed to be of the one kind – those that were of commercial significance, catering for handling cargo and complemented by the railways. The meagre infrastructure that passed for harbours and piers around Ireland, at the time, could only barely be described as adequate for subsistence living. The future, however, did not lie in fishing.

There were other harbours for fishing boats but very few providing any refuge, relying on the cover provided by large natural bays instead. The piers and harbours constructed around Ireland at this time were, in the main, to facilitate inshore fishing, some island ferries, supplies delivered

---

1   After 1922, this department of civil government in Ireland, Board of Public Works, became better known as the Office of Public Works (OPW) and was continuously petitioned by citizens, up and down the country, for improvements to public and private structures and for employment.

by small coastal vessels and mainly consisted of a small single pier, usually in a weather-sheltered position, the important principal being to land catches but not for berthing boats. Very few had two pier heads that could provide shelter for boats from the elements. Often tucked away in winding creeks and hidden bays, many relied on the use of the local geography to fend off the effects of bad weather and big seas.

It is probably not a coincidence then that William Campbell turned up in Ireland at the time he did, which was the same time as large sums of money were being appropriated to build harbours and piers, in order to provide relief works and to improve Irish fisheries during the time of the Famine. The same reasoning may also have prevailed later, in reverse, prompting the Campbells to leave Ireland just at the time this period of investment was coming to an end.

Well before Campbell arrived on the scene, the condition and suitability of the existing pier structure at Ballycotton had been the subject of considerable and justifiable criticism, as were many others around Ireland at the time. While Campbell was contracted on the improvement works at Ballycotton, criticism of the miserly intervention continued. And even after the work was completed and Campbell had left Ballycotton, the design of the harbour continued to be heavily criticised – and it remains a poorly designed harbour.

Campbell's arrival on the Public Works scene in Ireland appears to have been quite sudden. From relative obscurity he was appointed as a diver and stone-laying contractor at Ballycotton. His entrance to the world of Public Works (Ireland) came as a bit of a surprise to some public officials, not least to the administrative staff at the Board of Public Works. Something had happened however – someone had intervened on Campbell's behalf.

Barry D. Gibbons was born in 1798 in Kinsale, Cork. He managed the building of a new pier in Kilrush by the Department of Public Works in 1828-1829. In his early professional career, he travelled as a contractor, supervising works on several harbours around Ireland before he collaborated with the famous engineer, Alexander Nimmo and became Resident Superintendent of Works ("Resident Engineer" as per M.B. Mullins, Vice President of the Institute of Civil Engineers, Ireland) at Dunmore Harbour in 1832.[2]

Gibbons continued his harbour engineering, and collaborations on different pier projects with Nimmo, while supervising the development of

---

2   The Kilrush pier was upgraded in 1841-1843, with the use of a diving bell and consulted by engineers, Rennie and Walker. The Superintendent of Works was Mr Vignoles and the contractor was Mr M. Favell of Harrogate. There was no mention of Campbell during this project.

the harbour at Dunmore. He progressed to the position of County Engineer for Wexford in 1834, where he was much admired for his work ethic and capability.

Work at Dunmore harbour – or Dunmore East, as it known to many today – is said to have commenced in 1817 and became, not so much a 'white elephant' but more, a long-life elephant, needing constant feeding. Preceded by the engineer, Mr. Simpson, Gibbons left in 1833/1834 to take up his appointment as County Engineer for Wexford. After much good work had been completed, the harbour project trundled on through criticism and damage by storms. Gibbons' replacement reported, in March 1838, that "works at this moment had been completely finished."

That was just before a destructive storm, during the following December, promptly demolished the breakwater.

The progress at Dunmore had also suffered, at one time, from a popular Irish pastime, backstabbing, which seemingly emanated from the new hotel established in the harbour, the Dunmore Private Hotel. Bar room gossip, a rather unrefined 'squinting window' type of criticism began to do the rounds. Having had some disagreement with workers on the site, the Resident Engineer was described as, "a most excellent engineer of a glass of grog."

With apparently no basis for the 'tittle-tattle' and even if rumours had some ring of truth, the man might have been forgiven for succumbing to the temptations of the New Hotel, that had "cellars with the finest wines of the first brands and liquors of delicious flavours."

Strangely, perched on the waterfront of a bountiful fishing village, this hotel's adverts did not mention sea food in particular, even though the proprietor had purchased a crab of "extraordinary dimensions". Caught by a Dunmore fisherman at the Hook Tower, on the opposite side of the estuary, in County Wexford, it weighed in at "upwards of fourteen pounds".

You would imagine that if they weighed it, they weighed it – what was the 'upwards' bit about? It reminds me of the time when I was on holiday with a group of divers from the Marlin Sub Aqua Club and capturing an enormous crayfish in an underwater cave at Liscannor, County Clare. The giant provided a lovely starter for 'upwards' of twenty-six people! They don't come like that anymore and not because divers were catching and eating some of them, I might add.

Getting back to Dunmore, the work trundled on for another few years before the purse strings were pulled and the final tidy up of the harbour works began. I suppose you could say that the curtain finally came down on the harbour works at Dunmore when the Board of Works intentions became clear. The properties they purchased, built, and altered for their supervising staff and service people, began to be sold off. A wave of local enquiries for 'small plots of land' and 'little dwellings leaning against walls' flooded in to officials and, I daresay, descendants of the lucky ones in this beautifully situated harbour are still in occupation.

Although there had been earlier enquiries to purchase the large diving bell that had remained at Dunmore, it wasn't until 1861 that the Board of Public Works sold off their largest bell. Measuring, roughly 6 feet by 4 feet by 6 feet, the dimensions indicate, of course, that it wasn't a 'bell' at all – it was an iron box that could be pumped continuously with air. The term had become a generic one, used to describe any kind of diving chamber. Thanks to clever patents by the Catholic Emancipationist and part-time improver of the diving bell, Honest Tom Steele, some even had an airlock chamber with a voice pipe.

In some respects, the prolonged construction of such a fine and expensive harbour meant that its original need and design had been outpaced by progress.

Having become County Surveyor for Wexford, my impression is, Gibbons was glad to be out of the harbour, if only because of the stones! There were more quarries about the place than one could shake a pick at: big stones, little stones, flat ones and square ones, hard ones and softer ones, rubble and shingle, dressed ones and ashlars, and so on. Those who could show ownership of previously worthless outcrops of rock were on a winner. Stones had to be inspected, they had to be sorted and they had to be weighed. The amounts, the bills and the problems with them just kept coming.

So much quarrying and stonework inevitably led to accidents. Apart from the minor injuries to limbs and ears, three deaths occurred on 23 May 1833, when the quarrymen, Brenahan, O'Hara, and Delany were killed by a blast in a nearby quarry. There wouldn't be half the space for the houses in Dunmore today, only for the harbour and the removal of so much of the cliffy surround that was dumped around it.

Originally a fishing pier and a place where mails and coal were dropped off, a staging point for packets and pilots, it had been surveyed for the Commissioners for Public Works by Alexander Nimmo from as early as 1818. Serious money was later allocated and work began in the early 1820s. Unfortunately, there were a lot of 'engineers' offering a lot of advice and continually wanting to alter specifications.

There were the water borne commercial interests of Waterford City, early steam and railway packet companies, the Post Office, the Board of Public

Works, Revenue, the Waterford Harbour Commissioners, parish priests and politicians. The local MP, Francis Leigh, a marvellous and prolific letter writer, was amongst all those with ideas and requirements and all blessed with the powers of superior observation and clairvoyance.

The steam and telegraph revolution was delayed coming into Dunmore and then, all of a sudden, steamers (with the exception of the tide, as is the case today) could just pass the harbour without any need to stop or pick up a pilot. With an increasing number of ship captains obtaining their own pilot's ticket for the harbour, the station had almost become obsolete even before it was finished. It nevertheless became a wonderful and prosperous harbour for fishing and, as a refuge. Waterford Port remains a commercially driven maritime entity and to the surprise of many, relatively large ships still pick up pilots at Dunmore and navigate up the precarious river channel, with towering containers of deck cargo.

A sound surveyor and administrator, Gibbons eventually came to the notice of higher office and was head-hunted, almost simultaneously, into two appointments in 1838. He replaced the outgoing Resident Engineer, Mr Thomas at "Kingstown Harbour" and at the "Dublin and Kingstown Railway Co".

He worked with another great engineer of his time, Brunel. Gibbons was, in effect, double jobbing, which seemed to an accepted practice at the time. Being a Catholic, it is understandable how Gibbons' appointments may have irked others in the public service.

With the large sums of money being ploughed into harbours, roads and railway development at the time, Gibbons supervised a huge amount of works and public spending around Ireland and was eventually appointed Principal Engineer with the Board of Public Works.

As well as his work on piers and harbours, Gibbons ventured into the design of bridges and with the Kingstown Railway, the novel atmospheric railway system from Kingstown to Dalkey. With Brunel, he helped to develop and push the railway system through the difficult terrain of County Wicklow.

A self-thought and made man, more technically qualified engineers were known to disagree with some of his opinions, much to their chagrin on more than one occasion. The design and development of the mail boat pier in Kingstown Harbour being a case in point and addressed further on.

It seems clear that at some stage, and for very sound reasons, Gibbons took Campbell under his wing and in as far as records show, his first contract for the Board of Public Works, was at the Ballycotton Harbour in 1848.[3]

---

3 Later events suggest that it may have been at Dunmore, or nearby Duncannon, where Gibbons first made the acquaintance or established a connection with

The terms of Campbell's contract at Ballycotton were a little unusual and were similarly awarded in a subsequent contract at Bunowen, County Galway in 1849, where we will discover reasons behind Campbell's preference in this regard.

At Ballycotton, William Campbell was paid wages for himself and an assistant, who may have been his very young son, James. Wages amounted to "five shillings per diem" or thirty shillings per week. They were also paid two pence per cubic foot for worked stone. All materials, tools, equipment and diving gear were supplied. Even after the pier at Ballycotton was completed, additional remedial works were necessary, as the design was criticised as being unsatisfactory. In a strong blow from the southeast, Ballycotton Harbour walls provided sparse refuge for sheltering vessels, even today.

Ballycotton was also where Campbell got his first taste of service procedures, when he was instructed that he should no longer address his correspondence – requests for stores, labour and progress of works etc – directly to Mr Gibbons.[4]

Mr Gibbons had hired Campbell personally. Being a well-respected top dog, the appointment, although an unusual procedural intervention, was not questioned and was the making of Mr Campbell, who would never look back – literally.[5]

Campbell's progress through the ranks, ways and procedures of the autocratic monolith that is Public Works are well documented in the day-to-day letter books that still survive. He secured a friend and mentor in Gibbons and the work just kept coming. Although Campbell seems to have been paid a daily rate by the Commissioners for most contracts at the time, it appeared at times that he was almost a permanent employee. Records

---

William Campbell. There is a very clear example of the esteem in which Mr Gibbons held William Campbell. In 1852, when Campbell was bidding for a wreck dispersal contract in the Waterford Harbour, the harbour commissioners wrote to Mr Gibbons for his opinion of the man. Gibbon's testimonial reads in part, "... Mr Campbell...is particularly intelligent...and your Board may rely implicitly on his statements and reports.... I Believe him to be thoroughly [Gibbons emphasis] trustworthy as well as accurate."

4   William Campbell may have carried out minor harbour works, in other areas of southern Ireland between 1840 and 1848 but no details have been discovered.

5   It is also true to say that, from the volumes of correspondence on file, there is a tangible sense of adherence to propriety by the Commissioners for Public Works in their day-to-day affairs and a real sense of insisting on value for money can be detected.

show however, that he was also contracting for quasi-governmental and local bodies, such as councils and other harbour authorities, recommended by Gibbons and possibly 'on loan'.

The Famine and 'This fellow Campbell', Bunowen, 1848

Between the years 1847 and 1851, William Campbell moved around Ireland from one harbour to another on various contract work for Public Works and eventually, back to the mother harbour of Kingstown. From the earliest mention of him in Board of Works files for Ireland, 1847, William moved from construction work at Ballycotton, County Cork to work on the pier at Kilkieran, County Galway and the construction of a new harbour at Bunowen, west Connemara. With little mention, he also worked on a small harbour at Errislannan, south of Clifden, indicating that he may very well have worked on a number of other projects that have no surviving records of his activities.

Barry Gibbons had estimated that the cost of constructing the harbour pier at Bunowen would amount to the familiar £6,000 figure, which conflicted with another internal estimate for £3,000, which may have been for materials only.[6] Gibbons' estimate was not a particularly large one and, as with other harbours at the time, it was financed by a grant of three quarters from the government, through Public Works and the balancing quarter to be raised from the Irish Wasteland Improvement Society, local donations from landowners and taxes. The actual cost was reported, much later, as having been £15,000. Fitting estimates with costs for public works was, not unlike today, aspirational.

After finance was secured, property rights negotiated and acquired, notices of the intention to proceed with construction of the pier at Bunowen were posted around local public and private buildings, such as churches, hotels and prominent positions in market squares. In the case of Bunowen, the main construction contract appears to have been awarded to the Galway-based 'builder and engineer', John Semple.[7]

Awarding public contracts in early Victorian times was a bit like it is today. The man at the shoot, a dinner or two at the golf club or regatta might obtain it, or others by virtue of owning the land on which the construction was taking place. In the case of the harbour under construction at nearby

---

6   The two-figure estimates, one half of the other, became a familiar scenario when applying for public monies from central funds for local enterprise of all kinds. The practice remained right up to the 20th century.

7   It remains unclear to the author whether Semple submitted a competitive and successful tender for all of the work at Bunowen or, just oversaw the project for the Public Works.

Kilkieran, the Irish Wasteland Improvement Society had procured the land and then received specification, grants and loans from the departments of Public Works, Fisheries, and relief committees. The committee then designated an actual works contractor and supervising engineer. In these circumstances, this was their prerogative. Quite commonly, the work proceeded with technical oversight by the Department of Public Works. In the case of Bunowen, the Commissioners of Public Works managed the whole affair.

The Waste Land Committee (Headquarters in London.) was established to acquire land that was laying waste from neglect and want of drainage. The purchase price was based on the value of the land, which was low and could be compulsory purchased. The intention was to repair the land, offer it back to the original owner at an improved price, work it or to parcel it out to a number of small farmers. The scheme was supported by the government through grants and loans but became highly contentious when some of the land, reconstituted at taxpayer's expense and voluntary donations, landed back in the lap of the wealthy, with very little to show for the tax gathered and for ratepayers. Nevertheless, the committee's motives have been judged altruistic and a measure of success was achieved. Their stated aims were, to provide work, alleviate famine and provide a future, through agriculture and fishing, as were the intentions of Public Works and their programme of harbour works.

Archival material shows that Campbell was working at Bunowen from March 1849. Records also show he was working on other projects in the area during 1848. His appearance just then is an interesting coincidence, with the completion of another harbour at Tarrea, in Kinvara Bay, south Galway. Was Campbell there, did he move on? Did he make any contribution to the wonderful stonework of the harbour? Campbell is not mentioned in any surviving correspondence from this project. Some blasting of bedrock did take place at Tarrea, after storms had damaged the new construction but the man is not named. Maybe, poor old William took his earlier brush with officials, regarding his own correspondence, to heart and kept shtum. If he did, it was not for long.

There were similar works ongoing at the harbour in Kilkieran but again, Campbell is not mentioned in the file for that harbour project. However, he is mentioned as being there in the file of correspondence for works at nearby Bunowen, and by Semple. The correspondence on file between Public Works and Bunowen is detailed and revealing. An understanding and a mind eye's view of life there can be had from its content and reveals something of both men, Semple and Campbell.

With the exception of some opportune work at low water, Campbell's harbour work normally proceeded as follows. The main contractor for the completion of the harbour would complete all of the work down to the footings. That which was below the water line was awarded to Campbell, usually on a stores and equipment arrangement with the Board, combined with an hourly rate and some pieces of other work. His work often began at the early stages of a pier or harbour contract.[8]

Construction normally began from the land out, providing an extending platform for the lifting equipment and a way to shift and manoeuvre the large stones into position. Excavating and maintaining a trench for footings at low water and below, for the point of a pier, was often problematic. This was a reason for constructing a pier on existing and visible rock when suitable, which Campbell levelled with blasting powder.[9]

At Bunowen, there was an allowance of £1,200 made for work by a diver and diving bell. In a construction tender for the pier submitted by J. O'Brien, there was an amount of £40 set aside for the carriage of one of the Boards' diving bells from Kingstown. There was no indication, at that stage, as to who was going to dive in the bell. The total estimate for O'Brien's completion of the work was £4,460.

There was no subsequent mention of a diving bell being used at Bunowen. This is probably indicative of how, along with the reduced difficulties in transporting a marine diver's gear, the more flexible abilities of hard-hat helmet diving had been replacing the necessity for the cumbersome diving bells.

The stone, Roman cement, (not considered as good as Rosendale cement, which was also in use for underwater work.) blasting powder, timber, tools and some of the diving equipment was provided and delivered to the site by the Department of Public Works or the main contractor.

Given the constant agitated state of political affairs in Ireland, it is understandable why the sale of blasting powder was tightly regulated. Despite restrictions, it is surprising to read how, at times, the stuff seems to have grown legs. William Campbell was known to have purchased his own powder on occasions.

---

8   There were limitations but low- or below-water pier construction work was not always completed by a diver and a bell.

9   A diagram of the partially constructed pier, gantry, travelling bogie used in the Portpatrick harbour project is a fair representation of the construction method universally applied in pier construction. The diagram was produced in evidence during the case against Robert Young, in 1839. The diagram with that of Morton's Bell Boat is also of some help understanding machinery and method.

The work was physically gruelling and everything about this type of civil works demanded good health and physical strength. Despite this, to look at a picture of Campbell, he doesn't appear the 'big strong man' one might expect such a diver to have been. Interestingly, low-volume, wiry men seem to have been prolific in the trade. A very likeable diving buddy, Philip Ogelsby RIP, not unlike the picture of William Campbell, immediately comes to mind, who hardly consumed any air from his bottle when my own would be almost empty. His low consumption of the stuff attracting the memorable comment from another 'well known diver' that, "he only breathes when he has to."

Stone had to be cut and worked, above and below the water, in all weathers, while operating heavy cumbersome gear. Constant attention to equipment was necessary; powder had to be kept in good condition, as did the Campbells' diving gear. The dangers in priming and detonating explosives were obvious and strict routine was constantly observed. Big wheels were turned by hand and huge stones were hoisted up and down, often above a diver's head. Labourers on site were being paid one shilling and two pence per day. Any attempt by an official to pay more wasn't missed and invited rebuke or dismissal.

Considering the period that was in it, getting all of the equipment and stores to these remote sites was a major feat of logistics. It was, nevertheless, all taken in their stride by men who must. How Campbell travelled around the country is not known. In the absence of any mention of sailing his own vessel at this time, with the exception of two brief incidents referred to further on, we might presume he was transported to Bunowen by sea. Given that gear may have had to be offloaded, he may have landed further into the bay at the old pier in Kilkieran, nearer to Galway by a few miles to the south-east of Bunowen. Although horse and cart was somewhat feasible for the entire distance from say, Galway, it was slow and arduous through remote regions.

Despite the period and the remoteness of these places, a number of small, inter coastal town steamer services existed in some areas around Ireland. The east coast of Ireland was in a class of its own, with a plethora of steamer services to choose from: coastal, cross channel or even international. Finding it difficult to just survive in the west of Ireland at the time, low demand and affordability meant that there was little added incentive to develop any kind of regular transatlantic steamship service, although establishing new stations were mooted a number of times. Emigration and commercial sailings did originate from the west of Ireland at the time, from such ports as Galway and Limerick. The proposal for a packet station at Blacksod, County Mayo also gained some traction at one time. With aspirations for a direct rail link to follow from Dublin, linking England, the idea was mainly emigrant and postal driven. Suggestions of shorter sailing times from an all-weather, all-ship berthage for packets and naval vessels, in a magnificent bay, were lost on the wind.

With the exception of Clare and the River Shannon system, there were no such services on the west coast of Ireland – there was just no demand. The exceptions were occasional intercity steamers, serving migrant labour and the growing emigrant trade to the larger port cities. Completing a journey between Cork, Limerick, Galway or Sligo and local coastal villages or towns would have been by sailboat or horse and cart. The railway would not come to Galway until the early 1850s.

Travelling by road (or what passed for roads then) from Ballycotton, say or from Dublin to the west of Ireland, carrying diving and construction gear, required serious endeavour and lots of time. Transporting a large iron diving bell over poor tracks, for long distances was just not on. Campbell must then have reached most of these outline and often remote places, with his suit and helmet, by sea and onward, if required, by horse and cart.

The west of Ireland is treasured today for its underdeveloped pristine natural beauty, which is mainly derived and maintained by its remoteness and lack of industrialisation. That wonderful promotional slogan, the Wild Atlantic Way (WAW), was exactly how it was when Campbell travelled through it in the 1840s – wild and damn difficult. Despite the WAW being one of the most successful public relations campaigns ever, its phenomenal success required relatively little investment. And thank God that this coastline has changed little; apart from the plethora of holiday homes and a few layers of tarmac, it's pretty much the same as it ever was although, given the runaway success of the WAW campaign and the fickle tourist trade, who knows for how long?

Mr John Semple, the main contractor at Bunowen, was described as being a 'building contractor and civil engineer', living at Dominick Street in Galway City. There were few, probably only two civil engineers by that name in Ireland at the time. It is important not to confuse our Galway man with another, more famous civil engineer of the same name. The latter Semple was responsible for a number of contentiously designed churches around Dublin, who, as it happened, was up to his eyes with bankruptcy litigation at the time. Our Semple and the newspaper notice flagging his return to Dominick Street, Galway in 1850, made the difference clear when he advertised that he was resuming his profession as 'architect and builder'.[10]

---

10   This branch of the Semples have had centuries-long connections with Galway, right up to the present day. A well-respected family that has made a considerable

After the notices of intent to build the harbour and pier at Bunowen were posted around the county, Campbell attended a site meeting with Gibbons and Semple in 1848. After construction got underway, everything went well to begin with but Campbell soon had to report delays – not of his own making, however.

Campbell wrote to head office, reporting that the large flat stones required for the pier's footings had not arrived and that he was being held up. Semple then received a letter query, couched in familiar public service jargon that always commenced with the familiar, sounding like an invitation but more like and order, 'Please explain'.

After the bust up between Ireland and Head Office in Westminster many years later, this would see interrogation by correspondence preceded with, 'A Chara'.

Sounding weak, Semple's reply explained that the stone had not arrived from Aran (Islands, off Galway) and that the suitable heavy timbers and trusses, also required by Campbell, could not be found in all of Galway. He did, however, offer the possibility that he may be able to obtain the timbers from the auction of two recent shipwrecks and, that he had already demanded delivery of the stone.

Anyone who has visited the Aran Islands will undoubtedly recall the stone! It is everywhere: forts, monuments, and the unexplained. More importantly, the stone is to hand almost everywhere and can be wedged and layered off in small or very large chunks, snapped to length, leaving the only difficulty to be that of transporting it. The stone mentioned in the case of construction at Kinvara and Bunowen, was sandstone.

In a piece by Rónadh Cox in *Old Moore's Almanac*, reported in 2015, described the scattered stones and their movement to places where they shouldn't be, to be 'a wonder', suggesting that tsunamis were responsible or, not so seriously, that "...little green men from Mars were doing this on the quiet..."

He need not have suggested such a far-away place as Mars, as the little fellahs have been reported a lot closer to home for centuries. Yet another remarkable feat of marketing.

For some of the wonders, explanations were a lot simpler. The stone had been quarried by local people, for the construction of harbours and buildings on the islands and, all along the west coast of Ireland, before and after Bunowen. Getting it down to the boats presented little difficulty –

---

contribution to the social history of Galway and its county, professionally and in sport.

nothing that a good horse couldn't drag over wet flat stone and logs. The secret was to drag it down and not up.

Semple knew his onions and had his ear to the ground. The large stones were being quarried on the Aran Islands and supplied to a number of harbours under construction. Out of his control, delivery was subject to the mood of the islanders, vagaries of the tempestuous Atlantic and the availability of a suitable transport vessel.

There was, indeed, a shortage of good lumber in the west of Ireland, mainly because of demand – there were few who could afford to buy it. Even now, you couldn't expect to come away from a builders' provider in the west of Ireland with all that was required for a building project, on the same day.

The answer to Semple's problem may have been solved by his earlier suggestion. The lumber might be had from the shipwrecks that had occurred during the recent storms.

During the previous December, the Belfast schooner, *Gem* was sailing from Limerick to Liverpool with oats and was wrecked on rocks at Guilín (Golam) Head, Lettermore. Captain Fabis and his son, along with a man by the name of Quinlan, were drowned. Michael Flaherty of Lettermullen with others in two boats, rowed out in stormy weather to the scene of the wreck and rescued two men who were stranded on the rocks. One was the ship's mate, Robert Shaddock and the other, seaman, John McCleod. Flaherty and his fellow islanders were applauded for the brave rescue and it wasn't the first time that Flaherty had risked his life in similar endeavours, on behalf of shipwrecked victims (contrasting with the law- breaking, scavenging reputation often hung on sea folk over a bit of after-storm beachcombing).

In fact, worse contrasts can be read, side by side, in the newspapers of the period and are striking. One can read of large parties of lords, ladies and gentlemen landing from their yacht at the likes of Clifden, for a spot of game fishing and hunting in the local estates, alongside reports of dozens of bodies, 'just skin and bone', being discovered weekly in the same remote areas.

Though there had been large baulks of timber washed up much further south in County Clare, Semple was a bit economic with details regarding the actual state of affairs, if he had the shipwrecked timbers of the *Gem* in mind. Not a large vessel, she had been carrying oats for the port of Liverpool, where they and all manner of staple crops were achieving good prices, at the expense of the starving inhabitants along the length of the western seaboard. What's more, its remains would have provided little useful timber.

And as for the lost oats, these may have been the same as those seized, for default on Poor Rates in Clare, just days earlier. Despite "the oldest man living in Connemara not remembering anything like the quantities of timber and staves floating off the coast", the *Gem* just went to flitters on the rocks and washed up in useless pieces all along the coast of Connemara.

Semple may also have been referring to the very large sailing ship, *Forest Monarch*, if the reports had been accurate. Seemingly a much better bet, this ship was reported to be wrecked on the Inniskeas, off the adjoining and equally remote area of west Mayo, on 20 November 1848. She was carrying a veritable gold mine of valuable timber, and along with some other cargo, rigging and the remainder of its hull, these were not auctioned until several months later.

However, initial reports were not accurate; the *Forest Monarch* incident had actually occurred at Arranmore, County Donegal. Even so, the "lemons and the female bust figure-head of a Grecian Lady with drapery fastened by a clasp on the right shoulder" that were washed up on the Galway coast, may have been from the *Forest Monarch*, creating the false hopes.

A poignant and not unconnected anecdote to the *Monarch*'s misfortune lies in her previous voyage. Captain John Richardson and thirty-four of her crew (one having died) survived the wrecking of their ship at Donegal. Luck had been with captain and crew, as with the local inhabitants and coastguards. Luck, however, had eluded earlier emigrant passengers, those that had set out with the ship and its crew from Liverpool, bound for New York the previous year. Of the 240 men, women and children on that voyage, 117 died at sea. The conditions responsible for such dreadful statistics are just too difficult to imagine. In this case, some statistical columns and entries were dropped from the passenger returns. One significant omission was, "Country of Origin". The reason given for this was that they were "All from Ireland" and many of them were from its west coast.

Yet another shipwreck that Mr Semple may have had in mind was the French schooner, *Bonne Marie* of Bordeaux. Wrecked nearby at Mace Head, all four crew were saved by the water guard. Again, locally manned boats put out in terrible conditions and snatched four lives from a watery grave. A relatively small craft, it soon went to pieces and sank.

It isn't hard to find irony in the desperation of the starving population of Ireland during this period: this French schooner was carrying a cargo of wheat from Nantes, bound for Galway and could very well have been part of the same grain that was forfeited and sold a few days earlier, in lieu of rents. France was shipping it in, Ireland was shipping it out and the poor buggers in the middle were starving for the want of it!

A ship's hull – or what remained in sight after the wrecking – its cargo, rigging and any valuable material gathered by the authorities at the scene of a shipwreck, was usually but not always auctioned. Invariably, the value of the all the cargo and materials had diminished because of the nature of their condition. The cost of recovering and transporting them could sometimes be uneconomic. More often than not, owners preferred to take the insurance, auction the lot on the spot and be done with it.

Water guards, coastguards and any officials of the Crown were all entitled to claim their 'Droits of the Admiralty' – a share of the value of the spoils saved and were seldom shy of stepping forward. Landowners and anyone involved in the recovery of anything of value on their land or foreshore, were also entitled to claim a consideration for salvage, and weren't behind the door either. Any cargo washed ashore from a wreck could be saved and seized by the landowner, who could claim recompense. In much earlier days, he could claim and keep the lot.

The matter was complicated if there were survivors from the wreck and the goods landed could be subject to complex calculation or, depend upon a number of factors. If the wrecking occurred in a remote area that was beyond the reach of law, it was often the case that no calculation was required. Disputes about salvage awards or tax levies on salvageable goods could sometimes be referred to arbitration. Not well known, the Ouzel Galley Society, based in Dublin could be petitioned to arbitrate on such matters. The society, a little publicity shy, has been in existence since the beginning of the 18th century until the present day and is comprised solely of past presidents of the Dublin Chamber of Commerce.

Awards were not always a reflection of fairness. Those rescuing survivors might only get a mention in the paper, a slap on the back or even a commendation by the local landlord to the Royal Humane Society. A shipping company might express its gratitude and forward a couple of guineas, to be distributed amongst the brave souls. For those who have seen the movie, *The Field*, where a piece of land in the west of Ireland was being auctioned, set some fifty years after Bunowen, they might begin to understand that there was always an expectation by local people, that they were entitled to 'first refusal' – at the right price, of course.

Semple may have 'known his onions' but Gibbons was also familiar with a few himself and, a lot of varieties besides. Gibbons had become a well-known harbour engineer on his own steam, so to speak, and knew that you couldn't build harbours on the whims of an opportune shipwreck that might provide timber for trusses and the like. They may try it on in the west of Ireland but Gibbons was not building piers and harbours on the basis of a bit of old timber that might be had from shipwreck.[11]

John King, the construction supervisor at Kinvara, had a not too dissimilar issue with the availability of timber at his new harbour. Seemingly short of all kinds of handles – picks, hammers and wheelbarrows – he was purchasing 'scantlings' of timber from local people who were pilgrimaging to the site with all kinds of timber, including 'trees'. After being chastised for the minor unauthorised expenditure, he promised to keep better accounts in the future and not to make any unnecessary purchases.

John King is also credited with supervising construction of the pier at Ballyvaughan around the same time.

Being the foundations man, William was usually one of the first men to arrive on site – and one of the first to leave. The new road to the pier site at Bunowen had been cleared and prepared, and most of the construction equipment and some of the pier stones had already arrived.

In the high summer of July 1849, when days were long and weather was favourable, the big tides enabled work to proceed at a pace. One of the reasons why Campbell must have appealed to Gibbons was that he was a can-do man. Not wanting to hold up work, he got stuck in, completed and moved on.

Campbell began by blasting and clearing bedrock that needed to be reduced for levelling, providing low water clearance for vessels to come alongside the new pier. It wasn't long however, before Mr Semple grew anxious and was minded to write to the commissioners at head office, regarding a request from William Campbell in July.

It is believed that Campbell may have lodged at the premises of Anthony Gorham, in Clifden, for a short time and then drew down provisions from Gorham while working at Bunowen, in advance of being paid by the Board – "on tick". Already having written to Gibbons[12] to thank him for the work and expressing the hope that payment to him would not be unduly delayed, its tone suggests that Campbell was fearful of lapsing into bad debt again. Remoteness obviously being a factor in delay, Campbell became anxious and also requested that Semple write to head office on his behalf, seeking

---

11   The Semples were in Galway long before Public Works arrived and were there after they left – and they remain. Soon after the timber saga, maybe having learned a thing or two about supply and demand, John Semple established his own sawmill in Galway, the Atlantic Sawmills.

12   See photo pertaining to *Letter One* (dated August 1849) on page 44.

the advance payment of £15, in order that he might settle his account in Clifden.

It appears that the incident concerning the £15 was also playing on the mind of Anthony Gorham, who had earlier written his own[13] to his suppliers– John Scally & Company in Dublin. Gorham was worried that "this fellow" Campbell might not pay his bill and perhaps they (Scally) could check with the commissioners and encourage an advance or full payment directly, throwing in a sweetening offer of discount. Apparently misfiled, the letter from Gorham[14] turned up in the OPW's file for works at "Errislannan pier". The most logical explanation for its turning up where it did is that the letter and its sentiment had reached its target – the Commissioners of Public Works. It also suggests that Campbell was also working at another pier, Errislannan, at the time and that the bill was for groceries only. This 'making sure that everyone was aware of the same credit note' flurry of correspondence might also suggest that Campbell still hadn't shaken off a reputation for bad debt.

Deserving praise of the highest order, a wonderful account of this period in the west of Ireland in *Humble Works for Humble People*, written by N.P. Wilkins and published in 2017, recalls the forgoing incident of the £15, Campbell and Gorham's letter[15] stating, "Gregory was not the only one with problems at Errislannan. One William Campbell was a diver at the works. Anthony Gorham, a local shopkeeper, reportedly gave him groceries on credit, costing around £15, to be paid when Campbell himself was paid. It was not an unusual practise in Connemara at the time to extend credit in that manner. But Gorham, thinking the works nearly complete in January 1949, feared that Campbell would soon move away, leaving him, Gorham, unpaid. So he wrote to J. Scally & Company in Dublin (presumed to be Campbell's employer under contract.) requesting that they pay Campbell while he was still at Errislannan, so that Gorham would get what was owed to him. The records are silent on the outcome of this matter."

Well the record can be refreshed. Apart from what are seemingly minor discrepancies, the following appears to be what occurred, and is clearly outlined in the copies of Campbell's and Gorham's letters, included in the letter books.

Campbell had written to the commissioners at the Custom House seeking an advance of the £15 and authorised its payment to Anthony Gorham. Mr Gorham then instructed, in his own hand, on the same letter, to have

---

13 See photo pertaining to *Letter Two* on page 44.

14 See *Letter Two* on page 44.

15 See *Letter One* on page 44

2. Famine Harbours and Piers, 1848-1850

the £15 paid to Messrs John Scally, Pill Lane, Dublin (not Campbell's employer as speculated by Wilkins, but Gorham's supplier). This letter was countersigned, Anthony Gorham.

It so happens that John Scully (Scally) of 29 Pill Lane, was a wholesale merchant and was supplying Gorham with merchandise. Gorham was offsetting his own debt to Scally with the payment owed to him by Campbell and is an explanation as to why it might not have appeared in Gorham's accounts. Quite by the way, John Scally sat on the same Queen's jury panel with Mr Singleton, the vendor of Campbell's diving dress.[16]

Semple's outline of Campbell's predicament was despatched in correspondence and also included reference to the poor state of Campbell's diving dress, "only patching and mending it every day". He also expressed concern that, Campbell's debtors in Clifden might seize his "diving engine and helmet" and prevent him from leaving. They were being a bit previous, as Campbell had no intention of leaving just then.

The Commissioners replied to Semple, informing him that they could not intervene in William's private affairs of debt and that they should get on with the work. They also stated that they had forwarded a new diving dress for Campbell. It might seem from the reading that, the Commissioners had dispensed with habits of a lifetime, and had become Mr Campbell's benefactor, providing him with replacement new diving gear. This was not the case, even though it was Gibbons who had ordered the diving dress to be sent.

The receipt for the diving dress, issued by "Agent to the British Waterproof Company, Robert Singleton at 21 Wicklow Street" was clearly made out to William Campbell. It wasn't long before Gibbons intervened once again and Campbell received the advance requested and a further one for £60, in September, just before he left Bunowen.[17]

Seemingly attempting to show that, at all times, he was cost conscious, Semple also suggested saving 5 shillings a day on Mr Campbell, while he was just hanging around idle – the Commissioners might let him move him on to another job! With specific mention, he suggested the Irish Wasteland Society's agent and supervisor, Mr Thomas Hazel, at the pier construction project ongoing at Kilkieran.

---

16 A bustling area of markets and small mercantile establishments in the heart of Old Dublin, Pill Lane was in the parish of Saint Mary's, near Capel Street, Dublin.

17 William Campbell may have had owed monies to the Waterproof Company at an earlier date and this could, very likely, have been the reason for the earlier bankruptcy proceedings against him.

The poor man overestimated his importance and the lie of the land and received a reply directly from Gibbons, not so much chastising him but Gibbons was nevertheless emphatic. Campbell was not to be moved on and that he, Semple, was to get the stones and get the work done. A saving might have been made on Semple's budget but the department were still paying for Campbell either way and Gibbons had a little gem in Campbell.

Gibbons was a man with a vast experience in the vagaries of local contractors, with a special awareness for those not under his direct control. After the protracted operations at Dunmore still fresh in memory, he knew that if Campbell was moved on, it might be difficult getting him back on site at the appropriate time. Without Campbell and his expertise, the work could come to a halt, so it was imperative to keep him on site and to keep the pressure on Semple to deliver on his contract. The order hit the mark, and Semple later reported, "NB. The diver does not seem to be in any hurry out of this place."

Campbell had arrived in the area in March, blasted rock, chipped stones, donned his diving helmet and erected the new pier at Bunowen. He worked in the shadow of the ruined castle and forts at Doon Hill and Bunowen that still loom above the harbour today. Owned then by the Geoghegans, the fortress was the home to the marriage between the 'ferocious' Donal O' Flaherty and the infamous pirate queen, Grace O'Malley. One wonders if William Campbell took time out to walk the ruins while he was there. I did, and the view of west Galway is worth the easy climb. The pains go but the memories linger on.[18]

Campbell knew the value of 5 shillings a day – guaranteed, same deal as the one at Ballycotton and didn't depart until September. The contrast between Campbell's wages and that of the labourers, five times more, is just a recurring fact of life. A more startling comparison could be made with the generous travelling expenses paid to Alexander Nimmo, twenty years earlier, while contracting at Dunmore. About to take on a direct contract with HM Government, the Post Office offered him three guineas per day and a shilling per mile – a lot of money when travelling back and forward from London to far flung places around Ireland! Alexander Nimmo left the commissioners in 1826, to work directly for the Government, as well as consulting on a number of other works.

Travelling expenses were always a contentious issue in the public service, as any of its officials might reluctantly tell you. Recalling my own submissions for travelling expenses, while employed in the service, it was indeed a very

---

18 Geoghegans-O'Neills played a significant role in the petition for construction of the new pier at Bunowen.

welcome recompense, albeit a wholly justifiable one, I hasten to add. One was recompensed at agreed rates for travelling for the Service in one's own transport, plus an allowance for a meal if out all day. As the payment was not earned income, it was received free of tax. Somehow though, one always felt privileged, if I can put it like that. That is, until after my particular branch of the Service was transformed from state to semi-state and ultimately privatised. And when the private secretary of our newly head-hunted CEO left behind a copy of her boss's expenses claim on the photo copying machine, I never felt a thing after that.

I am not certain that all of Campbell's travel expenses were recompensed but, I suspect that if he was going from one job to the next, then they were, just as with others in the Service.

Such comparisons alone may suggest that this would have been the only inequality that existed then. We know now that great numbers of families were in unimaginable want and took work at any price, if ever they were lucky enough for a 'scheme to come to town'. It might seem like just a recollection of history, a reflection on the awful situation resulting from failing crops of potatoes – but it was more than that. The 'Famine', that awful time, contained much more crime than just wanton disregard or neglect of an unfortunate population, or a shortage of spuds!

The contrasts that existed at the time (ones we regularly read of today) were items of news in the contemporary press. You could keep up to speed with the course of the Famine by following the trail of dead reported in the press! Whole families were turned out of their homes, off their rented land, deprived of all their belongings in order to pay fines while an echelon of better off dined at long, immaculately set tables and sailed their fine yachts to Europe and the Holy Land. Ireland's landlords and fine gentry were ordering huge yachts that got bigger and bigger, competing in races for the leading positions in their royal clubs and in the pecking order of fine society. At the same time, whole communities were being ravaged and laid waste for the want of food.

Poverty, hunger and death remained even in the period considered to be somewhat after the 'Famine Years'. *The Advocate* reported in April 1857:

> *The Royal Irish Yacht Club will hold a regatta in Bantry Bay next Summer.*

The following social comment appeared directly beneath the above:

> *During the last week, an unusually large number of peasantry have left the west of Ireland for America.*

Disbelief can turn to distress when one reads of the terrible inequalities that existed, and of the terrible deaths that befell a section of the population, who literally had to 'eat their young'. Not an exaggeration, I hasten to add!

In the same newspapers, you could read a notice by the Widow Stokes, announcing an upcoming auction of all manner of exotic fruits, grain, sugar etc while on another page, there were accounts of cannibalism. Surprisingly, in 1849 such acts of total depravation were actual news items – during intervening years, this subject was buried. In recent times, details are re-emerging.

At the same time, Campbell was attempting to obtain payment for work he had completed, in order to clear his debts at Clifden and beyond. The Protestant rector and chaplain of the workhouse, in the not-too-distant town of Ballinrobe, was lambasting Lord Russell and the houses of parliament, with accounts of one hundred deaths a week from starvation and cholera. He supported his accusations with the following testimony:

> *In a neighbouring Union, a shipwrecked human body was cast on shore, a starving man extracted the heart and liver, and that was the maddening feast on which he regaled himself and perishing family!!!*

Now, one might be tempted to suspect exaggeration on the writer's part, if only to coax some sympathy for the sufferers. They were not all telling lies or exaggerating, however.

Three months later, the parish priest of the same town, Peter Ward, wrote to the Rev. Dr Spratt, chairman of the General Relief Committee at the Carmelite Convent in Dublin, on 19 August. He began by offering thanks for the £20 donated by a Protestant clergyman in Wexford before launching hardly believable accounts of the plight of his flock in the district:

> *"... More than 800 families cruelly banished from their homes ... upwards of 800 houses levelled ... poor wandering without clothes in awful distress. I did all I could to save as many lives as possible. I called on the government for relief – they refused. I implored the landlords to come to my aid and assistance – they did not listen. In the village of Drimcaggy, four were dead together in a poor hut – brother, two sisters and daughter. The flesh was torn off the daughter's arm and mangled in the mouth of the poor dead mother, her name was Mrs Kennedy. William Walsh of Mount Partree and his son were dead together, the flesh torn off their bodies by rats, and by each other, flesh was found in their mouths.*

Pat Shaughnessy declared that such was the agony of hunger that he would eat his own child unless relieved."

And there was more. Father Ward understood that it would be difficult for outsiders to comprehend or believe such acts and in order to somehow authenticate and emphasise his account, he concluded with, "These are true facts."

Even if they were only half true, they are still hardly believable. There was a lot going on that wasn't pleasant and a lot who didn't want to know about it. And it continued.

William Campbell was working in the thick of genocide by Famine. It seems impossible that he had not become aware of the starvation and death that existed all around him but we have no record of comment by him. Even in 1849, when hundreds were dying every week in north Mayo, getting kicked from sheriff to landlord in search of food and relief, they died from exposure and hunger and were buried at the side of the road where they fell. The effect of these death marches was similar to the forced marches of World War II and the resettlement campaigns to Gulags – you were not meant to survive. Even today, as erosion picks away at our coastline, the bones of unmarked graves continue to be discovered. How many victims are out there?

It is unfortunate that Campbell's descendants had no knowledge of his work and experiences in the west of Ireland at that time, not seeming to have passed down in any stories to his family. Then again, maybe it was not a period best remembered. I daresay, we may take a similar view when history judges our own attitude to present day victims of conflict and migration.

There was, however, a lot more going on at Bunowen and Errislannan than just unpaid grocery bills. The peninsula immediately south of Clifden is called Errislannan, after Saint Flannan. This saint's name, his holy well and an associated church have a recorded presence there from the seventh century. The most westward part, on the north side of the peninsula, is called Drimeen. There is a harbour there on the extreme western point called 'Boat Harbour'. Although it is another beautifully constructed stone harbour, it is believed that it was not commenced until the 1860s. The peninsula is a secret gem that the rusty WAW signs have not invaded.

On the southern side of the peninsula, there is another lovely stone harbour, called Curhownagh. On a visit there, some local boatmen have told me that a diver once visited there. His job was to blow away some rock from a natural breakwater, in order to improve access for the building of the harbour. This harbour was called Loughane Lea in the Board of Works files, and the civil engineer, George Gregory, was hired as Superintendent for Works there in 1847. Work continued in 1848 and it was at this harbour that Anthony Gorham had said that William Campbell was working, when he gave him the groceries 'on tick'. We must conclude then that William Campbell was the diver in question and that he was operating between the three harbours in 1848 and 1849.

The commissioners received a letter from the principal landowner at Errislannan, Colonel John Lambert, who had complained that their supervisor on site, Mr George Gregory "was frequently absent from work" and that he was "addicted to drunkenness."

Strong stuff and the Board sent the District Engineer, Roberts, to investigate. Having written to both men and informed them of his impending visit to the works and his desire to interview both men, Lambert absented himself. Nevertheless, Roberts interviewed Gregory and a number of workers on the site and completed his investigations. Roberts' findings were revealing and turned the tables on the accuser.

Roberts reported that Lambert had been pressurising Gregory and his wife, in her husband's absence, in attempts to deduct monies from the wages of a number of men (a highly unorthodox procedure even then) who were working on the new harbour. These were small tenants of his, with small holdings who, he claimed, owed him rent, grazing fees etc. Gregory summoned up the courage to reject Lambert's demands and then, the nasty letter arrived on the Commissioners' desk.

One might assume Gregory, a site supervisor for Public Works, was fairly alright for food and accommodation but Roberts reported that the "poor man was living at the site in a rough cabin."

Gregory's absences from duty had been to attend his own wedding and, his mother's funeral, and both had been approved in advance. George Gregory was exonerated by the Board and continued with his duties at the harbour.

Whether or not Campbell was playing both ends against the middle is uncertain but unlikely, in my view. Given the repetitive correspondence on money issues throughout his career with the Board of Works, I suspect William may have, at times, been inclined to push the envelope in a way the Scots have a reputation for.

It is quite often the case that, when you 'give a dog a bad name', it can stick. It was the case with Campbell's earlier brush with bankruptcy. Even though it was dismissed, the incident seems to have followed him and affected his access to credit. Talk, especially bad talk, can travel fast, even then, and appears to have been the case at Clifden. This unsubstantiated financial slight on Campbell's reputation, would return to haunt 'this fellah Campbell'.

The issue reared its ugly head once again, some years later when, in December 1863, officials reported that William Campbell had, 'absconded'. And as it was, with my own perception of the man, during early discoveries of official correspondence relating to this event, we were all nevertheless mistaken. William Campbell was not only an honourable man but he was also a man of his word. He was also a man with considerable courage.[19]

Correspondence indicates that Campbell was also involved in the construction of the new piers at Duncannon in County Wexford, which began in 1849 as well as at the nearby village of Arthurstown. They were completed in 1851. Just a short distance north and up the estuary from Duncannon on the same side, Arthurstown is situated in a beautiful little bay called King's Bay. The parish is Saint James and this is where the much-admired Lord Templemore resided at Dunbrody estate.

Both projects involved work below low water and Campbell's end of things would have been completed in a relatively short period. Campbell was contracted by the Board of Public Works and as before, worked to the engineer, Barry Gibbons. Although these were Waterford Harbour projects, it was not until sometime later that Campbell contracted directly to the Waterford Harbour Commissioners.[20]

Campbell and a Diver's Work

The work that was completed in the small harbours, dotted around the coast of Ireland, during this period is a magnificent testimony to the

19 William Campbell is noted to have been and to have carried out work at Bunowen, the nearby pier at Kilkieran and to some unknown extent, at the pretty little harbour of Curhownagh, Errislannan in west Connemara, during the summers of 1848 and 1849. The author was unable to locate any further reference to Campbell at Kilkieran Pier or at Kinvara, south Galway in the Board of Works files. It seems unlikely however, given the variety of Mr Campbell's skills and after his work at Ballycotton in 1848 was complete, that he was not employed on any of the works ongoing at other harbours. Campbell also stated that work was not finally completed at Bunowen until much later, in 1849.

20 Records of Campbell's work at these Famine harbours and piers have been gathered and compiled, in the main, from OPW letter books and correspondence in the National Archives, cross checked and supported by reference to newspapers of the day. It is quite probable that Campbell also worked at other harbours and piers, for which there are no surviving records.

artisans of stone craft. The sheer quantity of stone laid on stone is one thing; the beautifully cut, shiny step on step is quite another and remains a wonderful legacy. Moreover, there is a lot to be said for the determination and dedication of some officials, who got behind the spirit of bringing relief by development to so many remote areas of Ireland. On the other hand, we have arrived at a point in our history that, we believe, represents a journey of considerable progress while at the same time, we can display such a wanton disregard for the journey and its heritage. It is most regrettable that many of these structures have been neglected since, have fallen into decay, demolished and others just been tarred or cemented over, or replaced altogether with concrete.

There is little to compare with an idle moment spent sitting on the time-worn steps of one of these old stone harbours, eating your sandwiches as the sun sets on a summer's evening.

A qualified and experienced contractor, Campbell had come to the fore at a time that proved fortuitous for both men. Barry Gibbons was elevated from his position as County Surveyor for Wexford, to Resident Engineer for Public Works, based at Kingstown. And amongst a variety of public works, his position entailed overseeing the implementation of a programme of harbour construction around the coast of Ireland.

Earlier schemes were limited by the practical but sometimes difficult application of shuttering, pumping and so on. And in the past, construction had rarely reached out beyond the low water mark. This type of shuttering, excavation, constant pumping could be protracted and expensive. Consequently, the piers were often only suitable for fishing vessels to come alongside, closer to high water and depending on the incline of the seabed, with very little space.

The priority was to improve the capability of piers and harbours in order to facilitate boats alongside for maximum periods of time and tide. If fish catches and landings were to improve, harbour walls and piers had to be pushed out beyond the level of low water.

The extension of existing and the construction of new, longer piers became even more feasible with the aid of divers and diving bells. But diving bells and their support equipment were heavy, cumbersome and difficult to move around from site to site. Operations and the transport of men and equipment could also be weather dependent. When diving technology and equipment improved, the situation changed.

William Campbell's work on a pier was of a precise nature and could be of relatively short duration. If repairing, he could maintain and repair stonework that was already beneath the water. With new piers, he supervised the excavation and laying of cut stone for their foundations. In some cases, he prepared and laid the ashlars himself, a craft we will discover he had a talent for. He blasted and cleared rock beneath the low water mark and to some extent, other protrusions that were exposed at low water. It was work that was not specific to a diver but his presence on site meant that another explosives man was not required.

Campbell's skill and management of pier work was later described at Kilmore, County Wexford when it was reported, "We experienced a delightful treat in seeing Mr Campbell, the 'accomplished diver', going through some of his operations. He was arranging one of the basement stones at a depth of fifteen feet from the surface of the water and although it weighed upwards of three tons, it was so ingeniously hung from a framework devised for the purpose that he managed it with as much ease as a bricklayer would a bat on terra firma."

Hitherto, the use of roman cement had not been common in pier construction, previously using only lime. Campbell loved the stuff though and used it extensively, to great effect. As the name suggests, it is in use since Roman times, amongst its most valuable qualities being that it sets extremely quick and could remain strong and binding beneath the water for centuries.

It seems that Campbell was able to work a mix of the cement for various applications underwater. Using a 'concrete mix' of the stuff, filled into hessian sacks of various sizes, he was able to make large repairs and place others as 'bedding', before laying the cut stones. There is still evidence, in some old piers today, of re pointing with the mix from this period.

Campbell was a one-man operation – almost. A reliable man or boy was required to man the air pump and to lower the bits and pieces, such as tools that a diver required. He was talented, experienced and, like his boss, Gibbons, eager to get the job done. His gear was all portable: it could travel by sea and by horse and cart and it all fitted in with Gibbons' vision of getting the work done as best and as quickly as possible. They were skilled men of their time but importantly, they were honest and committed men.

From Galway, there is record of Campbell visiting piers at Tarbert on the Shannon, County Limerick, County Waterford and in County Wexford, before returning to Dublin.[21]

By 1850, a lot of pier and harbour work around Ireland had been completed but, by no means all of it. Harbour development is not unlike the nature

---

21   Kilrush and the Shannon was where Barry Gibbons worked, on what was probably his first pier project. It was also probably where he met the young lady who became his wife.

of all infrastructural development – ongoing. The nature of Campbell's input into this type of marine construction meant that he was one of the first on site. Clearing and preparing the seabed, blasting rock and laying foundations. Almost constantly supplied with work by Gibbons, he was also one of the first to move on.

Being widowed and unattached, with wide experience of all aspects of harbour development, were aspects of Campbell's life that proved a convenient partner for Gibbons own ambitions. He kept Campbell near to him and put him to work around Kingstown Harbour, on various tidying up jobs, before despatching him to the next project.

Although the substantive work on Kingstown Harbour and its piers had been finished for about eight years, a number of tasks remained. There were still large amounts of rubble strewn on the seabed, along the base of the piers, missing facing stones and a new inner pier to be erected. This would be a pier within piers, required for bigger and faster steamers – the mail boats.

All the equipment Campbell required at Kingstown was on site, at the huge Public Works complex opposite the harbour. The harbour had several diving bells in its yards and various pieces of diving dress and equipment. The extensive inventory of diving equipment belonging to the Board lay scattered all around the country and it too needed tidying up. After a national inventory, gear was sold, condemned or replaced and preparations for the new project, the mail boat pier in Kingstown, began.

Even at this early stage, Gibbons had either been approached by the City of Dublin Steam Packet Company (to whom he was no stranger) and was asked to consider the design of a new mail boat pier or, he may simply have been tasked by the Board of Public Works to the project. According to a speech made by this Protestant Catholic Emancipationist and part-time innovator of diving equipment, Thomas Steele, at a Repeal meeting in Kingstown in 1845, "his friend Barry Gibbons" had already been working on such a plan and had shown him the drawings. In the same speech, Steele recalled how he dived in the "Kingstown bell" to seven fathoms in the harbour, on the night of 31 December 1839. Steele was experimenting with his invention at the time – an "underwater lamp" – and was conveyed below with two "honest-hearted and good-humoured divers."

For good measure, he also brought down a bottle of port to celebrate the occasion. While on the bottom of the harbour, pouring out three glasses of the rich liquor, he addressed his fellow divers, "Now say I, my brother divers, what the blazes do we care about King George IV ..." after whom the harbour had been named, and proceeded to drink the health of the father of Ireland, "King Dan".[22]

22　"King Dan" was a reference to Daniel O'Connell, the Liberator, who died two years later. It is highly unlikely that Thomas Steele could have made his descent in the diving bell in Kingstown Harbour, during the dark hours of 31 December 1839, without the permission of its Resident Engineer, the recently appointed Barry Gibbons. He may also have been 'gilding the lily' somewhat, as it is extremely hard to find '7 fathoms' today, in what was Kingstown Harbour.

William Campbell's birth details, from entry in parish records of Old Monkland, Lanarkshire. Courtesy of *Scottish People*.

Pier at Bunowen, north-west Galway. Foreground by William Campbell in 1847/8. End was added much later. Author's collection.

Pier at Errislannan. A quiet, beautiful peninsula near Clifden, County Galway. Using underwater explosives, William Campbell cleared a safe entrance to this harbour and laid foundation stones for its pier in 1848/9. Author's collection.

Kilkieran Harbour and graveyard, north-west Galway, with famine grave markers. Situated not too distant from Bunowen Harbour. William Campbell also worked on the construction of this harbour, visible at the top of the photograph. Author's collection.

Market Square in Clifden, County Galway. William Gorham's premises have the stylised windows, centre frame. William Campbell obtained provisions while working there in 1848/9. Mr Gorham wrote to the commissioners for advance pay for William, in fear that he might have to leave without paying his bill. The bill was paid. Image is courtesy of the *Lawrence Collection* at the National Library of Ireland.

THE GLASGOW
MECHANICS' MAGAZINE,

CONDUCTED BY

A Committee of Civil Engineers and Practical Mechanics.

"Cased in thy iron walls, thou far-famed bell,
My faith in thee, O Art, all fears dispel ;
I with undaunted heart the scene survey—
Behold the finny brood in gambols play!"

| No. XCIX. | Saturday, 12th November, 1825. | Price 3d. |

PORT-PATRICK DIVING-BELL.

Fig. 2.

An illustration of the diving bell used by William Campbell at Portpatrick, Scotland in 1838. From *Glasgow Mechanics' Magazine*.

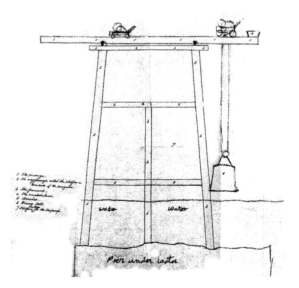

Section of Frame-work and Carriage.

Original drawing of the diving bell and gantry arrangement submitted during the court case that followed the fatal accident at Portpatrick.

Letter from William Campbell to Board of Works engineer, Barry Gibbons, on the progress of the pier at Bunowen, County Galway; payment of wages and stones from Aran etc, in 1849.

William Campbell's letter of instruction to the commissioners, for permission to settle his debt with Anthony Gorham of Clifden from wages due to him.

Images on this page are from Correspondence Ledger and files in Board of Public Works archives at the National Archives, Dublin.

Chapter 3

Diving Work at Duncannon and Kilmore, 1850-1852

Adventure at Kilmore, 1851-1852

As with many of the stone harbours that were built during the 18th and early 19th centuries, ongoing battles with the elements often led to serious damage, or even destruction and necessitated constant upkeep and repair. With no department responsible for these structures, many fell into ruin and became totally useless. Working methods, materials, machinery and innovation dramatically improved during the Victorian period and facilitated the construction of substantially improved piers and harbours around Ireland.

In 1843, the local fishermen of Kilmore, on the south coast of Wexford, formed a committee and met in the Wooden House bar and eating house on the Main Street, overlooking their old pier. When they rose, they had agreed to organise and collect donations from the surrounding towns and villages, in order to repair and improve the dilapidated pier that had been further damaged by recent storms.

Amongst many familiar local names on the original document of account, which still survives in the National Archives, an unusual contribution from the newly established Glasgow Insurance Company is recorded. A number of local donations were matched by small grants from the Board of Public Works and the Fisheries Fund, and the work commenced.

Work continued for about two years, under the supervision of the local committee, chaired by Andrew Furlong, who lived opposite the pier – in the Wooden House. A survey, reported to have been completed by Mr Frazer (Captain), suggested that the ongoing remedial works should be abandoned, in favour of the construction of a new and extended pier. This was Commander G.A. Frazer, who had sailed in the survey vessel, *HMS Lucifer*, and the ketch, *Sparrow*, plumbing the depths off the east coast and around Wexford, and a mighty fine job he did too.

Whether or not construction work in other counties began and proceeded in the same fashion as those at Kilmore, the Wexford fishermen were extremely astute in their record keeping. They had kept a detailed record of their own input into the works thus far: estimating values of unpaid labour, the value of work vessels (all named) and equipment that they had supplied. When it came to submitting their memorial for a new pier, they were able to use these values as part of the required 'matching funds'. The amounts justified the value of the grants and loans sought, which the Government of the day were disbursing for harbour and pier projects around the country.

Alleviating hunger and poverty, by improving fishing capacity and providing employment, were amongst the principal aims of these harbour projects and the money was not wasted at Kilmore. Improvements were intended to provide the coastal populations with the means to feed themselves; to catch and get their fish to market. The seas off the south coasts of Wexford and Waterford (in particular, an area known as the Nymph Bank) were highly prized fishing grounds.

With funding in place, a project that might be described today as a, Private Public Partnership (PPP), with significant support from the County Surveyor and Engineer, Barry Gibbons, got underway. Despite Gibbons' request for Peter Maher to become supervisor at Kilmore, the Department of Public Works turned him down at first. Although Maher was described as 'not local', he did live in a house at Kilmore, described as 'Maher's house'. For anyone who knows country folk and their ways, they will understand just how many generations it takes to become known as 'local'. Nevertheless, Gibbons' wishes prevailed and Maher headed up the project.

The first stone of Kilmore pier was laid on 8 May 1849. Amid the sounds of 'feux de joie' and the explosions of some ordnance on the beach, a celebratory dinner was begun in Mr M. Furlong's Wooden House bar and restaurant, Main Street, Kilmore Quay. After a dinner, claimed to have been "the most fastidious middy ashore could wish to see", numerous dignitaries stood and performed lengthy speeches, matched with recurring toasts of 'Success to the Kilmore Fishery Pier'. Glasses rose on numerous occasions and special thanks were toasted to their favourite engineer, Barry D. Gibbons, who had sent his regrets at being unable to attend. One of the final orators was James Rainer, who had led the Taghmon Amateur Band from the pier.[1]

---

1 It is interesting that the expression, 'middy ashore' was used in this way, at the time a little more than ten years after the farcical play of the same name was written and performed. 'Middy' was understood to be the naval rating, midshipman. Later, it was also used to describe a girl's blouse. It was represented in the play as being the character influence a sensitive young man might experience at sea.

By this time, Gibbons' reputation and the broad extent of his capabilities had become well known. His opinions grew in confidence and influence. Maher had become the supervisor at Kilmore but the quid pro quo may have been that Maher also had to supervise the outstanding and remaining works at Fethard and Slade harbours, simultaneously. Gibbons' faith in Mr Maher proved to be well founded. Despite opposition from officials, Gibbons had arranged for Maher's wages to be increased from 27 to 30 shillings per week while he supervised at the construction work at Slade Harbour in 1847. Despite some begrudging local opposition, both projects were completed to everyone's satisfaction, proving Gibbons to be a man of sound judgement and Maher to be a reliable and competent supervisor. It might be noted that, although Maher was erudite and extremely competent, his wages were only a fraction of Campbell's remuneration.

Maher was another of these admirable, can-do persons, and brought the 800-ft pier at Kilmore to a successful conclusion in 1850/51, after the foundations for the last portion of the footings were laid by William Campbell, at low water springs, in 1850. The cost was reported by the local committee as having been £6,000. The sum allotted by the government schemes did not please everybody and was described, by some, as 'miserly paltry'. The final arbiters, in these instances, must be the users and they were well pleased with the finished pier, reserving opinion nevertheless, that an additional spend of £8,000 could have improved it to 'packet station' status.

It would appear that a diving bell was not in use at Kilmore and William Campbell would not seem to have travelled to any of these coastal projects with one. By then, he was thoroughly proficient with his 'marine gear' – a rubber suit and helmet with air delivered by hose from a pump on the surface.

Campbell arrived at Kilmore in 1850, when the seabed was being levelled and some of the early foundation stones were being laid. Begun around the same time, he also dived and inspected the pier at Duncannon, in January 1851, for Public Works. So it would appear that, while Campbell might not have been at either of the sites for the whole time of construction, it was more that, once more, he was moving from one project to another in counties Wexford and Waterford during these years.

During his work there, he witnessed a number of shipwrecks that occurred around the harbour. The day the foundation stone was laid, in May 1849, the remains of the American brig, *Saint James*, wrecked on Saint Patrick's Bridge, were auctioned ashore. Some ships were badly damaged and brought in to the partially built, new pier and many others were totally wrecked on the infamous reef, Saint Patrick's Bridge. This dramatic reef, hugely visible but invisible at high water, extends for several miles from the shore just east of the harbour, almost right out to the Little Saltee Island. The shore, all along this stretch of coast, is strewn with acres of huge stones and Campbell was never short of granite.

The pier was more than half completed in May 1851 when Campbell encountered his first shipwreck at Kilmore. It was the *Lyepa Zaritza*, a 500-ton Austrian ship that set out from South America with guano. She ran up on the rocks of Saint Patrick's Bridge and became a total wreck. The cargo and ship's equipment were offloaded and saved onto the new pier, where it was auctioned by John Walsh. Campbell was hired to blow up the remains of the vessel that lay on the rocks.

A few months previous, the large brig, *Horatio* was wrecked and driven onto the shore on the opposite side of the harbour. She too was auctioned by John Walsh, where she lay on the Ballyteige Murrough[2].

In June 1852, the 860-ton Dublin ship, *Malabar*, property of John Martin & Son, had been heading for Dublin from Saint John, New Brunswick, carrying a cargo of timber when she lost her rudder off the Great Saltee. Holed and filling, she was towed into Kilmore, where her cargo was saved and her remains dismantled as a total wreck. Again, the new pier was put to good use, where the wreck, hull, fittings and cargo, were all auctioned by John Walsh.

Wexford wrecks were John Walsh's bread and butter and few on the shores of the county escaped him. John Walsh (not Kilmore's parish priest of the same name) was an auctioneer and probably one in the same as the Lord Mayor of Wexford, a public-spirited man with offices at Crescent Quay.

Another incident involved the large American mail steamer, *Atlantic*, that ran onto the bridge in exactly the same place as the *Lyepa Zaritza*. The stranding occurred in fog, while the *Atlantic* was heading for Liverpool in April 1852. Having heard her bell, Peter Maher dropped what he was doing and rowed out to investigate. Out of the fog, the big vessel loomed and Maher rowed up alongside. He boarded the stranded vessel that had a valuable cargo and a number of passengers. The captain hadn't known where he was until Maher told him and pointed to the ship's position on the captain's chart. Further relieving the captain of worry, Maher also told him that if he waited for the tide, the ship would float off again. Despite the good advice, the captain ordered a tug from Waterford, which didn't arrive until well after the ship had floated off.

Eager to get out of the area known as the Bay of Shipwrecks, the *Atlantic* took several surprised men from Kilmore with her – and they weren't

2 More commonly known as *Ballyteigue Burrow* in modern usage.

volunteers. Having to make his own way back to Kilmore in darkness, Maher was annoyed and wrote a complaining letter to Gibbons. The lone rescuer had been invited aboard by the ship's master and effectively saved the valuable ship but got short shrift for his efforts. On a human level, it was disappointing. On a legal level, Maher could have taken it further.[3]

In between dressing harbour stone, laying foundations and blowing up wrecks, there was a serious storm. It occurred in October 1851 when a lot of stone lay on the quay wall at the time, for one reason or another. The force of the waves breaking over the pier washed the stones off and into the harbour. The men set about rigging up a crane and chains to hoist a steel basket, which was repeatedly lowered into the harbour to be filled. When it was filled by a diver below, it was hauled up and emptied into a floating barge. The stone was then floated outside the harbour and dumped. Filling the steel basket below was done by Campbell, in shallow water about twenty feet deep. During the recovery operation, an underwater escape occurred, the like of which must go down in the annals of diving as a first and maybe a one-off at that.

The bucket, full of stone, was being hauled by the crane but the barge was badly positioned directly under the crane and over the lift. Campbell's diving helmet became caught between the keel of the barge and the rising bucket, which itself was being wedged against a pile of stone on the bottom – he and his helmet were trapped. The men above were ignorant of the danger and continued to winch. The helmet began to squeeze and Campbell was immediately in danger of either having his head crushed or drowning. Drowning was a distinct possibility in Campbell's case, as his son, James, later revealed that his father never learned to swim.

How he did it, I do not know but he unscrewed himself out of the helmet by revolving his body. With his suit filling with water, he then had to remove his own weights and extricate himself from the lifting chains before he could get to the surface. Astonishing stuff![4]

An erudite observer wrote up a letter and submitted it to the *Wexford Independent*. These are the last few sentences:

> *... fully aware of the fearful death he had escaped. Had the public been deprived of such a servant, it would, I might venture to say,*

---

3 Artefacts from shipwrecks are still found by strollers along Saint Patrick's Bridge at low water.

4 A helmet that could be unscrewed from the breastplate, which was secured to the suit, was invented and patented by Siebe Gorman in 1839. I suspect it was never thought that it would be used for such an escape.

*be an impossibility to find a substitute for him, in the business he
is engaged in, he being a most ingenious man. It is owing to an
improvement he made on his helmet he attributes his miraculous
escape.*
I am, Sir, your very obedient servant,
J.T.C

William Campbell would seem to have had a number of admirers, some
seemingly reluctant to give their names. It was recently discovered that
J.T.C. was the prolific Kilkenny poet, John Thomas Campion (Dr), and
probably the same man who later described himself as "a constant reader
and a real friend of progress" during some later work by Campbell in
the harbour at Kilmore. Campion trained as an apothecarist but did not
become a medical man until 1860. He was a regular contributor on literary
and philosophical matters, a fine poet and was considered a 'true patriot'
or an 'ardent Irishman', as he also described himself.

Whatever demons William Campbell faced with his near-death experience,
when his boots hit terra firma, he took himself off to Dublin and got married
the following month, for a second time.

Building the pier at Kilmore was quite a different feat of engineering than
the larger project at Dunmore. Its successful completion, without any
undue delay, was mainly due to Superintendent Maher's approach to his
work, to the workers on the project and, from the active support that
they received from the community and the county's favourite engineer,
Gibbons.

These harbour works were generally a great success and just like the
intervention at Ballycotton, where the privileged classes were pleasantly
(I presume) surprised to discover that a "rude seacoast population could
also manufacture woollen and linen textiles when encouraged", the public
investment at Kilmore also proved well spent. Not peculiar, in any way, to
Dunmore or any of the other pier work in County Wexford for that matter,
the fact that there was so much money sloshing around in the development
of harbours and piers at this time meant that the usual hangers-on
managed to find their way to the honeypot – but not at Kilmore.

On successful completion of the works, the proud people of Kilmore
and Wexford held a banquet dinner in Maher's honour. Returning to the
hospitality of the Furlongs in the popular eatery, the Wooden House on
Tuesday, 30 December 1851, the committee and friends gathered once
again. At the hostelry, well known for its "fortified cuisine", and sometime
appearances of the Taghmon Band, the celebratory public dinner was
held in honour of Mr Patrick Maher and his successful completion of an

"Improvement of Ireland". Attended by a large number of community and public representatives, the accolades and toasts were endless. What is striking, from reports of the festivities, is the apparent genuineness of the communities' admiration and their gratitude, not only for Maher but Gibbons too and those other professionals employed on the project. Strikingly, senior figures of the Catholic and Protestant faiths were present on both occasions. A well-remembered night was had by one and all after they toasted, "Success to the Pier".

It was the second such toast in recent months. Maher had occasion to attend another similar function in Mrs Doyle's Hotel, Duncannon, during the previous May. On that occasion, it was Patrick Cavanagh, the Superintendent of Works, who had brought the construction of the new harbour and pier there to a successful conclusion. Everyone was toasted. Once again and most loudly, it was to Mr Gibbons along with the 'generous' Lord Templemore who, reportedly, for a second time secreted a small gold object in the foundation for good luck. The pier had already benefited from a gold coin he had placed under one of the foundation stones when it was begun.

These harbour projects were hugely popular and all the same nice things were toasted to Mr Patrick Cavanagh. Again, it was reported that he was not a "local man" when he was presented with an inscribed gold watch and chain.

Despite having been ravaged by famine in previous years, it is striking how happy and cheerful the local population of Wexford appears to have been at these 'get togethers'. They had succeeded in securing state funds for their communities' new harbours and piers and one can detect a sense that they no longer felt they were being left to wither on the vine for their previous rebellions, and that a new dawn had awakened. They clearly laid the reasons for their good fortune at the door of Barry Gibbons, whom they almost idolised.

Campbell was not finished in Kilmore and would be recalled two years later, for further improvements to the harbour there. He would experience and report a rare event and once more, he was very lucky to survive it.

Having recently changed ownership once again, the Wooden House has probably been the best-known pub and restaurant in the county of Wexford. The Lobster Pot in nearby Carne being a close second, it too was put up for sale after a long ownership in the one family. The quayside, the Wooden House, the fishermen and the divers' pub, Kehoe's and the village are my all-time favourite places to be, and I still visit.

It was believed that the Wooden House got its name from the time an Austrian ship, called the *Neptune*, wrecked nearby and one of its two "wooden deck houses", which were auctioned locally, was purchased or recovered and added on to the Furlong's house, making it the 'Wooden House'. This particular incident can no longer be taken as being the origin of this pub's name, as the wrecking of the *Neptune* did not occur until 1860, almost ten years after Maher sat down to his banquet there. The Wooden House on the Main Street of Kilmore Quay is believed to date from as early as 1700, and maybe for some time before that.

New Wrecks, Old Wrecks, and Very Old Wrecks

Described as a widower, Campbell's only known family in Ireland, at this time, was his son James, who was thirteen years of age.[5]

Having escaped drowning at Kilmore, Campbell returned to the altar for marriage once again, on 23 November 1851. The ceremony was performed by the Reverend Drury at Saint Bridget's Church of Ireland (also known as Bride's or Brigit's), which stood in the shadows of its two great mother cathedrals, Saint Patrick's and Christ Church, Dublin, being annexed to both at separate times. Having shaken off his reputational status of near bankrupt, William is recorded on the marriage certificate as being a "gentleman" and the son of a farmer. As was the practice, no profession is recorded against Mary Charles, his intended but her father, James, was described as a "carpenter".

How William and Mary met is unknown to us but they both roomed at nearby Golden Lane prior to the ceremony. William's profession would have seen him amongst many other men in the carpentry trade, including those at Teall's shipyard in Ringsend.

A question arises, where and under what circumstances might William Campbell have met Mary, and a family mystery also begins at this point. It was later declared that Mary was endowed with musical and teaching skills and was considered to have some business acumen but later, when young James marries, one might imagine that these qualities were meant to be ascribed to his wife, when we discover her position and education.

Also nearby, William's son, James, would marry at Saint Peter's Church, twelve years later. Saint Peter's was situated closer to William's recorded address, Golden Lane, at the time he married Mary but Peter's was more 'fashionable'. Saint Bridget's was considered a beautiful little church but unfortunately, it was demolished in order to make way for a revolutionary

---

5   It is not known whether either of his siblings, his father or his mother, were still alive at this time.

development of housing in 1896, known as Iveagh Buildings after their principal sponsor, Lord Iveagh, better known as Edward Guinness, of the famous same name brewery nearby. Saint Peter's suffered the same fate later, when the number of devotees declined and property prices rose.

William was recorded as 'full age', which was thirty-eight years in his case and Mary as "minor", in her case being fifteen years.[6] Only two years difference between Mary and William's son, James, and you may say what you like but the fact remains, such marriages were not rare and this match stood the test of time and travel. They remained married to one another until death, almost half a century later.

As there were multiple tenancies in many of the houses in Golden Lane and directories did not individualise tenants in the house(s) or boarding house(s), the actual residence that Campbell and Charles resided or lodged in has not been identified.

The conjoin of the Campbells with their respective spouses would prove to be life changing, in the real sense of the phrase. James, still only a teenager, would eventually prove to be the driving force behind remarkable family adventures. His father, a rock, was always by his side until many years later, when James finally went his separate way in a new land.

In spite of Campbell's work earning him a reputation of some merit as a contractor, together with the reputation of Scots for thrift and steadfastness, he was having his own difficulties adjusting to his new masters. Accounting for every nut and bolt he was acquiring while working at harbours, unrelenting official correspondence with instructions for adhering to proper practice, demands for explanations, were the other side of the public coin new to him. His upsetting habit of writing directly to Gibbons was of particular annoyance to the staff at headquarters in Kingstown but he just wasn't familiar with civil service procedure or, maybe it was just that he had no time for it. It would get him into trouble, nevertheless.

William and Mary Campbell's first child, William's second, was born on 8 October 1852 and christened William. The christening took place in the parish of Saint James and Dunbrody, County Wexford – but what were the couple doing so far from the capital? The remains of the old parish church and graveyard, Saint James, are perched over the cliff road leading from Arthurstown to Ballyhack. It was replaced by an architectural gem, All Saints Church, built in 1875 between Arthurstown and Duncannon.

---

6 Sixteen years of age was also recorded later.

This area of south-east Ireland, from Carnsore to the Waterford estuary, has remarkable connections with seafaring, reaching back over a thousand years. Its geographical location in north-west Europe remains an important maritime milestone and was one of the first places that ancient mariners, journeying from the south of England and Europe, expected to see. South of the coast are the Tuskar and Saltee Islands, which have a terrible but well-deserved reputation for shipwrecks but the coast also provides numerous sheltered and sandy areas with long, safe tidal fetch for landing. Foreign armies, such as the Normans and Cromwell landed there and some reports indicate that it hadn't escaped German planners, as a staging post for the invasion of Britain during World War II.

Duncannon, a beautiful seaside town, where various religious communities and the Knights Templar settled in the 12th century, is also famous for its impressive five-hundred-year-old fort. Still very much intact, housing a museum, visitors centre and small craft units, it attracts a constant stream of tourists to the village during the summer season. It too has a modern slogan touristic signpost – The Norman Way. Duncannon remains a beautiful small harbour village, steeped in a rich history but it was, after all, a rather out of the way place.

In the first instance, it was a recently acquired contract with the Waterford Harbour Commissioners that had brought William there. He was also working on the development of the new pier at Kilmore, further east along the coast, where he had blown up the remains of the wreck, *Lyepa Zaritza* on Saint Patrick's Bridge. The efficient manner in despatching this wreck came to the notice of the harbour commissioners in the adjacent county, and they sent for him.

Secondly, Duncannon had also been undergoing improvements to its harbour, and Campbell spent the guts of two years working in and about County Wexford.

There are also some indications, which suggest that his recent young wife's family, the Charles, may have been from this area and that she thoroughly enjoyed being there. It was a very happy time in the memory of the family, so much so, that their son, William, would name his own house and their large property, 'Wexford' many years later. The choice was obviously a sentimental attachment to the 'old country' but might have had more to do with his mother's memories of the place.

The border between the counties of Waterford and Wexford runs down the middle of the Waterford estuary, after the rivers Suir and Barrow join. Notwithstanding the county boundary, the Waterford Harbour Commissioners' responsibility to preserve the shipping channel leading to the port of Waterford extends over to the Wexford side, and clearing obstructions are their responsibility.

Campbell's contract with the Waterford Harbour Commissioners had kicked off in September 1852. After an earlier but brief return to Kilmore in the same year, this seems to have been about the time he finished that particular stint in the county.

Campbell and his wife, pregnant with their son at the time, were presumably in lodgings, or perhaps staying with some branch of Mary's family, when William travelled down from Duncannon in one of the Waterford Harbour's service vessels, and moored over the wreck of the collier, *John and Hannah*.[7]

Laden with coal, the 290-ton brig, *John and Hannah* had sunk the previous March on the Wexford side of the fairway, just off Broomhill. She entered the estuary (The 'estuary' was included in the catch-all description, 'Waterford Harbour'.) from the southwest, running before a WSW gale, and missed the pilot at Dunmore. Wary of the breakers nearer to Creadan Head on the west side of the estuary, the master of the *John and Hannah* kept too far east and ran up on a sandbar opposite the shore of Templetown, on the Wexford side.

The Waterford pilots, stationed at Dunmore, had been getting a lot of bad press that year. Just before Campbell arrived, the very large American ship, *Columbus*, came to grief at the Hook Tower and thirteen passengers and crew died. An inquest and an enquiry were held in the city and the pilots became the target of a lot of criticism. It was reported that the pilot boats failed to go out from Dunmore, to speak with or render aid to the vessel when it could clearly be seen in distress, attempting to tack back and forth in the estuary before she eventually went on the rocks.

It was low water and it was reckoned that there had been about a foot to spare between the keel of the *Hannah* and the seabed before she grounded. This might not have been so serious if the brig, when she grounded, hadn't fallen over, preventing her from getting off again. All the crew climbed into the rigging and were rescued by two pilot cutters. One of the pilots had been stationed at Dunmore and the other was sheltering under the well-known set of smugglers' steps near Creadan Head, on the west side of the estuary. The position of the wreck was reported as being

7 Even though there are some indications throughout Campbell's life that he had sailing experience, it remains unclear as to how he travelled around the country or, arrived at Duncannon with his gear. A service vessel seems to have been supplied by the Waterford Harbour Commissioners for his work there. A journey by steamer from Dublin to Waterford would not have been a problem in this instance.

three miles inside the Hook Tower, which is about halfway between the Hook and Duncannon.[8]

Rightly or wrongly but once again, pilot shortcomings were blamed for the loss of the vessel. The wreck became a nuisance and was either not worth raising or considered too difficult a task, when the commissioners decided to have it removed. An advert inviting tenders for the work was published in local newspapers. A number of tenders were received and after Gibbons' testimonial mentioned earlier, Campbell's was accepted. A competing tender had been received from the earlier owner of the wreck, Mr Aspinal. Master of the smack, *Mullet* of Duncannon, Mr Aspinal had sold the wreck where it lay and was now offering to remove it for £90! A feat of financial dexterity we now call a win-win.

William arrived on site in September and was soon being gawked at by curious on-lookers, crossing over from Dunmore on the opposite side of the estuary. Thrilled with their excursion, they reported that the water was so clear that they could see the diver walking around under the water, in his "brass helmet and India rubber apparel".

Finished his initial survey, Campbell told the Waterford Pilot Committee that a lot of the collier was still intact and would require a number of charges to complete the job.

After William's son was born, on 8 October, his father left the shores of Broomhill and Templetown for a brief period, to celebrate the birth and have a well-earned break.

News of Campbell's return and his operations spread and sightseers travelled downriver in the little steamer, *Duncannon*, for the "grand blow up". He placed three sealed containers (metal tanks) under the wreck, connected up his wires and galvanic batteries and from a safe distance, blew it up – half of it anyway. Bad weather and maybe the demands of his new son postponed the blowing up of the remainder.

As in other cases, Campbell's modus operandi was usually a lump sum and a rate per day. In keeping with this, the harbour provided him with a service vessel and all the equipment and labour he required. He received a £10 advance and £1.12s per day for at least three weeks.

He no sooner had the *Hannah* dispersed when he informed the harbour commissioners that there was another "very old wreck" lying inside of the *Hannah* at Broomhill. An ancient place, described by the journalists covering the story as "a tomb of many Capulets", a reference to a 'very old' wreck in this area, it is very interesting and we will come back to it.

---

8 A more detailed position appeared in the tender advert for the removal of this wreck.

Campbell was given the go ahead to blow up the very old wreck and was also contracted to blow up yet another wreck. This third wreck, the remains of the brig, *Emma*, which had lain sunk for a considerable time further up the river at Woodstown, would become the subject of litigation.

Campbell was reported to have used 400-600lbs of powder to disperse the *Emma*. The *Hannah*, probably blown up with a similar charge, erupted huge columns of water and "among other debris", delivered a multitude of concussed fish to the surface. It was rumoured later that everyone in the locale were sick of eating fish by the time Campbell left Duncannon.

Christmas passed and it became clear from the commissioners' reports that all was not well with the *Emma*. They were minded to inform Campbell of the distinction they had made between a contract to "blow up" and disperse the wreck and one of "removing" the wreck. The latter was clearly their intended requirement in the case of the *Hannah* but less clear in the case of the *Emma*. Devils lurk in detail and both parties knew that you could be there for a month of Sundays collecting all of the debris from a wooden collier that had been splintered into thousands of fragments with a large amount of explosive. An almost identical situation occurred ten years later when his son, James, was hired by the same Board to "blow up" – "remove" the wreck, *Spankaway*, lying in the river. Once again, the vultures in suits and wigs were dipping their quills.

William Campbell had received £50 for the *Hannah* job. No rate per day was offered and he supplied all the powder. It is unclear if this included work on the "very old wreck". His price for the *Emma* was £25.10s., the Board providing the powder on this occasion.

The Waterford Commissioners appeared to have come to the conclusion that they were somehow short-changed on the powder earlier and decided to provide the explosive themselves in this latter contract, and to have Campbell stick it under the wreck and light the fuse. It strikes me that the price, representing three day's work, was low and I wonder if Campbell had snuck his usual little rider in: price per day in the event of overrun.

The Board remained unsatisfied with the outcome of the *Emma* contract and wrote to him seeking completion of the removal of the wreck. Campbell sought an advance, in order to 'remove' the wreck the following spring. In March 1853, the commissioners duly reported that an advance of £10 had been forwarded to the marine diver, William Campbell, for the completion of work on the *Emma*.

Campbell may have pocketed the advance but his old acquaintance, the shipbuilder, Mr Teall in Dublin, had another job lined up for him. Teall had been contracted by the Dublin Ballast Board to raise the recently wrecked mail packet, *PS Queen Victoria* in Dublin Bay and by comparison, the £10 for collecting matchwood in the River Suir was probably hovering in the elevated pan of the scales.

In June, the Waterford Harbour Board was still waiting for Campbell to return and finish the job. To their credit and sense of public spirit, the minutes of the Waterford Harbour Commissioners were reported extensively in their local newspapers for many years and have provided great insight into the development of Waterford harbour.

Another interesting aside was also reported. Immediately below a report describing Campbell's blowing-up jobs in Waterford, another mentioned that the battery used to detonate the explosive charges was one invented by and described as the "Reverend Dr Callan's Preparations". It was also known widely as, the 'Maynooth Battery'. The article in question also reported that the "Office for the Protection of Priests" was collecting petition signatures (1,423) for the abolition of the Royal College of Maynooth, that college being where the good Dr Callan was supplementing his clerical duties with his work in the sciences (electricity in particular) and for which he was already highly regarded and become world famous.

The seminary college for the education of Catholic priests was under fire from "The Protestants of Ireland", at the time, calling for the repeal of government grants to the college and for it to be closed to "Maynooth-bred ecclesiastics". Good sense eventually prevailed and the college remains a functional seat of learning for the whole of Irish society, and beyond its national borders, to this day.

Catholics in Ireland were recovering from so many years of repression, and the Repeal Bill was thrown out. One wonders nevertheless, just how invidious and to what extent were anti-Catholic policies prevalent in civil governance and the professional classes at the time?

That "Very Old Wreck"

Returning to the reports of a "very old wreck" in the Waterford estuary, we must take into account who it was that originally used this phrase. There is legislation in Ireland (and in many other countries) that considers a wreck of 100 years or more as being historically 'old' and worthy of protection. To use the phrase today, a 'very old wreck' would certainly be considered to be more than one hundred years old and probably more than two hundred years. For a diver of Campbell's reputation and intelligence, to report that there was a very old wreck "nearby" was significant, especially if you consider that it had not previously been reported as an obstruction. For Campbell to say that it was 'old', then this might mean 18th century. For him to consider that it was 'very old' would suggest 17th century or earlier.

During the siege of Waterford by Cromwellian forces in 1645, a number of ships were in the estuary attempting to land. They were repelled on this particular occasion and one of Cromwell's large ships – his flagship, the *Great Lewis* – suffered some damage. She sank between Duncannon Fort and Creadan Head in January, on the higher side of the estuary, just to the north of Dunmore. There were few survivors.

Among the Waterford Harbour Commissioners' responsibilities is one to keep the navigable channel to Waterford Port clear. In order to do this, dredgers are constantly employed, removing deposits of silt and obstructions. The dredger, *Lesse*, employed in 1999-2001 – as per Kevin Downes in *The Great Lewis and the Siege of Duncannon, 1645* – clipped an obstruction on the edge of the channel and managed to raise some timbers to the surface. A diving team from the heritage authorities, Dúchas arrived and confirmed that it was indeed, a very old wreck. An extensive video and archaeology survey was completed (which included a visit by the television series, *Wreck Detectives*) and arrived at an opinion as to the identity of the wreck. Given the armaments, timbers and items that were visible and examined in situ, the wreck was determined as being from the 17th century and probably the wreck of the *Great Lewis*.

So the question arises. Is this the same wreck, 'the very old wreck' that Campbell put the charge under in 1852? The very thought of such a thing, would shiver the archaeologists' timbers, who consider that 'the historical and archaeological value of this site cannot be over-estimated' and quite rightly so. For the time being, readers will have to judge whether the location of wrecks indicated on the chart[9] might be the important archaeological site that Campbell, with some assistance from the Reverend Callan, put his explosives under. Perhaps upcoming surveys by INFOMAR and Dúchas will reveal more details and the identity of these shipwrecks.

There may be some other 'very old wrecks' in the frame, such as *The Pretenders*, the name suggesting something similar or, maybe the same wreck. Or the 'unknown' French East Indiaman from c.1758. Another 'unknown', a 'bomb vessel' from which a number of items were reported to have been retrieved earlier, may also be a possibility. Dr Connie Kelleher from the Underwater Archaeological team of Dúchas has excavated and

---

9 See page 72.

studied this shipwreck and is doubtful about which shipwreck Campbell might have been referring to.[10]

---

10 Some readers may agree with critics of the Dunmore pilots, after they failed the *Columbus* in January 1852. After so much money had been spent upgrading Dunmore East Harbour, it was regrettable that they were still unable to provide adequate pilotage to visiting or distressed vessels in all weathers. It must be remembered however, that although this southern part of the estuary is very wide and navigable at nearly all stages of the tide, this is not the case from Creadan Head northward. The estuary still appears to be very wide but the all-tide navigable channel is quite narrow and shoals dangerously shallow quite quickly on both sides. The pilot boats were relatively small, sail-only boats and their claim that they could not get away safely is probably well founded. The estuary is sheltered from a westerly wind but from southwest right around through south to northwest, it remains much exposed to weather over low lying land and totally exposed to open sea to the south. During *Columbus's* battle with the elements, the wind blew, WSW, and also from the south.

Chapter 4

Up to Dublin and Back to Wexford, 1853-1860

Campbell returned to Dublin in the beginning of 1853 and began diving at the wreck of the paddle steamer, *Queen Victoria*, which sank in Dublin Bay. Mr Teall, the shipbuilder in Ringsend, was appointed Superintendent of the wreck and operations to raise it for the Dublin Ballast Board.[1]

Seemingly on foot of his earlier relationship with Mr Teall, William Campbell was hired as the diver to attend the wreck of the *Queen Victoria* and may have worked with another diver(s) not mentioned by name. Despite a number of vessels put at their disposal and all the gear they needed, they found diving at the Baily challenging, what with overfalls, unusual tidal anomalies, strong currents and being dangerously exposed to winds while close to shore. After a number of attempts to raise the sunken packet, the project failed.

Some of the cargo and personal belongings were recovered from the wreck. The ship's silver plate was recovered by Campbell before the wreck was finally abandoned for good. Diving can still be difficult there but for curious sport divers, well worth the effort. The newspapers gave a running commentary on the inquests and subsequent inquiry on the loss of the *Queen Victoria*, elevating Campbell into the limelight, becoming "The Celebrated Diver", for a while anyway.

Later in 1853, William Campbell was put to work preparing the seabed just east of the watering wharf that served steamers situated in the south-west corner of Kingstown Harbour, opposite the Royal Saint George Yacht Club. The Board of Works had been petitioned by the Dublin Steam Packet Company to improve the berthing facilities for existing and future design of mail boats, and Barry Gibbons was tasked with the design and construction of a new pier to facilitate these requirements.[2]

After work had commenced, Gibbons' design and method of construction were contested very publicly by his peers. Construction had already begun

---

1   As the steamer, *Queen Victoria* is mentioned elsewhere in this book and extensively in *Between the Tides*, I will confine remarks to items of the incident not covered before and repeat just a few others that are pertinent to this story.

2   It may be recalled that Thomas Steele claimed to have been shown these plans by the engineer, Barry Gibbons as far back as 1845.

but after objections were raised by a number of important figures, it had to be suspended. The Board of Public Works hired Mr James Rendell to produce a report on the existing proposal, and on any alternative one he might consider to be more suitable than Gibbons'. A number of professionals were heard, including the harbour master, William Hutchison who, having initially expressed reservations for Gibbons' proposal, could not agree with alternatives suggested either. After protracted delay and two serious counterproposals, the Admiralty got the hump and commissioned Captains Frazer and Kellet for an opinion. Gibbons' proposal got the thumbs up.

During its construction and even for a time after it was completed in 1859, the pier was affectionately known as "Gibbons' Pier" and maybe someday, the man's name might return to the pier. Given the ease with which the names of public officials can appear on bridges and roads today, a fitting and lasting memory to this great Public Works engineer is a long time overdue. However, with many administrative buildings and roads in Kingstown named after monarchs, lords, and great military figures of the Empire, a pier in the Great Royal Harbour with a name like Gibbons, and a Catholic moreover, wasn't going anywhere – Repeal or no Repeal. The Lord Lieutenant of Ireland was placed in the centre of the Royal Harbour when they named it, the Carlisle Pier.

One of Rendel's main objections to Gibbons' design was its length and suitability for the growing length of steamers. It may have been a genuine concern but the proof of the pudding is that, even well after it was completed, it continued to handle all kinds of steamers, that just got bigger and bigger and the same pier handles cruise ships to this day. As it has proved, the pier and its size are directly related to the depth of water in the harbour. It could not and still cannot handle very large vessels.

Concealing the beautiful stonework beneath, a horrible mantle of concrete was subsequently perched on top of the pier in later years. The Victorian ironwork has been removed and everything above the deck has been removed but it is still a pier. The mail boats are gone but beneath the gaudy and rusting iron and concrete overhanging add-ons, the remarkable cut-stone structure remains. The splendour of this example of Victorian masonry is partially concealed in the shadows now but it only rests, waiting for its next debut. The Carlisle Pier is 'vacant' and the space has become one of the most sought-after pieces of sea frontage on the Irish coast.

A Return to the Southeast and The Lings

Campbell visited Ballycotton again towards the end of 1853, to assess complaints about the state of the pier. Not having been originally constructed to the recommended design, Campbell was having a time of it with complaints from local people, who claimed that there was no use "tinkering and patching a bad design and worse execution". The wall had sunk and in bad weather, the sea was coming over the walls and smashing boats, reducing some fishermen to sinking their boats in the harbour to save them. The pier had deteriorated to the point that a public enquiry was being demanded.

Campbell returned again in March 1854 and between his work there and another repair job at Ballinacourty, County Waterford, he was able to finish up substantial repairs to the pier at Ballycotton in August. The Board of Public Works handed it over to the county for a bill of £1,700 – and I'm sure they were glad to take what they could get for it.

1854 would prove to be another busy year for Campbell and his son, James. A contract early that year involved construction and repair works at Ballinacourty Pier, or Wyse's Pier as it is known today. Situated on the east side of the entrance to Dungarvan, County Waterford, Wyse's Point and its diminutive pier face southwest into the broad expanse of the partially sheltered bay. It is, nevertheless, also somewhat exposed to wave and wind from the SSE.

There is little correspondence on file that explains the extent of Campbell's involvement at Ballinacourty and, one might expect his input to have been similar to previous contractual operations on these piers: blasting rock for foundations and laying the first course of stone blocks. A little digging however, revealed that Gibbons had sent Campbell to Ballinacourty to complete and oversee repairs to an existing pier – another that had been badly built twenty years previous.

After being first mooted and consulted by the engineer, Nimmo in 1824 and the land at Wyse's Point donated by Sir Thomas Wyse, a contract was awarded to David Power of Cork to erect a modest pier on the east side of Dungarvan Bay, for landing fish and manure. Wyse was an MP and ambassador to Greece and Italy with a colourful history and best known in Ireland as a great pioneer of education and Catholic emancipation. Hidden away in the dusty files of the National Archives in Dublin are some beautiful watercolour pen-and-ink sketches of the intended pier, just screaming out for an appreciative wall to hang on. In fact, there are quite a number of similar beautiful works in OPW files that could easily populate a 'collection of civil art'.

No longer remote of course but once these out of the way bays and piers Campbell travelled to were much more than that overused adjective, 'beautiful' suggests. Often missed by travellers confined to main routes, they were rarely visited by anyone but fishermen and often well sheltered from the wind and the extremes of weather. They were silent and calm places, where the sun sets on still waters and midges dance in the still air of a summer evening. Heavily weeded in the shallows, they produce that special 'sea smell' and a sense of peace, broken only by the sounds of fussy seabirds and echoes of the wooden thump from the fishermen's oars. Ballinacourty Bay was once like that and its charming old lighthouse and the bay beyond are still like that and, whether or not it meant something special to William or Mary Campbell (which, I suspect, it did) they both loved this part of Ireland.

Of the very few registered 'Charles' in Ireland at this time, James Charles, Mary's father's name, is one that is recorded in this staunchly Catholic area. He married Mary Murphy in 1820, at "Stradbally with Clonea and Ballanheen."

Ballinacourty Pier got off to a flying start with the help of Mr Wyse, the Fisheries Board and the Commissioners for Public Works. Sadly, Mr Power died in 1829 and the contract had to go to tender once more. Two brothers, Alexander and Jervis Deane from Cork, a well-known family of architects and engineers, won the contract and work on constructing the pier recommenced in 1832.

Everything seemed to have been wrong with this pier. The design was inadequate, the stone used was not correct, supervision was lax and so on. The Public Works engineer, Mr Gibbons, working at Dunmore East at the time, became involved, after the brothers began to look for money for work on a pier that he did not believe came up to scratch. After the to'ing and fro'ing, claims and counterclaims, the brothers were paid off in 1834 but Gibbons insisted on short payment for extras he did not believe were warranted. Freemen of Cork, financial difficulties caught up on the brothers and they were declared bankrupt the following year – and not for the paltry price of a diving suit, as in Mr Campbell's case.

After a very short period for a new construction, in 1843 the chickens came home to roost. The weather and the sands of Dungarvan began to claim the infill of the pier, badly laid on poor footings.

In 1846, the Wyse estate entered into further agreement with the Commissioners of Public Works and their engineer, Barry Gibbons and donated additional land for an extension and repair to the existing pier. Today, the pier is just a fair-weather jetty, with a charming but boarded up old lifeboat house. It is a place for summer activity and, sadly, once more it is showing signs of neglect.

Campbell rectified the faulty aspects of the earlier construction and added a small extension. When he finished at Wyse's Pier and Ballinacourty,

Gibbons arranged for him to return to the neighbouring county, Wexford. The new quay at Kilmore, more commonly called Kilmore Quay today, had been completed but further rock blasting was required to provide safe entry and berthing for boats at low water.

The pier grant and other moneys were all spent but the job was not fully complete. Maher had attempted to remove the last rocks that were obstructing a clear passage to the quay but without a diver and specialised equipment, he could only get down to the level of the lowest spring tide. Not to "spoil the ship for a ha'worth of tar", Gibbons arranged for his old stomping ground to get a further leg up, in the form of a maintenance grant and sent Campbell and his son, James to remove the final obstructions. William and son, James commenced work on the pier at Kilmore Quay in August 1854 and their arrival was heralded in the 8 August edition of the *Wexford Independent*.

Collectively known as "The Lings", the offending group of large rocks, situated just outside of the entrance to the harbour, were individually known as The Great Ling and The Big Shane and were the scourge of Kilmore fishermen. When returning to harbour in poor visibility, losing sight of their land transits, there was a temptation to head straight for the pier, many striking the rocks during anxious moments attempting to make an entry.

Known to favour rocky ground, the name reflects the fish called ling, once caught in abundance there. A species almost like an eel in appearance, it has a lovely cod like texture. They were caught in large quantities seasonally, dried and salted, packed in barrels and shipped down to parts of western Europe – still a popular destination for Kilmore's catch but few ling these days. How Big Shane got its name remains a mystery.

The Lings remained above the surface after high water and consisted of substantial amounts of large boulders roundabouts and with several metres below the surface. Some of the rocks were enormous and if the article below can be believed, individually weighing as much as 70 tons. Campbell's method in removing them are best described in this part of the article, penned by "A Constant Reader and a Real Friend of Progress", in the *Wexford Independent*, 30 August 1854.

> *"... the rocks had previously been bored and at one o'clock, Mr. Campbell (better known by the name, "The Talented Diver") proceeded to apply the charge, to me a most interesting proceeding. The fuse being ignited[3] we took our departure to a civil distance and almost immediately, a grand explosion took place.*

3   The reader will notice that a battery was not mentioned on this occasion.

> *We then went to see the results and to my astonishment, this huge mass of rock was divided into four quarters, as even as one would cut a griddle cake. … Mr Campbell and his son have removed the most dangerous obstacles to the entrance to the pier, as far as regards to the fishing boats…"*

It is difficult to determine who the "Friend of Progress" actually was but he was rowed around the harbour by Campbell and shown all the other rocks that could do with blowing up. Given the suggested commentary by both Campbell and the author, and that the pier would benefit from a dog-leg extension and breakwater, you might be tempted to conclude that he was also a friend of Campbell. Well, he may very well have been and he also might have been the earlier press contributor, J.T.C. – John Thomas Campion mentioned earlier.

Still in view of the Wooden House, the pier did get a dog-leg extension, an additional breakwater and supported by Irish and European funds, a marina and many other improvements since, making it another fine harbour for fishing and pleasure vessels.

The Campbells seem to have stayed on for another month or so and carried out some additional tidying up at and below the water line of the new pier – and whilst so engaged, a remarkable phenomenon occurred. An account of the event is given in *Between the Tides* but for continuity and context, some extracts from the Wexford newspapers in September and October, relating to Campbell's account of the incident, are worth repeating here.

Extraordinary Phenomenon

> *"… I was in one of our boats, seeking after some implements and not looking seawards when, of a sudden, I heard a mighty rush of water against the back of the pier and in a moment, it came sweeping around the pier, head full three feet high and abreast. It was within one half an hour of low water at the time. The inner dock was crowded with the small sailing craft of the place and quite dry, the tide being four hours on the ebb. In less than five minutes every boat was afloat and we had high water. In five minutes more, the water ebbed again to the lowest spring tides. This was repeated seven times in the course of two hours and a half. St Patrick's Bridge was alternatively dry and covered to the extent of a mile and the sea formed a cascade from end to end of it. The influx appearing to come from the east … the current was running at the rate of ten or twelve miles per hour. … Had the occurrence taken place at the period of high water, the result*

would have been the complete overflow of the land in the district and consequent immense loss. We have often heard old people of the place say that on a Sunday, after Lisbon was destroyed by the earthquake of 1st November, 1755, the day being remarkably fine, the sea at Kilmore suddenly rose and fell in like manner. ... The phenomena are not unknown on the Waterford coast and are known as 'death waves'."

Campbell and the locals were spot on.[4]

The disturbance, an earthquake, had taken place off the south of Wales and caused the "phenomenon". And similar to the effects of the Lisbon earthquake that occurred one hundred years earlier, it too was the cause of a tsunami that ran along the south coast of Ireland.

It was while diving on one of Campbell's old stomping grounds – the wreck of the *Queen Victoria* in Dublin Bay – in 1984 that a couple of divers and myself experienced a very similar phenomenon, caused by a similar earthquake emanating from the same area off Wales. Not a pleasant experience and lot of cleaning up in the boat afterwards. This area of the British Isles remains well known for such occurrences and the coincidence has remained a striking event in my memory.

Underwater operations had not stood still in Kingstown during Campbell's absence. About the same time that Campbell was working in Kilmore, the Harbour Master at Kingstown, William Hutchison, invited another diver to Kingstown. It is unclear if he had run his intentions by his own commissioners first or, any other Public Works' official, the latter being clearly established 'in charge' at Kingstown and having overall responsibility for the harbour at the time.[5]

An incident occurred in December of 1853, after the schooner, *Victoria* berthed in Kingstown to avoid a storm and came to grief. A number of other ships had also run for refuge into Kingstown. Unfortunately, the

---

4 With some qualification, scientist now report that this earthquake occurred on 15 September. Campbell reported that, its effects at least, were felt on 16 September.

5 William Hutchison was a retired lieutenant in the Royal Navy, on half pay before he took up the position of Harbour Master at Old Dunleary in 1817. He assumed the position of Harbour Master of the Royal George Harbour at Kingstown in 1823. Reporting him as 'Lieutenant' led to confusion at times, as his son was also addressed as "Lieutenant William". Further complication was also added when William senior was sometimes also addressed as "Captain". The Board of Public Works referred to the harbour master, William Hutchison, as "Lieutenant" in all of their correspondence with him.

Victoria sank after she was struck by the brig, *William*, while entering the harbour. A case arrived at the steps of the Admiralty Court and the owner-master of the *Victoria*, William Raymond, won the first round of the legal joust. Revealed at the hearing was the fact that the *Victoria* was not showing any lights while at anchor. The owner-master of the *William*, John Richardson, detecting a bit of wriggle room, appealed. Despite the fact that the *Victoria* was at anchor, unmanned and not moving anywhere, Justices Crampton and Perrin found its master partly responsible. They reduced the original award of £1,367 by half and ordered no costs.

Appointed that year as Government Surveyor of Emigrant Vessels, our old friend, Mr Teall was contracted to raise and move the wreck into the old harbour. Teall apparently could not rely on Mr Campbell on this occasion, as he was in his beloved Wexford at the time. Neither is it believed that Mr Teall hired the diver, William Moses, who had been summoned to Kingstown to work on another wreck in the harbour at this time.

William Campbell, an experienced diver under contract by Barry Gibbons for Public Works, had been sent to Kilmore to blow up and remove submerged rocks at Kilmore Quay and no apparent attempt had been made by the harbour master before, during or after the *Queen Victoria* operations, to tackle the wreck of the *Argyle* that had lain wrecked for some time against the lighthouse, on the inside of the east pier at Kingstown.

Hutchison was having a free hand at the time in this respect and, despite instructions from the Board to have the sunken schooner raised, he delayed. Obviously, Campbell was contracted by Public Works to work in the harbour and wherever else they chose to send him. As Campbell could not possibly contract to do all of the available work about the place, it nevertheless seemed a little pointed to hire a contractor and diver from the south of England and invite them to do the very work that the harbour's own usual contractor was already performing, just when he happened to be elsewhere.

The schooner, *Argyle* had been anchored in Kingstown during the winter gales of 1852/3. Her moorings were snagged and broken by another vessel and she was wrecked near the lighthouse, against the east pier of Kingstown Harbour. Tenders from various parties were submitted to the Board for the raising and salvage of the wreck but Hutchison was slow to proceed with the work. A tender from the diver, Benjamin Harris for £60 was accepted in principle by the Board and despite notifying Mr Hutchison on how he should proceed with the work and charges, Mr Harris did not get the go ahead. It took another year of correspondence and procrastination before William Hutchison arranged for the demolition and dispersal of the *Argyle*, where she lay against the end and inside of the east pier, in July 1854.

Within a harbour master's authority but seemingly unusual to reject the advice of the senior Board of Works engineer, Mr Hornsby, Hutchison contracted with Captain Abbinett of Gosport, to blow up the wreck. Abbinett, a celebrated diver himself, one of a well-known family of salvage divers (father and two sons), took the diver William Moses with him to Kingstown to do the job. After several attempts and over 400lbs of explosives, they succeeded in demolishing it but not before causing considerable damage to the pier. Described, as being like an "earthquake" that was felt all along the pier, it created a twenty-yard long "chasm" in the structure.

Board of Public Works were apparently livid when they ordered a halt to the work. It was quickly announced that the harbour's chief engineer's permission had to be sought before any further charge could be placed. Gibbons was the engineer responsible but had been away when Hornsby stepped in and Mr Atwood was the works superintendent. It is unclear whose permission was sought, if any, but the next explosion saw more red-faces and an even larger chasm in the pier wall. It is highly unlikely that they had asked Gibbons.[6]

Campbell was by no means overpaid while a contractor and often quoted prices well below his counterparts in the same game. Unlike much of the opposition though, he was a 'one-stop' operation, capable of performing several tasks, mitigating the need for additional contractors. A man with many talents, this is where his 'per day' price paid off. Hiring Campbell was really a win-win for both himself and Barry Gibbons.

On Barry Gibbons' recommendation, William Campbell replaced Mr Atwood as Superintendent of Works at Kingstown two years later – a significant post with attractive opportunities.

Campbell returned to Dublin later that year and a second son was born to the couple on 30 December 30. His name was Charles James.[7]

Possibly with a view to beginning his career in Public Works, William's son, James, at eighteen years of age, accompanied Barry Gibbons to Donaghadee in 1856, to survey the ongoing harbour works. The excursion

6   The allocation of ship's names, referred to further on, reflects many things. A method of identifying and differentiating vessels, a reflection of their owners' likes and allegiances, and today, pretty much the same but much more 'faddy'. During this period, it was saints and Queen Victoria. Within the space of a couple of months, there were three schooner-type vessels lost at Portrane, Dalkey and Kingstown with the name, *Victoria*. The naming of racehorses provides somewhat similar curiosity.

7   Details of Charles's actual place of birth and baptism are unknown. There is a belief, amongst descendants, that Charles may also have been born in Wexford.

proved positive and James was later hired to work on the harbour at Donaghadee. He was despatched, with diving bell and equipment, by steamer to Belfast in August 1858, to carry out repairs and to increase the overall depth of the harbour.

In his later position as Superintendent of Works at Kingstown and by arrangement with Gibbons, William purchased two new diving dresses and an air pump for the project. William supervised the inspection and loading of all the gear on the steamer before his son left.

Even though James appears to have been hired as a temporary contractor by Public Works on his own account, his father, William, wangled it so that he too went to Donaghadee and worked alongside James for several months before returning to Kingstown – giving him a 'leg up', so to speak. Unfortunately, records concerning James at Donaghadee are wanting and although "divers" are mentioned in official correspondence, no specific naming of young James thereafter appears in the actual records.

In addition, James Campbell was reported to have accompanied Barry Gibbons in the winter/spring of 1858-1859 to Waterford Harbour, where they examined shoals in the estuary and surveyed the riverbed for a suitable graving slip, by boring. This visit and James' introduction to the Waterford Harbour Commissioners by Gibbons may have influenced their choice of contractor the following year, when they recommended James for the dispersal of wrecks in the harbour.

OPW hard-hat divers in Donegal, early 1900s. Courtesy of the National Archives, Dublin.

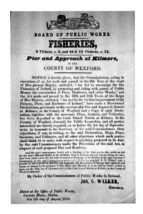

A notice of intent by the Board of Public Works, to build a new pier at Kilmore in 1848. Image from Board of Public Works archives at the National Archives, Dublin.

PRESENTED
TO
Mrs. Grogan Morgan,
OF
JOHNSTOWN CASTLE,
BY THE
KILMORE PIER COMMITTEE.
SAMUEL GREEN, Esq., J.P., Chairman,
Rev. RICHARD KING, Clk., } Deputation.
Rev. JAMES WALSH, P.P., }
Rev. P. MAYLER, Secretary,
With grateful thanks for the
Honor conferred on them,
By Her Laying the First Stone.
MAY 8, 1849.

First stone laying ceremony at construction at Kilmore (Quay) pier in 1849. William Campbell made a number of professional visits during construction of the harbour. Blasting wrecks, rocks and laying foundation blocks. News item from *Wexford Independent*.

Kilmore quay pier today. Original construction with overlay of cement. The Wooden House Inn is beside new houses construction in top, right-hand corner. (Holiday houses extension to Wooden House). Author's collection.

Cannons discovered in the Waterford Estuary, 1999. The guns are believed to be on the wreck of the *Great Lewis*, flagship in Cromwell's invasion fleet of 1645. Image courtesy of archaeologist, Connie Kelleher and staff at the Department of Arts, Culture, Heritage and the Gaeltacht.

The site of this wreck (see chart) is where William Campbell was dispersing shipwrecks for the Waterford Harbour Authorities in 1852, which included one "very old wreck".

Wyse's Pier at Ballinacourty, County Waterford by Wyse in 1832. Author's collection.

Later upgraded by William Campbell in 1854. Author's collection.

William and Mary Campbell

Photograph of William and his second wife, Mary (née Charles) Campbell. Despite being stamped "Adelaide", the photograph is believed to have been taken in Dublin prior to their departure for Australia in 1864. There are indications that Mary Charles and father, James may have been from the Waterford Estuary area, Duncannon as her first son, William, named his farm in Australia *Wexford*. Courtesy of Trevor Dowling.

Chapter 5

The Lords of the Committee of Privy Council for Trade authorised the Master Mariner, Thomas Crosby, to issue Mr Richard Brickley his certificate of competency, his Master's Ticket, on 7 April 1860 at Dublin. It is also recorded that one Richard Brickley of Port Leaven, Cornwall, received his "only mate" ticket at Dublin on 6 December of the same year. This later entry records his date of birth as 25 February 1840. The issuing ticket number is also different. The entries are confusing and it is unknown if these two awards refer to the same person. The "only mate" certificate also means a master's certificate. The muddle presented by these reports and official entries was only the beginning.

Richard Brickley was born in County Down in 1822 and was living adjacent to Kingstown at the time he received his ticket. Brickley was married and lived in the village of Glasthule with two young children: a son, Richard and a daughter, Anastasia both baptised at Kingstown's Catholic church, Saint Michael's. The church stands high over the harbour, an elevated site at the junction of Sussex Parade and the main thoroughfare of George's Street.

Glasthule is a small coastal enclave that nestled amongst a speckling of granite quarries, about a mile equidistant from Kingstown and the coastal village of Dalkey and was considered a predominantly Catholic area. It fronted to the seashore with a number of well-to-do 'villas' and fishermen's cottages and some fine houses on the rising slopes landward. These climbed with prestige as they elevated and reached the surrounding heights of Dalkey, Killiney and Glenageary.

Before the construction of Kingstown Harbour got into full swing, this area consisted of modest cottages and some huts occupied by local fishermen. By the time the trains, steamships and all the fashionable business fraternity had arrived, the local fishermen had been joined by migrating contractors to the industry that was 'the harbour' and established themselves around the place. The Royal Harbour required enormous quantities of stone rubble and cut granite, and many of the fishermen also took on the work of quarrying it, to replace or supplement their existing livelihood.

The rock was quarried locally, almost everywhere, including along the seashore. One can still see the unfinished remains of partially worked stone along the seashore, the steps and the stone landing places put in place to facilitate rafts and flat bottom barges to carry away the large pieces of cut stone. The clearance was another case of win-win. In the first instance, it provided the stone for the construction of the new harbour and other civic buildings, and also cleared the coastline for many of the beautiful 'villas' that were built afterwards. I daresay, very few fishermen were able to produce any title to their meagre dwellings and shore-side huts and were ultimately moved on.

Fish and fishing in Dublin Bay were both bountiful and rewarding. There was a large variety of fish species that could be caught inshore and a plentiful supply of crustaceans and shellfish from the bays and rocky inlets, stretching from Merrion Strand to Dalkey. A number of famous eating houses sprung up around the bay that established significant reputations serving seafood, such as the 'Conniving House' in Sandymount.

Amongst the coastal villas looking out to sea was 'Bellmarino (Bellamarine) Cottage', situated close to the boundary of Sandycove a few hundred yards from the centre of Glasthule Village. Richard Brickley lived there with his family for some time. The house proper, *Bellmarino,* was situated on the east side of the property, on the seashore and to the rear, fronting on to the Glasthule Road. There were two cottages.

Creating utter confusion in attempting to keep a bead on Richard Brickley during research, he was sometimes referred to as *Richard Brinkley* and even *Bringly*. Quite surprisingly, a man with a similar sounding name, William Brinkley, was also listed at the same address, seemingly in the other cottage. As Richard was to become something of a celebrity himself, the press, either by design or mistake, or acting on false information, constantly confused the two men, or their names at least, until Richard and his children emigrated to Liverpool. After his departure, Richard did not become a stranger to Dublin and kept a foot in both cities for many years to come. As many cross-channel sailors were known to have done, for one reason or another.

William Brinkley, often listed as mariner or sea captain, was a coxswain of the Dublin Port Authority lifeboat, originally based nearer to his own accommodation at "Bellamarine" – i.e. near to the lifeboat house in Sandycove but moved later to Kingstown Harbour. He was retired on a pension in 1862, after the Royal National Lifeboat Institution (RNLI) took over the running of the lifeboats in Dublin Bay. Brinkley is listed at several other addresses, including at a small cottage ('Harbour Cottage') in the Kingstown Harbour complex of the publicly owned buildings at Quay Road. Brinkley was coxswain of the Kingstown lifeboat provided by the Ballast

Board but, whilst employed as such, he obviously wasn't always at sea, saving lives!

As the harbour master, Lieutenant Hutchison ran the marine show at Kingstown Harbour, an appointment made by the Lord Lieutenant and administered through the Ballast Board at first. (Hutchison's tenure is addressed further on.). Brinkley was sometimes cited as his 'coxswain'. The fact was that he and Hutchison operated the lifeboat when required but Brinkley was otherwise a 'boatman' under Hutchison. Brinkley rowed the harbour master around his harbour and ran various errands: issuing berthing instructions and making various checks on visiting ships in the harbour. And it must be said that both men jumped into the lifeboat, without a moment's hesitation, on numerous occasions to rescue sailors in peril.[1]

After obtaining his ticket, Captain Richard Brickley seems to have moved to nearby 23 Corrig Avenue for a short time. The avenue is a long spinal road running down from the heights of Glenageary to Kingstown. Maybe his improved status warranted the move; whether it had anything to do with the Catholic association of his old address might be considered further on. Although the two men, Brinkley and Brickley, appear to have been Catholic, no birth connection has been established between them. The reason for explaining the confusion that is presented between the pair will unfold soon after the Campbells became acquainted with Richard and/or William.

The 1860s were the 'heyday' of the Kingstown Regattas. In the high summer months, the prestigious yacht clubs, Royal George and Royal Irish, would alternatively sponsor a series of yacht races in the bay and an ocean race, which included sister clubs like the Western and the other Royal in Cork, as well as rowing races at Kingstown. Visiting and competing yachts came from all over Britain and Ireland, and further abroad, including the famous *Royal Squadron* at Cowes.

The history of 'Royal' yacht clubs in Ireland is turbulent: flags, crowns, ensigns and seemingly highly politicised. This author and possibly some

---

1   The pair are recorded together when they ran Ireland's earliest lifeboat at Sandycove. William Hutchison, twenty-four in 1817, was Harbour Master of Old Dunleary Harbour, with a house at Bullock. This was probably one of the small 'Pilot Cottages' on the southern side of the harbour, a couple of which remain today. Along with lifeboat duties from Sandycove, he also supervised shipments of stone that were being recovered from a number of areas on the foreshore and from local quarries. Hutchison lived at Bullock with four children for a number of years, before he was appointed to the position of Harbour Master of New Dunleary – the Royal Harbour of Kingstown.

readers may well be forgiven for not being able to fully comprehend the 'big picture' of this particular sport at this time.

The races were hotly contested each year and the results gave the rich gentlemen good cause to order bigger and faster boats to be built, in order that they might 'get one up' the following year. Designs and sizes were improving and escalating annually, in every respect, culminating in some of the largest, swiftest and most expensive yachts ever seen. Needless to say, such yachts needed lots of crew and professional masters to complement the big spend, in order to sweat the maximum performance from these magnificent specimens.

This was the world in which Richard Brickley moved and, by all accounts, one which he seems to have relished. He does not seem to have owned a boat himself but he did become an accomplished ship's captain, sailing yachts, sail and steam at first and deep-sea steamers to follow. There is little doubt that Richard Brickley was a kind of 'man's man' and was well liked amongst the wealthy yacht owners. He did, however, demonstrate an early trait for what seemed to be a high-handed approach to those 'under' him and maybe because of it, gaining the respect of his wealthy masters.

Mentioning the competitive boat owner and their crews, Richard first came to the attention of the public in the reports of sail races and regatta performances.

After he got his Master's Ticket in 1860, Brickley took command of the wealthy landowner, George Powell Houghton's yacht, *Leonara*. The yacht was a 116-ton schooner, a fine example of marine craftsmanship and the type of vessel making Kingstown the most popular venue in the world for yacht racing at the time. It was July 1860 and the *Leonara* had just returned with a party of celebrated guests from a cruise in Norway. Damage had been done to the bottom of the boat after striking rocks and she put in to Belfast for repairs. Admired by yachtsmen and journalists, she was considered to have been the best-looking vessel to have docked there. Some of the crew were left to travel on, without the boat, from Belfast to Dublin.

When Richard Brickley (reported as Brinkley) returned to Kingstown, a crew member from the *Leonara*, John Dumphy along with two others, were unable to get satisfaction from him during the course of claiming their wages for the voyage. After Brickley abused and assaulted the sailors, they brought the case before the court. Richard was found at fault, and fined one shilling, with one-shilling costs, for the assault. There was no mention of wages being paid.

George Powell Houghton's only son, also George, was injured in the Charge of the Light Brigade and was invalided to the hospital at Scutari,

Istanbul where the young lieutenant was put under the care of Florence Nightingale. He died from his head wounds in 1854. Broken hearted for the remainder of her life, his mother, Anne Coote, died in 1859. And they said that Houghton himself never fully recovered from the double tragedy before his own death.

George put his considerable estate at Kilmannock, County Wexford up for sale and threw himself into yacht racing and cruising. He owned three magnificent and very large yachts: *Countess*, *Leonara* (116 tons) and *Red Gauntlet* (150 tons) with some interest in the yacht, *Amphitrite* (53 tons). *Leonara* and *Red Gauntlet* were built at the famous yard, Innmans of Lymington. His three daughters would marry in quick succession before he relinquished ownership in his last yacht, *Red Gauntlet*.[2]

It was reported that Richard Brickley also sailed in the yachts, *Maraquita* and *Water Kelpie* for their owner, Captain Henry.[3]

Two prominent men would pass away in 1862 and cast adrift two other men who had been closely associated with them. Though they were from very different backgrounds, to some degree, they had come to rely on one another. Neither of the four were blood relatives or professionally connected but, probably all knew of each other. The two who lived on were then thrown together in unlikely circumstances and their meeting would alter the course of their lives.

I believe that it is no exaggeration to state that the harbour master, Lieutenant William Hutchison, ran a 'tight ship' around his harbour. It was, after all, his responsibility to maintain the safe flow of vessels in and out of a very large harbour – a demanding responsibility. Originally mooted as a harbour of safe refuge, it quickly became a harbour of some commercial interest and a postal and passenger packet station. What made Kingstown Harbour different was that it had also become a very popular public amenity. And this remarkable enterprise in the history of Public Works has become even more popular today.

---

2   The sale of Houghton's estate, Kilmannock, was put in the hands of one, M.W. Knox, while still the land agent for Lord Templemore and residing at *Glendine*, Arthurstown but instead of selling the estate, Mr Knox bought it, moved in and moved on after things got a bit hot around Arthurstown. This followed the fallout from a prominent scandal. No stranger to controversy, this particular one was created by the actions of his wife, Bessy with the Bird's Nest in Kingstown. Details are further on.

3   Some of these beautiful and well-known yachts, from England and Ireland, found their way into yacht clubs all over the world, including Australia. Having finished their racing career, some were put trading in the South Sea Islands.

One needed all kinds of interpersonal skills to perform the day-to-day, smooth operation of such a harbour – keeping everybody happy. Times were also changing for Mr Hutchison and he would experience a run of bad luck in his endeavours, which at a casual glance, might seem to have tarnished his impeccable career somewhat.

His misfortunes probably began in June 1860, when word got out (and was wrongly interpreted, as it would transpire) that a licence to sell beer and liquor to 3rd class passengers at the refreshment rooms in the railway terminus at Kingstown, had been applied for. The existing lessee, Mr Polson, apparently happy to serve alcohol to 1st class passengers without any objectors, took umbrage when the harbour master, William Hutchison, expressed his objection to the application by writing a terse letter to *Saunders Newsletter*. In a reply, the lessee, Mr Richard Polson, objected to the tone and inaccuracy of Mr Hutchison's claim, stating that the article was libellous and sought a retraction and a reply. Polson maintained that there was no third-class room now and that no licence to sell beer and liquor had been sought but, that a licence to sell wine was being sought. Sounding familiar?

Polson's appeal was to the harbour commissioners, which it was assumed, were Mr Hutchison's superiors but it seems that the chain of command had become somewhat blurred at this point.

After exemplary testimonials, Hutchison's original appointment in 1823 would seem to have been made by the Dublin Ballast Board. This was after Hutchison competed for the post with Mr Toutcher. Mr Toutcher's role in the harbour, at that time, was ambiguous. He was referred to as the "works superintendent" for the ongoing harbour works. He was also considered, by the harbour commissioners, to be their de facto harbour master for that part of the new harbour already completed and the harbour commissioners were happy for him to continue as such. If only for a short period, this situation became an oddity thrown up by the staged development of the new harbour – the east and then later, the west pier. There was a harbour master of Dunleary (old harbour), and an acting harbour master of the new harbour, Kingstown Harbour.

Hutchison rolled out the big guns, and wrote to the Lord Lieutenant of Ireland, Marquess Wellesley, presenting an impressive curriculum vitae. After an audience no less, he reminded those who should know that he had been a serving officer in His Majesty's navy with distinction, that he was the nephew of Viscount Frankford(t) and that his competitor, Mr Toutcher, was neither and a non-national to boot – a Norwegian. Hutchison's uncle had just died but William got the job by Royal Warrant.

A sum of £300 pounds had been the figure considered appropriate as salary by the harbour commissioners but was reduced to £200 on the appointment of Mr Hutchison. It might seem like the commissioners had a dose of sour grapes, seeing that £300 was the reported salary for the Harbour Master at Howth but the figure was £50 more than his counterpart at Holyhead.

Ten years later, a New Board of Works was constituted and pruned a lot of the excess labour from the harbour works at Kingstown. A lot of jobs were lost and some serious reductions were made to the wages of senior staff. Mr Toutcher's money was halved, from £200 to £100 per annum. It was reported that Richard Toutcher (also referred to as Captain) had been the "original Projector and Founder of the Royal Harbour" at Kingstown and had fallen on hard times towards the end of his life. It was also widely reported and recorded in Board of Works papers that through his innovations, he had saved the state a large fortune during the building of the harbour. A collection was established and a petition was made to parliament for a pension. Captain Richard Toutcher died at Kingstown in 1841, aged eighty-four. He departed in "neglect with a small pension from the Crown."

One reader of the *Dublin Evening Packet* claimed, "Captain Toutcher died of a broken heart". He was Norwegian by birth but had spent the last sixty-five years in Ireland. Nevertheless, he wasn't 'local', one might add. Captain Toutcher's pension had been terminated with his death and articles about his destitute widow fell out of print after 1842. There were no announcements of any outcome from the petition made on behalf of his widow.

Clearly appointed by Royal Warrant, under the oversight of the harbour commissioners, themselves appointed by the Ballast Office in Dublin, a sub-department of the Dublin Corporation, it was, nevertheless, the Commissioners of Public Works who wrote to Lieutenant Hutchison, three days after his own 'beer' letter had appeared in *Saunders Newsletter* and laid it on the line for him. Paraphrasing, they informed him that he had no business interfering in matters that were not included in his terms of responsibility and to desist from any further comment forthwith. Quite surprisingly, Hutchison's own letter was published with his representative signature, "Hutchinson", spelt with the 'n'.[4]

---

4 The administration and control of royal harbours remained somewhat obscure, fading in and out of contentious disagreement right up until 1899. The matter had arisen during Hutchison's tenure in 1855, when legal clarification was sought by the Board of Public Works. It was reaffirmed that this Board was in administrative control of royal harbours (Kingstown and others) but that the Lord

Storm Warnings at Kingstown, 1861

Several ports on the east coast of Ireland had trading twins on the west coast of Britain. Dublin to Liverpool or Holyhead, Larne or Belfast to Stranraer were as Dover is to Calais, except that in the former, the territory was British on both sides. Ireland had always been a troublesome possession but it was Britain's and she traded with it in the same manner as the remainder of the kingdom – with some exceptions regarding taxes and so on. Because of the relatively short distance and given fair weather, sailing vessels could make a return journey within a day or two. As commerce with Ireland began to fast track after the turn of the 17th century, so did the number of sailing vessels carrying passengers and goods.

Notwithstanding progress, for almost the whole length of the east coast, there were few places that a sailing ship could seek refuge from dangerous weather. Harbours existed of course, such as those at Wexford, Dublin, Belfast but one had to negotiate the shallow sandbars that lay in their entrances or along estuaries. Smaller ones existed but they were just that – too small and unsuitable for one reason and another. Far too many ships had been wrecked, attempting to make for the safety of a suitable harbour in heavy weather, far too often.

Given the geography and the bathometric conditions that prevailed up and down the coast, with the exception of Larne and Belfast to the north, there was little safe entry and refuge for sailing ships during dangerous gales that blew from the north, through east to south. A harbour of refuge was needed, and a magnificent one at Dunleary (becoming Kingstown and now, Dún Laoghaire) was constructed. And apart from two additional internal breakwaters to protect the new, privately owned marina, it has remained largely unaltered since.

After its completion, initial figures gave the impression that it became responsible for quite the opposite to the desired effect – it had become a magnet for shipwrecks. The truth was, more were using it, fleeing to it and it was that sailors were just beginning to become familiar with it. Following improvements, the installation of good lights and the passage of time, the pattern of losses eased. Nevertheless, criticism of the new harbour lingered, emanating mainly from those who had sunk a lot of money into the development of its competitor (the unsuccessful packet

---

Lieutenant reserved the right to make an appointment to the office of harbour at his pleasure. The Board of Public Works would administer the office and any appointment. Interestingly, the harbour master had originally been empowered to appoint a collector of harbour dues. The proviso of HM's privilege seemed to be more related to asserting and maintaining the Royal Navy's right of berthing and use of these harbours.

station hopefully being constructed at Howth) and those commercially wed to the docks at Dublin, who were wondering which way to jump. Criticism erupted, for the last time, after a bad storm in February 1861.

During the winter of 1861, between the 8th and 10th of February, sixty vessels were wrecked in the vicinity of Dublin. Sixteen were reported to have wrecked in the new harbour itself. One in particular left its mark in the bay, when a hurricane of snow and sleet, the likes that had never been seen before, blew through Kingstown Harbour and along the east coast, creating havoc. Not the first with the description, The Great Storm, "wreck after wreck presented in every state of destruction."

There were a significant number of fatalities, both inside and outside of the large harbour of refuge at Kingstown. Ships that couldn't clear the lighthouse outgoing and those had been driven from across and down the channel, unable to negotiate an entrance to the harbour, came to grief on the stone slopes of the east pier.

Captain Boyd and fourteen of his shipmates from Kingstown's guardship, *HMS Ajax*, were lost when they attempted a brave rescue of crew on some of the stricken ships. Their heroism is a matter of record now and remembered in harbour folklore. A splendid monument to the heroes of the day, Captain Boyd and his crewmates, resides on the pier to this day, erected on the very spot where the incident occurred.

The harbour authorities took a pasting after the incident, when the public and the press blamed them for the lack of foresight and a lack of due diligence regarding some safety aspects of the harbour's construction. The design of the harbour and its exposure to bad weather from the northeast was also questioned. The 'well docked' Kingstown lifeboat and its failure to respond in time was another target of the critics. The latter was probably more an emotional response to the terrible loss of life, than one might have considered to be fair comment. It may just have been a lack of understanding of the lifesaving measures that were practical at the time.

Nevertheless, the Dublin Bay Lifeboats, the first such lifeboats in the world since they were established in 1803, funded by the Dublin Ballast Board, came under scrutiny and were taken over by the RNLI in 1862. The Kingstown lifeboat and its coxswain, William Brinkley, were retired. William was awarded quarter pay and allowed to stay on at his small cottage in the harbour complex on Quay Road, off Sussex Parade. A new lifeboat was built, supplied by the RNLI and was housed in a new boat house at the east pier in 1862.

The bad press was brief and criticism of the commissioners faded after it was generally accepted that the storm had been one of rare violence, and the harbour had stood them well otherwise. The final arbiter has been time and an excellent record of harbour refuge and lifeboat service established ever since.

Constantly recurring, was the pervasive criticism of local people, when ships were cast on the shore, often in pieces. Men were shot taking away pieces of timber; women were sentenced to hard labour for collecting lost and discarded clothing and youngsters were transported to the colonies for collecting (judicially described as stealing) anything that was cast upon the shore and not belonging to them. Maybe it was the case that, in the far-flung remoteness of the countryside, it was considered necessary for the law to be enforced with rigour in order to maintain it.

In contrast, the coastline from Dublin to Bray during the 'Great Storm' was strewn with wreckage and nowhere more so than in the harbour of Kingstown. Much of it cast on the shore in front of the two Royal yacht clubs, Victoria and Traders wharfs, and the Coastguard building. The townsfolk fell on the harbour in their droves and took away all they could carry, without any reprisals. The goose and the gander are not always treated the same.

The first transatlantic telegraph cable effectively failed, almost immediately after it was laid in 1858. Although other underwater cables were succeeding to some degree, the America-UK cable was not successfully replaced until after the American Civil War had ended. Transatlantic communications becoming almost instantaneous over a cable might have made a significant difference in the outcome of the American Civil War, beating the mail delivery service by a best ten days. Historians and strategists continue to theorise just how transatlantic communications might have affected the outcome of the civil war, just as the same cables famously did during the 'Zimmerman Affair' in World War I. In all probability, lots of young men were going to fall in any event and probably would only have shortened an atrociously bloody war by about the same ten days.

In other places, the picture was different. Telegraph communication was being successfully installed, in tandem with development of the railway, throughout the British Isles and Europe and just as with the mobile phone many years later; everyone was soon 'connected'. A message from London could be transmitted to Dublin and relayed to Kingstown in jig time.

The Kingstown Harbour Commissioners had seized the advantage presented and, not unlike in other ports, they installed a weather warning system that relied on the new electric communication on top of the clock tower – the tower that sat on top of the centralised building, the offices of the Kingstown Harbour Commissioners.

Dated 12 March, a month after the catastrophic storm that struck the east coast of Ireland, a "Notice to Mariners and Others" appeared. Headed, "Storm Warning Signals", it was posted at Kingstown and informed all those who could see the apparatus and interpret it that, on receipt of a telegraphic signal from the Meteorological Office in London, weather warning signals would be displayed on the staff of the Clock Tower in the Harbour Commissioners' Yard.

It was a new invention, the Fitzroy Signal after its inventor, Admiral Robert Fitzroy. As a captain, he sailed with Charles Darwin on their circumnavigation in *HMS Beagle*. Coincidentally but by invitation from Fitzroy, the voyage also included his friend, the Irishman and hydrographer, Francis Beaufort of the still-with-us measure of wind force – the Beaufort Scale. Beaufort also invented a method of semaphore that could transmit weather warnings over long distances, from station to station, which had been adopted by the coastguard service. Between the two men, they pretty much represented the beginning of what is now the metrological forecasting service.

The notice outlined in detail how, by positioning a drum and a cone in various positions on the Fitzroy apparatus, could warn of the imminent probability of a 'Dangerous Wind'. As radio was a long way off yet, this was a significant advancement – for all those who could see it. Hands might have reached to the heavens to exclaim, "So much for London but what weather can we expect here?"

Notwithstanding the fact that harbour masters' offices and many sea-going vessels may have had their own barometers, which could help indicate a 'probable dangerous wind', or the modern telegraphic communications that existed between many other parts of the United Kingdom, barometer readings at Dover might not tally with weather blowing at Kingstown. During the Great Storm of 9 February 1861, when the weather conditions had been described as 'hurricane', it was also stated that the mercury hovered at 'fair'.

After due consideration, it is only obvious that the weather in Dublin or wherever you are, is apparent. However, if you were setting off up or down the Channel, it is more useful to know what to expect after rounding Land's End or Rathlin. It was early days. Having laid the foundations of a Meteorological Office, the collection of data had begun but weather forecasting, even twenty-fours in advance, was still hit and miss.

Fitzroy, a great thinker, was ahead of his time but his great invention, albeit with some 'behind-the-curve' predictions, was derided. In a fit of depression, he committed suicide just a few years later, in 1865. Quite extraordinarily, his friend, Francis Beaufort predeceased him, also by suicide, in 1857.

The Fitzroy signalling system was ingeniously simple. A telegraph message would arrive in the Harbour Master's office and the apparatus situated over his office and alongside the clock was adjusted to indicate the fair or foul weather expected but, was it more than that?

The well-maintained, stoutly armed, *HMS Ajax* was stationed in HM's Royal Harbour and messages received from the mainland moved Fitzroy's balls and drums, perched over the offices of the Harbour Commissioners that looked down on the King's harbour. The population of Kingstown could see at a glance that Queen Victoria, on the mainland, was in constant communication with her subjects.

The commissioners at Kingstown, seeing the value of the invention to seafarers at the time, were not seen to be sitting on their hands, or rooted in convention.

1861 was a busy year for the Campbells and probably the only time, while in Ireland, that William and James worked together on a professionally equal basis. It was July that same year that William Campbell, Superintendent of Works at Kingstown Harbour, already well established in Public Works at this time, was able to throw some harbour work the way of his son, James, a works contractor in his own right by then. The arrangement, as official correspondence suggests, was not to everyone's liking however and these privileges remained infrequent.

Notwithstanding all of the wreckage strewn around the harbour since the storm, a timber vessel remained lying derelict against the wall in Dunleary harbour for four years and was clogging up berthing space.[5] After due notice had been given to the vessel's owner, a local merchant named McCormack, to remove the derelict vessel, *Louisa* (a man by the name of Price was also referred to as being the owner of *Louisa*) and had expired, the harbour commissioners instructed their superintendent, William Campbell, to blow it up.

William contracted his son, James to place the explosives and father, William supervised. A small crowd, which included some of the commissioners,

---

5　The original harbour of Dunleary, also spelt "Dunlary", was still being called by its old name even though it was within the piers of Kingstown Harbour. It was also known as the, "Inner", or "Coal Harbour", as it is to this day.

the harbour master and William Hutchison (who may have had the earlier incident with Moses, the diver and the *Argyle* weighing uppermost in his mind) cheered when the three charges were electrically detonated and erupted a large amount of timbers and seawater into the air.

James cleared up some other outstanding derelict and wrecked vessels in the harbour, as well as recovering the chains and anchors from the wrecks, *Industry* and *Neptune* on the east pier.

No connection to the diver, Moses already mentioned, the brigantine, *Moses* from Troon had been dashed up on the rocks in the storm, right in front of the windows of the Royal Saint George Yacht Club and had become "anything but an ornament in the harbour". The Campbells were tasked with raising her with lighters and chains and successfully re-floated her into the Coal Harbour.[6]

The Badger is Sunk – Send for Mr Campbell, 1861

In a way, the salvage of the armed revenue cutter, *Badger* marked the beginning of an end to the Campbells' fortunes in Ireland. William Campbell senior had not been actively involved in any shipwreck 'salvage', that we know of, before this time. A technical exception might be made, with his almost reluctant operations on the wreck of the City of Dublin Steam Packet, *Queen Victoria*, in Dublin Bay in 1853. After being suited up in preparation for his first dive on the wreck, he was lowered twenty metres straight down into the remains of her smokestack. Not the primary goal of raising the vessel, he did salvage artefacts and cargo from the sunken paddle steamer.

William and his son, James to follow, mainly contracted to public bodies, such as harbour authorities, for contracts that were civil works of one kind or another: piers, harbours, clearance and dispersal of obstructions that sometimes included sunken wrecks and the discarded remains of their invaluable cargoes.

In the 1853 case of the *Queen Victoria*, the ship was owned by the City of Dublin Steam Packet Company (CDSPCo.) but as it was a mail carrier, risk of damage or loss was borne by contract with the Post Office and thus, no underwriters were involved. And as she sank in Dublin Bay, the Dublin Ballast Office contracted the Dublin shipbuilder, Mr Teall, to raise the vessel. Teall, in turn, contracted the "well-known diver", William Campbell. The project to raise the vessel failed and the wreck was abandoned in situ,

---

6 Some of the wrecks shown in the "Plan of Wrecks" in the harbour, presented with the proposal for the new mail boat pier in 1854, were also mopped up by the Campbells.

after a substantial amount of items were recovered from the wreck. Thanks to their failure, it remains a protected wreck today and a very nice dive.

Shipwreck salvage can be a rewarding business. It has also broken many an over-optimistic salvor. Performed now with someone else's money in the most part, it was both financially and physically a very risky line of work. William did well during his diving career to steer clear of the risk, completing any work on sunken wrecks under the same terms as his other civil contracts. A price for the total job, by the day or by time and materials, supplied or not, or sometimes a combination of all the above.

There is no record that either William or his son, James purchased a wreck from its owner or underwriters, in order to work or to raise it.

Purchasing a wreck where it lay on the seabed or stranded on shore could be very profitable. The number of such cases had been growing with the advent of steam and emigration but, there were still few men or diving companies around, with the skills and equipment to exploit a shipwreck and its cargo at short notice. That would change sooner rather than later.

Being in the right place at the right time has often proved to be a crucial factor in the success of a salvage venture. Having got the wrecked vessel to the shore and its ownership clearly established, it was then just a simple matter of selling or auctioning the wreck or part of it. Given that shipwreck was a fairly regular occurrence in some areas, a local auctioneer could do well during a bad winter.

A serious bidder had to first determine who owned what and who was owed what, from the first moment the wreck occurred or was abandoned. He also had to be aware of all the costs that were due for any assistance that had been rendered to the stricken vessel, while it was being saved on shore or, to the point where its wrecked value could be exploited.

Many cases ended up in the Admiralty Courts and everyone who thought they had a claim — assistance given to stricken vessel by lifeboat, by coastguard; provision of equipment; earlier salvage agreement (even if only verbal); fishermen and the general public, owners of land on which the ship lay and so on — always turned up. The list is long, from those who were first to spot the ship in distress and alerted authorities, to those who rediscover abandoned wrecks, even centuries later. A procedure often so unpredictable that an unwary salvor could at times, do well to save his shirt.

The rediscovery of wrecked Spanish Armada ships from 1588, on Streedagh Strand, County Sligo, by wreck hunters in 1985 is a case in point. Believed, at first, to be a straightforward 'salvor in possession' claim, any rights believed to be had in this regard were defeated in court by the Irish authorities in

1987. After a further ten years of protracted negotiations and a second judicial hearing 'finders'' awards, costs, and permission to re survey were made to the salvors. These shipwrecks remain in the possession and under the protection of the Irish authorities.

A contemporary contract agreed with American divers on the wreck of the *Pomona*, sunk off the coast of Wexford in 1859, would seem to have been a financial success for the contractor and the divers but included yet another aspect of salvage seemingly quite rare. It was agreed, apparently on site and reported that divers could keep fifty percent of any value recovered from the body of a victim brought to the surface. This may seem distasteful but their original contract on the ship and cargo did not include recovering bodies. As there were hundreds of bodies still trapped in the wreck, some with hundreds of pounds on their person, they were nevertheless impeding ingress to the wreck and the salvage operation. The deal was said to have been struck for the sake of the grieving relatives. A thousand dollar note from the wreck was found on the beach!

Another interesting but much later salvage agreement was struck when the giant bulk carrier, *Kowloon Bridge* sunk at the Stags, off Cork Harbour in 1986. A class of ship with controversial design history, she had been in trouble earlier and while avoiding bad weather, she berthed in Bantry Bay, Cork. Her mooring broke and she was forced to return to open water. The enormous vessel got into further difficulties along the coast before striking on and sinking at the Stags Rocks off Cork.

With a worrying potential for pollution from her fuel oil and the enormous cargo of iron ore pellets she was carrying, the wreck became a serious concern. It was reported that the underwriters took 'sharp' action and relinquished ownership of the stricken vessel to a colourful diver, who was residing locally. Part time salvor, Shaun Kent, was reported to have purchased the huge wreck for £1.

The point being, in this case, sometimes the owner of a ship (The *Kowloon Bridge* was reported to have been owned by a syndicate of banks.) and its cargo, or an underwriter's contractual obligations, can be conveniently transferred for a nominal sum. Put another way – got rid of! The lessons of Shell and BP's *Exxon Valdez* being a salutary lesson for underwriters and owners alike.

Whether or not such a ruse was contrived in the case of the 90,000-ton *Kowloon Bridge* is both clear and yet unclear! And unfortunately, in the first instance, the cost of cleaning up the extensive damage to wildlife and the coastline environment caused by her 1200-ton spill of bunker oil, fell at the feet at the Irish government – the taxpayer.

There does not appear to have been any widespread pollution from the iron ore that is still in situ, even though, in the case of iron wrecks from the Victorian period, fishermen have reported that crustaceans caught in and around them, appear 'rusty'. Whether or not they taste 'rusty', I couldn't say but I can say that any iron objects taken from the same wrecks give off a reviling, pungent smell when they reach the surface.

It remains unclear if any restitution payments were ever recouped by the Irish government from Mr Kent, or the real owners of the wreck, for the damage done, or might be done in the future by the remains of the *Kowloon Bridge*.

Getting back to James Campbell and the *Badger*. When it was reported that the *Badger* was sunk outside of the entrance to Kingstown Harbour and was to be raised by James Campbell with his schooner, *Lively*, they also threw in a remark about an earlier wreck. This was announced in a lengthy article in the *Freemans' Journal* of 9 February 1861.

> *The Harbour Commissioners of Waterford recently made a contract with Mr Campbell of Kingstown to blow up the collier brig* Spankaway.

Sunk in the River Suir, the wreck presented an obstruction and James duly blew it up, dispersing the blockage but the wreck resurfaced to haunt James. James was also reported to be "an old hand at this sort of work, being employed with his father about nine years ago ... near Duncannon Fort."

These were the wrecks that were blown up and mentioned earlier.

The article was in praise of James but did not tell the whole story. The issue of the *Spankaway* began in September 1860, when the unrivalled illusionist, Professor Hartz, Wizard of the World, was performing at the Waterford Town Hall. Modelling himself on the French illusionist, Robert Houdin, Hartz became famous around the world for such unrivalled tricks as 'The Incomprehensible Canary' and 'The Column Glove', which were performed for six nights in Waterford City. The tricks would entertain and defy discovery, for seat prices of between two shillings in the favoured front rows and somewhere at the back for six pence.

The *Spankaway* contract had become a protracted disagreement between James and his ex-employers, the Commissioners of Waterford Harbour and led to the dilution of Campbell's favoured status with the Waterford men. The affair was still unresolved at the time of the article and marked another milestone of technical progress, which was indicative of the changing times.

The Waterford Harbour Commissioners had determined that there were a number of obstructions in the Suir, near the bridge in Waterford and hired the Wexford Diving Company to investigate the extent of the problem. The Wexford Diving Company was represented by the marine diver, Francis Hore (also referred to as "Francis Moore") who reported that there were two lighters, with cargoes of rock and some coal, lying on the bottom. He also made a report on the wreck of the collier, *Spankaway*.

The Harbour Board invited Mr Hore to remove the obstructions. The limestone and coal cargoes were removed but there was trouble removing the remains of the lighters themselves. Some salvaged items from the *Spankaway* were also removed but the harbour commissioners were then minded to invite competing tenders for its demolition.

The collier brig, *Spankaway* was still causing an obstruction near the bridge. Having been informed that ownership of the wreck had changed, the commissioners then approached a Mr White, inviting him to remove the wreck and its cargo for the sum of £400. It didn't happen and an invitation to tender for the job was advertised.

Campbell submitted a price and not unlike his father's practice, it included a weekly rate and a lump sum. The "marine diver Mr Francis Hore" and the Wexford Diving Company also tendered at a lower price, which was defeated. James' own abilities and the satisfactory nature of his father's earlier work for the port were duly noted and James secured the contract. The fact that his father, William, had been hired by their old engineer, Barry Gibbons, was also mentioned but Mr Gibbons and his influence had moved on and James Campbell only succeeded by a whisker.

James had tendered to supply all the divers, materials and powder and to disperse the wreck. Having received an advance, he duly blew up the offending obstruction. However, after inspection, the commissioners contacted Campbell to tell him that they could not complete payment, as the wreck parts had not been removed. In reply, James submitted a new tender to remove the wreckage and for it to become his property. The offer was rejected, and the thing went back and forward. Campbell threatened law through his solicitor, John Lalor of York Street (now, York Road), Kingstown for the recovery of £61 owed to him.

When the *Badger* sank, both matters – the lighters and rocks and, the *Spankaway* – were still in contention and despite the fact that a *Spankaway* in the same river was being 'fitted with a new foremast' in 1862, the issue with Campbell remained unresolved until 1865. The little wreck had continued to provide concern to the Waterford Harbour Commissioners and a living for the employees of the Wexford Diving Company. This relatively obscure diving company worked the coast of Wexford and Waterford, even as far as Ballycotton in Cork. Some salvage projects by the Wexford Diving Company are mentioned in local newspapers for a number of subsequent years and some others that are not mentioned. The company finally went out of mention in the 1870s.

The "talented" Campbells never returned to Wexford or Waterford to dive. The thing about it was, Campbell's earlier favour at the port was at an end. One could imagine the local diver, Mr Hore, being sent down to report on Campbell's work and then, the commissioners happy to unnecessarily begin splitting hairs. There were new divers on the block, in the form of Mr Hore, Mr Armstrong, Mr Peare and the recently constituted Wexford Diving Company, who could be contacted at 3 Main Street, Wexford.

Another two men mentioned in connection with the Wexford Diving Company were Mr Thomas Byrne, manager (probably of Wexford) and Mr Terry of Ballymacotter, Cloyne. The schooner, *Samuel Dickson* was used by the company during their salvage of the American ship, *Tiger* in Moore Hall Bay, in 1862. It would appear that Mr Terry joined the men of the Wexford Diving Company during collaboration on the wreck of the large sailing ship, *Eugénie*, which had wrecked on his own doorstep in Ballycotton, in 1865.

The salvage of the *Eugénie* was another quite important case of shipwreck and salvage ending up in the courts. The ship was owned by J & R Martin in Dublin and management of their wreck was put in the hands of an organisation cited as The Protection of Wrecked and Damaged Goods, who invited tenders for the salvage. This was probably the forerunner of the company that became famous as the Liverpool Salvage Association (later, the Liverpool and Glasgow Salvage Association). The Wexford Diving Company did not secure the contract but Mr Terry, in Ballymacotter, was put in charge of the wreck.

Another father-and-son team of divers, in northern Ireland, Richard Clegg and his son John, a pair with another interesting track record, were awarded the contract. They (or at least the son, John) were later charged with larceny from the wreck – salvaged goods were said to have been siphoned off for personal profit and John was tried at Fermoy, County Cork in January 1869. Some important points of law surfaced, but John was found guilty, and sentenced to three months imprisonment.

Some of *Eugénie*'s cargo was sold locally and laughter erupted in the court when the local buyers, at pains to understate the value of the goods, in a manner only a Cork native can, decried that they had been done! Knowing only too well that they too could be prosecuted if the sale was found to be illegal, they described the items of tin as "rotten" and that the "blades fell off the knifes", etc.

Anyway, it was clear that the Cleggs had dirtied their bibs and that Terry had kept his clean. The Wexford Diving Company obviously mopped up the balance of the salvage work and a "Wreck Auction" notice appeared on the front page of the *Cork Examiner* in June 1868, indicating that Mr Terry was now in some kind of arrangement with the divers from Wexford.

A number of important shipwrecks had occurred. The list of emigrant boats piling up around the coast was growing. Diving apparatus had improved considerably and had become more widely available. Men willing to step into a diving suit when opportunity presented, were increasing. At the same time, many out-of-work divers involved in harbour work throughout the British Isles were being laid off. Others were coming out of the navy with diving skills. Good divers and companies were surviving, some on opportunity and luck while others just faded away.

The Wexford Diving Company and other divers from Wales were beginning to work the valuable wrecks around the "Graveyard of a Thousand Wrecks" on the coasts of Wexford and Waterford. Terry was well in with the organisation (the Preservation of Wrecks people in Liverpool) and Hore had influence with the Waterford Harbour Board. And amongst other positions, William Armstrong was a harbour commissioner with the Wexford Harbour Board. The names, Hore and Armstrong both appeared on the list of jury members that presided in Wexford, at the inquest of victims from the wrecking of the emigrant ship, *Pomona* in 1859. I reckon that the Campbells didn't stand a chance.

So, it was just progress; just a case that, you have had your day. After all, in a small pond, it is often about who you know at a particular time and the rest is up to yourself. The Campbells had lost favour in the southeast, but they were still 'top dog' at Kingstown.

The idea that the newly constructed harbour at Kingstown would act as a harbour of refuge only had long passed. Its two massive, long arms, all-weather walls, each almost a mile, not only gave succour to fishing fleets, commercial traffic and naval vessels but had become an important railhead. A civil and commercial port was established there, as well as it becoming a fashionable and desirable place to live.

In the original plan for the harbour, there was little consideration given for the commercial – just refuge. Development of the harbour at Howth, during the early years, had been progressing simultaneously and some envisaged that it would become the mail packet station for Dublin.

When the railway came to Kingstown in 1836, it stopped short at Salthill, Seapoint. Pressure from opposing commercial interests to facilitate sailing passengers, mails and 'progress' eventually drove the railway on to the centre of the new harbour, just at the junction of the 'Forty Feet Road' (now Marine Road), Quay Road and the east pier.[7]

Quite tastefully, the rail line was extended further south, much of it below ground level, by a series of bridges, tunnels and deep cuts in the rock, from which only smoke and steam could be seen rising, as the train ploughed otherwise invisibly through Kingstown. A cut was made under Quay Road that facilitated the mail and passenger train onto the new Carlisle Pier.

Almost below ground level for the entire distance from where Mr Gibbons moved to in Connaught Place, through Kingstown to Killiney, the panoramic vista of the bay remained uninterrupted by the rail line but it would seemed to have had unintended consequences. As the line was laid between the bottom of the town and the seafront, it had the effect of separating the harbour from the rest of the town and its development. The Royal Harbour and all its glory were now on the other side of the tracks or vice versa, so to speak.

On that other side, there were Public Works buildings and yards and some buildings occupied by the harbour authority plus, the grandiose atmosphere of the Royal yacht clubs. Combined with the authority of the two boards of commissioners and their harbour, this part of Kingstown appeared to have become separated from the town by the railway line. It somehow seemed to have become more British and then, railings began to rise, almost creating a demarcation of the social classes, between upper Kingstown and the lower.

Indeed, it was not so long ago when it was mooted that gates should be put on the piers, in order to restrict access and that a charge could be levied for a perambulation on the great walls. As if this would not make it exclusive enough, it was also suggested that angling from the piers and the shoreline in the immediate vicinity of the harbour, should be prohibited. A new regime might want to concentrate on the more positive aspects – like improving access.

---

7 The Forty Feet Road has also been called Forty Foot Road, Sussex Parade and Royal Marine Road and now, just Marine Road. Name changing of streets in Dunleary/Kingstown/Dún Laoghaire has been a perpetual reflection of the different shades of its administrative authorities. The origins of the name put on the popular bathing place, "The Forty Foot" at nearby Sandycove remains a constant source of curiosity to Dunlearyians – how did it get this name? The answer might seem to lie not too far from the Forty Feet Road.

Access to this magnificent linear construction, an important social and leisure facility, was restricted somewhat along the seafront by the development of the prestigious yacht club houses and the hard standing for their yachts. The buildings themselves are beautiful, thankfully, having resisted almost all temptation to modernise them. And although the cross-channel ferry service has terminated now, the space, the empty terminals, are off limits to the public, with some exceptions. Some frontage is already occupied by commercial interests and not for the first time, opportunities for extending private commercial interests onto the new and old piers are continually probed.

Unfortunately, the last remaining undeveloped space – Old Dunleary, Old Harbour, the Inner Harbour, the Coal Harbour, all the same space – has to remain under constant guard by the local inhabitants and users, for it too, increases in value by the day. With a value that is hard to overestimate, this last bastion of public access to harbour water, the 'bag-end' space of the harbour, still lying under the 18th century 'Coffee House', has been put under threat of capture a number of times by commercial developers and constant vigilance are local watchwords.

Within the confines of the new piers, safe berthage was provided for sailing ships, railway and commercial steamers. The Admiralty vessels stationed there were either moored off the inside of the east pier during peace time or, alongside the shore at Victoria Wharf (also called Saint Michael's Wharf and the Admiralty Wharf during time of war).

Numerals and 'broad arrow' carvings, representing the position of individual moorings for ships, were etched into the large granite stones along the inside of the east pier, probably chiselled there by someone like Mr Campbell. These denote the mooring positions of the various vessels and can still be seen during a pleasant walk along the pier. The Traders Wharf came later and was built more northerly and just outside the confines of the old harbour.

Today, there are three yacht clubs in Kingstown, one motor-yacht club and a sail training school. The two premier clubs in Campbell's time were the Royal Saint George (established in 1838, work on the clubhouse at Kingstown was completed by 1843), its name leaving no ambiguity about the loyalty of its membership, and the Royal Irish (established in 1831, the clubhouse at Kingstown opened its doors in 1850), which suggests, like some British army regiments, a membership attempting to make a distinction – Irish but loyal to the Crown.

The two Royals had the best seats in the House of Kingstown, a third going to the National Yacht Club in 1871. The Kingstown Yacht Club would seem to have existed beside the Royal Slip since 1864 and appears on early maps. Also called the Kingstown Royal Harbour Boat Club, it later underwent a series of name changes to become The National. Another clubhouse was not built until the twentieth century. Situated in the old harbour, this was the Dún Laoghaire Motor Yacht Club, which catered for all comers, just as the others have aspired to in more modern times.

High in the architectural and social pecking order were the great Georgian squares and terraces of Dublin City but Kingstown and its arteries, lined with pseudo-Romanesque villas, had become the "most fashionable town in all of Ireland".

Immediately surrounding the harbour, acres were given over to administration buildings: the offices and yards of the Harbour Commissioners, Public Works, Revenue, Board of Trade, Admiralty, Railway and Marine, Coastguard and a public park on which the famed Pavilion was later built. Merchants, the trades, all graduating down in importance as they radiated up and out from the important centre, creating a town that came to represent a British home from home, its suburbs were full of grand mansions.

The town's heights were dominated by the spires of Saint Michaels' Catholic Church at the top of Sussex Parade (Marine Road) and the Protestant Mariners' Church, situated a couple of hundred yards across the park to the south. It overlooked the Harbour Master's house and reservoir that supplied water to keep steam up on the cross-channel steamers.

The coastguard cutter, *Badger* had arrived back at Kingstown from a preventative cruise to the north, under the command of Captain Bones (Banes) on Saturday, 28 December 1861. A heavy, freezing fog descended and prevented her from negotiating a safe entry, through the piers, to their berth in the harbour. The *Badger's* crew, eager to go on festive leave, had to drop anchor about a mile to the northeast of the entrance. Her navigating lights still burning, the crew bedded down for the night to wait for morning and clearer skies.

During the night, the commercial screw steamer, *Leda* left Kingstown and rammed into the cutter, sinking her immediately. There was a scramble from the bunks and up the masts. Badly shaken, and all their possessions lost, all fourteen crew were nevertheless saved by boats put out by the *Leda*.

It was reported the *Badger* had been cut in two and that the harbour master, Captain Hutchison, immediately sent for Mr James Campbell. Well known to the harbour master for a number of reasons, the Campbells had been busy all year, raising and clearing wrecks around the harbour, after the Great Storm of the previous February. The *Badger* was now sunk in the approaches to the harbour and would have to be moved or destroyed pretty smartly.

James Campbell arrived in his schooner, the *Lively* and assessed that he could raise the badly damaged cutter. The Campbells do not seem to have owned a vessel, of any kind, up to this point. There had been reports, during salvage operations on the *Queen Victoria*, that William senior operated from "his sloop, the *Pride*" but ownership has never been confirmed. A possible explanation is that William was supplied with the sloop by Teall, who had been awarded the contract. Ownership of the schooner, *Lively* seemed to have just come out of nowhere and appears to have belonged to James.[8]

Maybe not quite out of nowhere – during his work in the harbour after the storm, one of the vessels that James raised and repaired was the schooner, *Lively* from Bridgewater, owned by Mr Duddridge. The owner had the cargo insured but the schooner was only partly so and the poor man was reported to have already been in dire straits. Although the *Lively* went up for auction, I suspect that Campbell defrayed his expense and his bill for the work in part settlement, during a successful bid for the vessel.

James Campbell, for whatever reason, only held on to and operated with the schooner for about eighteen months. No record of it being registered in his name was found but, James seems to have developed a taste for 'coasting' at this point, with some cross-channel voyages carrying timber recorded to him and the boat. Not long after, James purchased a not too dissimilar vessel from a man living an unusual life in Kingstown. The purchase would involve the aforementioned Richard Brickley and would alter the course of the Campbells' lives.

Under the command of Lieutenant Dyer from Kingstown's guardship, *HMS Ajax*, it took almost two weeks for Campbell to place chains under the *Badger*'s hull and, with the help of the coastguard cutter, *Wellington* and the tides, they tightened up on her sufficiently to haul her off the seabed. With the aid of a tug, they eventually bumped her into the inner Coal Harbour.

The *Badger* was a favourite in the town. She could be seen during regatta season, decked out with flags and competing in the cutter races. So, when she was described as having been "cut in two", it was probably a description that had more to do with shock than a less obvious reality. The damage was bad but Campbell got her safely into the old Inner Harbour and was able

---

8   The sloop, *Prude* of Dublin was auctioned in Belfast soon afterwards.

to make a temporary repair, before she was towed off to Dublin for full restitution. Lasting repairs seem to have been finally completed in England and the *Badger* returned to service, with new rigging, the following year.

The incident highlighted a number of shortcomings with Kingstown Harbour, the lack of a dry dock space being just one. The difficulty large sailing vessels were having negotiating the entrance to the harbour during contrary weather conditions, was yet another.

The diving and works contractor, James Campbell, now twenty-four years of age, had become well known in the town. His father, William, now aged 49, had two more sons by this time, in his second marriage to Mary Charles: William, 10 and Charles, 8 years. It appeared that father, William and son, James and the whole family were thriving and well on their way to becoming a respected force in the fashionable town of Kingstown. Their fortunes in the town would continue to prosper but, within twelve months, everything would change and 'Kingstown Intelligence' would never again report on any member of this Campbell clan.

It was a year when everything seemed to be going well for the Campbells. The family grew and prospered after the promising promotion in Public Works, which came with a house. The work was steady and a salvage vessel had been acquired by James. It had become clear though, that an increasing number of divers were mopping up important salvage and clearance opportunities in Wexford and elsewhere, and the Campbells had lost their edge in that county. Competition had outpaced them in the game but, they still had a number of other strings to their bow.

Civil works was their forte and Kingstown was their base. They built above and below the water and James had secured a contract with the City of Dublin Steam Packet Company, to keep the hulls of their steamers clear of marine growth, by scraping their bottoms while they lay alongside. Avoiding dry-docking and keeping the speed of the steamers constant was an important element in maintaining speed, enabling the CDSPCo to hold on to their valuable mail contract.

Chapter 6

Campbell, Gibbons and Hutchison, 1861-1862

The engineer Barry Gibbons lived at 2 Connaught Place, a very nice two-floors, above-basement, terraced house with an unobstructed view of Kingstown Harbour. This pleasant example of Georgian architecture overlooks the Grand Harbour and remains in constant occupation. Separated by a very short distance, the Board of Public Works supplied William Campbell and his family with a less eye-turning house within the Public Works complex. An interesting aside, the value of perks that came with the job, at the time, can be gauged by the shuffling of various senior employees from one prestigious bit of property to another.

A large house – a grand building, in fact – situated in the centre of the Public Works yard opposite the harbour, was designed by George Smith and completed as the House of the Harbour Superintendent. It became known as the Harbour Master's Lodge. Ornately decorated with granite carvings, the entrance is formed with a portico supported by two columns and the roof carries a domed tower, housing a large clock. Despite original intentions, it became the seat of the Harbour Commissioners. Some harbour masters, in modern times, have thought fit to actually live there but it is mainly an administrative office now, with meetings held by the commissioners from time to time.

The harbour master, Lieutenant Hutchison's house, was situated further south along the promenade beside the Mariners' Church, along with what was listed as his offices and the "cottage of the chief coxswain". It would seem that somewhere along the way, the original designation of the Harbour Superintendent's accommodation was altered and his grade of accommodation got the heave-ho down the line.

Gibbons was a well-respected engineer, consulted for a number of companies and had done well for himself. You might call him a protégé. William Campbell, by any social measure of success, also appeared to be well-placed at this point, as was his son, James. James Campbell had his own diving service vessel by then, a contracting business with several employees and would soon reside at York Street in Kingstown. Not the same fashionable status as dwellings along the promenade, it was a little further back up the town ... but getting there.

Winters on the east coast of Ireland can feel very damp and bitterly cold. February, a notably treacherous month for shipwrecks, fierce winds, snow, and freezing temperatures, saw repeating accounts of damaged ships, wrecks and dismasted vessels occurring off Kingstown in 1862. One of the more notable incidents of that year occurred on 24 February, when the large sailing vessel, *China* struck the Kish Bank, just six miles east of Kingstown. Described over the top as "one of the most remarkable escapes from shipwreck that has ever occurred off our coast", the *China* struck on this notorious sandbank and Dublin pilots went to her aid in two tugs. The crew were taken off and were no sooner aboard the tugs when the large ship rose on the tide and floated off. She was taken in tow by a pilot boat and brought into Kingstown with sixteen feet of water in her!

Lieutenant Hutchison took charge of the vessel and grounded her alongside the coal quay in the old harbour – and at almost 1,000 tons, she left very little space for berthing other vessels. James Campbell was called and was tasked by Hutchison to give a written assessment of the damage to the bottom of the ship. Very little damage was reported, apart from needing re-caulking in a number of places.

A subsequent enquiry found that the captain should not have left the ship so soon, as she soon floated off and should have been capable of being managed by her own crew into the harbour without a tow. The tow cost £250 and was shared amongst the crew of the tug and the port pilots. It struck me as being a little like, 'witch testing'. If they drowned when dunked they were innocent; if they survived, they were guilty and burned. It had been a no-win either way for the *China*'s master, James Lennerton. The captain had saved the crew but trial by his peers had found him guilty of mismanaging the ship. Not having been drowned or burned, he nevertheless had his ticket cancelled.

In July, there was an incident (seeming to be only minor) involving a horse and cart on the newly completed Gibbons' Pier. To the general public it might have appeared minor but behind the scenes, William Campbell had to swallow a stern reminder of his proper station.[1]

Another very similar horse and cart incident occurred on the same pier sometime later and reminded Campbell of the reprimand he had received

---

1   It was a royal harbour with royal slips, so one might have expected that the designer and builder of the new pier and the public at large might not have been surprised when "Gibbons' Pier" was honoured with a more 'appropriate' name. So, henceforth we'll stick with its present name, the Carlisle Pier.

on the earlier occasion. As the two were connected in Campbell's own mind, we will take both incidents together further on.

The Kingstown Lifeboat House

There are times when there is insufficient information to make a satisfactory judgement of a person, and we resist. Sometimes though, it may be necessary to form some kind of rounded opinion, for one reason or another. My opinion of the harbour master at Kingstown, William Hutchison, is that he was an admirable and honourable person. He was undeniably brave and a man who thought of others. His dedication to the life-saving service, from its inception, is beyond reproach. He put to sea in life-threatening conditions on many occasions and performed difficult rescues. He was honoured with a number of commendations of bravery for his service in rescuing and saving lives at sea. He was one of the few recipients of the Gold Medal presented by the RNLI for life saving. His impressive testimonials are still on file at the National Archives.

Hutchison could walk down the pier and call on harbour, lifeboat or coastguard staff to help launch a boat and proceed to sea at the drop of hat. No one would entertain the notion of replying that it was "too rough" or "not my job" and refuse. He was a leader of men and well-respected about Kingstown Harbour, the town and beyond.

The RNLI (Royal National Lifeboat Institution) received its royal charter in 1860 but at the time, there was no RNLI lifeboat based between Dublin and the one at Sandycove. There was a lifeboat based in Kingstown Harbour, at the behest of the Dublin Ballast Board and Hutchison was active with it and the one that had been at Sandycove. The Kingstown boat was the same one that had been criticised, following the disastrous losses in Kingstown Harbour during the earlier storm. The coxswain of the Kingstown Harbour lifeboat, William Brinkley, who had lived earlier at nearby Glasthule, was retired in 1861 when the service came under the control of the RNLI. It had been mooted (even before the criticism that had been levelled at the performance of the Kingstown Harbour lifeboat, after the February 1861 storm) during earlier consultations with the unfortunate Captain Boyd that, a new boat house should be built for the lifeboat and that it should be taken over by the RNLI.

Agreement was reached between the RNLI, the Dublin Ballast Board and the Board of Public Works for the erection of a new building, in order to house the lifeboat at Kingstown Harbour. A few months later, in September 1861, William Campbell reported to the commissioners that the new 'shed' for the Kingstown lifeboat was finished. Receiving hardly a mention and downgraded to a 'shed' (albeit by Campbell's own hand) it remains a most beautiful building of cut granite. A fine example of contextual architecture that continues to blend seamlessly with its surroundings. It is as if, it was always there.

The site chosen for the boat house was on the Royal Slip, which Campbell was also responsible for widening and is situated where the east pier meets the road. While keeping a perfectly level aspect, its base descends with the slope of the slip into the water, just like the boat that launches from within it. The finest cut granite, worked with great skill, it is still admired today by thousands of passers-by and is guarded by the local inhabitants and the crew of the nearby, more modern RNLI lifeboat station, from those who would have it removed. The premises are adjacent to the National Yacht Club, once the Kingstown Yacht Club.

Construction of the boat house was overseen by William Campbell, and probably involved a number of other stone masons at the time. Despite the fact that the harbour master, Mr Hutchison, was not in favour of the position of the new lifeboat house and even had reservations regarding the particular new class of lifeboat to be housed there, their professional positions in the same harbour must surely have meant that William Campbell interacted with Hutchison on the project to some degree. Despite petition, the position of the new lifeboat house remained unchanged and the new lifeboat, *Princess Royal*, was delivered into service the following year, May 1862.

The lack of a suitable lifeboat and rescue or pilot tug service in the bay drew criticism of the Ballast Board, from a number of important quarters, including the respected civil engineer, Barry D. Gibbons. In the light of the tragedies in the harbour's recent past, losses in and outside of its confines, Gibbons wrote to the various commissioners and to newspapers expressing his annoyance at the lack of the appropriate marine services. He included the unsuitability of the existing 'small' lifeboats that were available but also took the space to praise the bravery and willingness of the men who launch them in difficult conditions.

While the row puffed on, the lifeboat station had remained without a suitable boat through the winter of 1861-62, during which a number of ships were lost. For want of a tug, the barque, *Colleen Bawn* was banged up against the inside of the west pier, and with help from *HMS Ajax* and harbour crews, she clawed out of the harbour, where she hooked up for a tow to Dublin. The tow parted and she was wrecked at the entrance to Dublin Harbour on the North Bull, in January 1862.

Malcomson's (of Waterford) new steamer was lost after she struck the Muglins Rock, Dalkey, coming off and floating to a sinking position several miles east of Bray Head. Despite the evidence later given that there was no service from the coastguard on this occasion – and except for the loss of two dogs – there were no human casualties. The passengers and crew managed to get off in the ship's boats and they all reached the shores of Bray and Greystones safely. The crew hadn't given up on the vessel so easily though and rowed after the drifting but sinking *Adonis*, until she finally disappeared from sight. The loss was reported as having been five miles off Bray Head and the vessel was never seen again.

During a survey of the area, in pursuit of the wreck of the East Indiaman, *Comte de Belgioioso*, lost on the Kish Bank in 1783, a small group of amateur wreck hunters and diving enthusiasts discovered the remains of the *SS Adonis* on the outer Codling Ridge, about eight miles off Bray Head, County Wicklow. It appears that the vessel had sunk beneath the surface but had continued to drift with the wind and tide, until it finally got stuck on this very shallow sand ridge. Our surprising find could only be confirmed by a process of elimination and identification comparisons made of the remaining engine parts.

Mr Hutchison became honorary secretary of the RNLI and remained active in the service, as it was his harbour, after all. They all worked and lived so close to one another, that one could hardly get out of bed without seeing the other.

This was a critical juncture for the administrative line of authority in the operation of the Kingstown Harbour complex. The RNLI had instigated the building of a replacement boat for Kingstown, after the earlier catastrophe and the resulting criticism that was levelled at the structure of the life-saving service in Kingstown. The Ballast Board arranged for the building of a new boat house for the RNLI boat and its suitability immediately came under fire from the Kingstown branch of the RNLI, led by the harbour master, Lieutenant Hutchison. Their argument was that the boat should not be housed at the Royal Slip but, at the end of the pier. However, William Campbell had to proceed with instructions and built the new boat house where it remains today.

Again, it was the times that were in it: they were changing and personalities were caught up in conflicting attitudes of old and new. Steam and the new engine, was the elephant in the room and everyone knew that a lifeboat or rescue boat should be fitted with an engine in order to be most effective.[2]

2   The lifeboats stationed at Dublin and other ports were routinely towed by port tugs to the scene of shipwreck.

Hutchison was probably correct in his opinion, that the boat house was in the wrong place and that it should be nearer to the action. However, Gibbons was also correct, in that the lifeboat crews would have to get out to the end of the pier in order to man the lifeboat, whereas a powered boat would eliminate both disadvantages. The combination of a steam tug and inshore boat was the answer they were seeking. Today, the combination of a powered vessel, moored and ready to go and the smaller inshore rescue boat, housed in the beautiful old lifeboat house, seems a perfect combination for the present.

Sent to maintain it irregularly it was, nevertheless, the clock and the tower, just like the boots at Kilmore, that was beginning to get to Campbell. The boots incident was a petty one but demonstrated two things. One, William's ignorance, or possibly cheek, to try it on with a government agency and the other was this agency's ability to monitor expenditure and stick to departmental rules. And when you think of the size of the task, with enormous expenditure countrywide, this was no mean feat.

William had deposited his boots and shoes with a local boot mender, John Devereaux in Wexford. They sent the bill to the Board and they sent it back with a letter to William and Devereaux, suggesting they should sort it out between them. Boots and various pieces of protective clothing were being provided to divers employed by the Board of Works at the time and William obviously thought he was also entitled. He was possibly pushing it however, with repair of the shoes.

On the recommendation of the engineer, Barry D. Gibbons, William Campbell filled his shoes. He was finally appointed Superintendent of Works and Collector of Harbour Dues in the Royal Harbour, Kingstown in May 1861. After presenting the necessary guarantors for the job (James Twamley, member and caterer in the Royal Saint George Yacht Club and Puliford Batley, another esteemed member), William was able to write to the commissioners and thank them for the confirmation of his promotion and permanent employment in the harbour.[3]

1861 was a busy year for the Campbells but it was also a busy one for the harbour master, William Hutchison. Two royal visits to the harbour took place that year. One in June, when the Prince of Wales landed at the

---

3 Collector of Harbour Dues was a position that fell under the administrative umbrella of the Revenue Commissioners but was farmed out to Public Works staff at Kingstown. A trustworthy and responsible position, as it involved considerable amounts of money, the Board of Public Works made the appointment and not the harbour commissioners or harbour master, as had been thought to have been their privilege.

pier (which was still being referred to as Gibbons' Pier) to visit the large military establishment at the Curragh in County Kildare. Gibbons was also responsible for designing the gallery and under-cover seating arrangements for the comfort of the spectators. First however, the Campbells, father and diver son, had to remove all the sunken rubble that had been discarded during the construction of the pier, just to be sure there was no royal grounding. A ticket-only event, the visit passed off without incident and the harbour master was more than relieved when the consort boarded the steam train 'special' for Dublin.

The next visit, this time by Queen Victoria and her family at the end of August, did not pass off so smoothly. Again a ticket-only affair and under cover, as before, on the same pier, which was, by this time, being unmistakably referred to as the Carlisle Pier. What transpired was a moment in the harbour master's life that I'm sure he regretted ever after but, as an ex-naval officer, it was a matter of honour, which demanded satisfaction and was one he could not let pass unchallenged.

Shortly after the visit of the Queen, William Hutchison was berated in the street by Mr Thomas Meekins, who wanted to know why he had not received tickets for the affair. He accused Hutchison of preferential treatment and of making a botch of the distribution of the tickets that had been supplied by Board of Public Works. Hutchison cried "false" (which apparently, we would translate today as, "you're a liar") and Meekins took offence. He placed a feather (obviously one that had just been floating around at the time or kept in his top pocket for such an occasion.) on Hutchison's shoulder and said, "consider yourself horsewhipped."

It came to blows and unfortunately, Mr Hutchison was struck in his blind eye, one he had 'lost' after being struck by a ship's boom during a sea rescue in 1838. Hutchison preferred charges and the case was first heard in the Kingstown police court not long after. It drew considerable attention from the press and the general public, who packed the court to have a gawk. After a hearing, the case was elevated to the circuit court and despite impatience by the judiciary and advice to settle, it continued.

Mr Thomas Mossom Meekins, as it happened, was a barrister of some reputation and counter charged that the Hutchisons, father and son, both known as Lieutenant William Hutchison, had assaulted him. Pressured by the judge, they settled the 'affair of honour' in October, Meekins paying Hutchison's costs.

An interesting aside to the case was revealed when Hutchison told Meekins, in the street, that it didn't matter how much money he had: he couldn't have got a ticket and that even the officers in the *Ajax* didn't receive any.

Despite rank or religion, there was a serious pecking order in the Royal Harbour of Kingstown.

Mentioned earlier, the schooner, *Argyle* had been anchored in Kingstown during winter gales 1853/4. Her moorings were snagged and broken by another vessel and she was wrecked near the lighthouse, against the east pier of Kingstown harbour. After the harbour master, William Hutchison contracted with Captain Abbinett of Gosport and the diver, William Moses, to blow up the wreck, they only succeeded after several attempts and not before causing considerable damage to the pier.

The incident had not escaped jibes from at least one scribe, Terry Driscoll, in a jocular anti-establishment piece in the *Commercial Journal*, 8 July 1854. The Great Summer Exhibition of the Royal Horticultural Society had just been held outdoors at Salthill, Kingstown, and had been badly affected by wind and rain. Driscoll stingingly wrote, "the show was 'blown-out' for 'divers reasons'. They had been blasting a sunken ship, and givin' the sea wall a crack into the bargain."

I'm sure that this embarrassing piece of dirty washing did not escape the attention of its target, the harbour master.

This area of the east pier was a well-known 'blackspot'. The distance between the pier heads was criticised as being too close, as well as their angle presenting difficulties entering during a contrary wind. Changing times and the new steamships were hardly affected at all. Even though the criticism was genuine, it was coming around the last furlong a bit too late though. The ferocity of storms that had wrecked so many vessels earlier, repeating but waning in subsequent years, eventually became a thing of the past – the steamers managed fine.

William Campbell, an experienced diver working for the Board of Public Works engineer, Barry Gibbons, was busy blowing up submerged rocks at Kilmore Quay at the time and no apparent attempt was made to contract him for this particular piece of work on the *Argyle*. The demarcation line that skirted the boundary of harbour authority had suffered another wobble.

Notwithstanding William Hutchison's impeccable career, the harbour's letter books and correspondence that are on file in the National Archives leave me with the impression that Lieutenant Hutchison, for whatever reason, did not seem to get on with the Campbells. Their relationship seemed official and curt only, and from William Campbell's point of view, maybe it was the increasing frequency of having to perform what could be described as 'more menial tasks' (policing stall holders, discovering the unauthorised users of the commissioners' water supply, unregulated effluent discharge and investigating incidents of encroachment onto Public Works property) that irked him. Although not answerable directly to Hutchison, it was a ménage-à-trois with no upside for Campbell at the time.

William also had to interface with a number of unsavoury characters around Kingstown and Dalkey during the normal course of his duties: trespassers, fractious dealings with men unloading coal lighters, tongue-lashings from spectators under the influence of excess liquor during summer regatta or moving on unlicensed stall holders. However, there was only a single recorded case where an incident ended up in the courts.

While superintending work at Dalkey Quarries for the commissioners in May, William was assaulted by the local woman, Margaret Healy. She was arrested by policeman 57F and charged at the Kingstown police office. It appears that the commissioners were clearing huts and occupiers at the quarry when the assault took place. Unlawful occupation of commonage on Dalkey had been an issue from time to time but, it is unclear, in this case, if the huts were legally established or not, as some financial compensation was later awarded to their owners. A police guard remained at the quarry until the work was completed and the site secured. Margaret Healy was unable to produce bail and she was sentenced to confinement for fourteen days.

Administrative Duels

There was never any hint of conviviality, or anything other than propriety in official harbour correspondence from this period, and it was the stark bare words of instruction, the lack of any tone, except one of seniority and control, that might have done it. It is always regretful when one is reduced to seek an explanation for acts of discrimination, of any kind, in a person's religious beliefs. No matter how thoughtful or carefully crafted a summation, the outcome always smacks of bigotry. Nevertheless, it is sometimes necessary, in order to explore why something happened in a certain way and when another, more obvious or logical reason cannot be found.

The majority of the population of Kingstown were Protestant at this time, and more pronounced amongst the positions of civil administration and professions. So much so that the Royal Harbour and its well-ordered streets and houses, with names seemingly straight out of Kipling, became known as 'West Britain'. Equally noteworthy are the number of Kingstown Town Commissioners who had the same name as some of their streets.

A change in the fortunes of this section of the population was underway after Catholic Emancipation, exemplified by the self-made engineer, Barry Gibbons – a Catholic, rising as he did to meteoric heights in his profession and harvesting the respect of colleagues, with his disregard of religious norms of preference or association. As he progressed through his career, he elevated the Protestant, William Campbell up behind him and it might have been no wonder if it had gone against the grain with some at the time. Times were changing; I think practices were too.

The rot would seem to have set in after the admonishing of the harbour master by the Commissioners of Public Works, in June 1860, over the drink licence issue. Small but antagonistic, a number of incidents erupted between the harbour master and the Department of Public Works – Gibbons and Campbell. The smooth running of the harbour, from the marine point of view, was clearly Lieutenant Hutchison's responsibility. The physical maintenance and improvement of the harbour was clearly the responsibility of the Board of Public Works. If the harbour master required work to be done on the harbour, he contacted Public Works, not the harbour commissioners – you would imagine. He would certainly report at his meetings of harbour commissioners but, to get the work done, he simply had to toddle across the yard.

Another issue of some concern was the collection of monies due to the State, such as licence fees and harbour dues, which was carried out by officials of Public Works on behalf of the Revenue Commissioners. So, one can easily see how duties might continually overlap. In such circumstances and for staff not to see eye to eye, only meant trouble.

A seemingly simple and mundane matter, timber planks, provided by Public Works for boarding vessels to load or unload coal, had to be paid for – they were hired. The job of providing and hiring the planks fell between the recurring two stools and Public Works had to deal with it. This and other minor frictional interfacing were handled by issuing duplicate hymn sheets to their own officials, Gibbons and Campbell on the one hand and on the other, to the harbour master, William Hutchison. Maybe it was the growing relationship between Campbell and Gibbons, two men who had travelled and worked together for fifteen years and were now living almost side by side in Kingstown. An acquaintance that was more than just master and worker had apparently developed by this time, and this is possibly where the trouble lay.

Then there was the trouble with the flags. When Barry Gibbons died the following year, 1862, his funeral was one of the largest the county had seen. Although official correspondence suggests that some care was taken to inform William Campbell that he could have time off to attend the funeral, support for the sentiment was not in evidence at Gibbons' old workplace at Kingstown Harbour on burial day. While the citizens of Kingstown and Dublin mourned the passing of a well-respected engineer, a great man who travelled throughout Ireland during the worst of the Famine years to get the work done, some manner of 'protocol' had muted the reaction of officialdom. The begrudging display was not missed by some of the press. The Monday edition of the *Daily Express*, 27 October 1862, ran the following article under "Kingstown Intelligence":

> *The Late Mr Gibbons. – Throughout the entire of Saturday and Sunday the flags of the City of Dublin's offices, and the few yachts still remaining in the harbour, were borne at half-mast high, in recognition of this gentleman – the flags of the Royal St. George and the Royal Irish Yacht clubs, of which Mr. Gibbons was an honorary member, exhibiting the same sign of mourning ... It has been remarked as singular that the Government shore establishments at Kingstown, with which the deceased, as harbour engineer, was so intimately associated, have not shown the usual sign of respect by lowering their flags.*

It cannot go unnoticed that the Royal yacht clubs were to the fore in their respect for a decent man, Protestant or Catholic. The most prominent of course and maybe true colours, were visible in the flag at full height, alongside the clock over the Harbour Master's office.

It might appear that both men, Campbell and Gibbons, sinned in faith and association. Perhaps it was Campbell's relationship with Barry D. Gibbons, a colleague and a neighbour in Kingstown, as was the harbour master himself. They were each fine upstanding men, dedicated to their work and maybe it was time that just overtook them and marched on.

Barry D. Gibbons, RIP, 1862

Born in Kinsale, Cork, 1798c, Barry D. Gibbons died on 24 October 1862. He and his wife lived at Connaught Place, just off Quay Road, Kingstown. Being a childless couple, I suspect William Campbell and his family, who lived almost beside Gibbons, represented something more than an employer-employee relationship and that they had lost a good friend. The funeral to Glasnevin Cemetery was a massive affair; time off to attend was granted to some Public Works employees at Kingstown.

It was undeniable that Gibbons was 'a man of progress'. There is no doubt, that even during his lifetime, he was considered an outstanding practical minded engineer. He travelled the country extensively, proposing his own designs, supervising projects large and small, consulting and adjudicating on competing infrastructural designs. He had a distinct knack of involving and supporting local communities and gave generously of his time and expertise to their needs and advancement. Despite his numerous civic achievements – and the fact that so many turned out in the streets of Dublin to pay tribute to him in his death – he has somehow failed to attract any significant attention from historians.

My own belief is that Barry Gibbons was a man who loved his work and by virtue of being both very capable and inventive, he was able to demonstrate, at this important juncture, that a Catholic engineer was every bit as competent as a Protestant one. He never wore his religious persuasion on his sleeve but admired craftsmen who could work on their own initiative – and demonstrated that slackers were not confined to any particular religion. He was admired by all classes and creeds for his work throughout the counties of Ireland and for his interest in local communities, particularly in Wexford.

In his professional capacity, Barry D. Gibbons climbed through the ranks of his profession as a civil engineer and became Resident Engineer with the Board of Public Works, eventually elevated to Chief Engineer. He also consulted with and was employed by a number of steam packet and railway companies. He was a member of the Institute of Civil Engineers and served as ordinary member, council member, and vice president. He was a member of the Council of the Geological Society of Dublin. He was a member/agent of the Art Union of Ireland and a staunch supporter of promoting Irish art and an appreciation of culture and education. Both his wife's and his own name consistently appeared in publications against generous donations to multiple charities.

Barry Gibbons and his wife Anne (née Brew), sister to the gifted authoress, Margaret Brew, were apparently childless. Barry Gibbons was not residing with his wife at Connaught Place, Kingstown at the time of his death but, was reposed from 13 Dawson Street, Dublin, listed as a premises owned by Mary Anne Nolan, selling groceries, tea, wine and spirits. Advertisements for the same address would suggest that there were a number of occupancies in the building, which also provided some kind of post box arrangement for job seekers. It was reported that Mr Gibbons was staying at this address in order to be close to his doctors during his illness, which was reported to be pulmonary related. Both Mr and Mrs Nolan died at this address shortly after Mr Gibbons.

Barry Gibbons and his wife, Anne were Catholic. Anne's father was a Protestant minister in Kilrush and no record of Anne's marriage to Barry could be found. Barry Duncan Gibbons was buried in a prominent vault at Glasnevin Cemetery and its inscription reads:

Sacred to the memory of Barry Duncan Gibbons Esq., Engineer in Chief to the Board of Works, Ireland. He died 24 August 1862 aged 64 years. He was good, wise, and noble in thought and act, a good husband and warm-hearted friend, his hand ever open to the poor, his assistance ever ready for the lowly. May the Lord have mercy on his soul. Amen.
Erected by his affectionate Widow in faith, in gratitude and undying love.

Not recorded on the headstone, his wife, Anne was also laid to rest in the same vault when she died in 1899.

Barry Gibbons left his estate to his wife, Anne, recorded as being under £4,000. Fashionable and sought after but not considered in quite the same class as 'Millionaires Row', as it is today, Anne moved later from Connaught Place to 5 Sorrento Terrace, Dalkey and lived there with her sister, Cornelia, who died in 1876. Anne was also reposed from there, when she was ninety years of age, in 1899. No will was found for Anne.[4]

After the incident with the 'flags' mentioned earlier, Campbell might have suspected that the wind about the harbour was about to get a bit chilly but, might not have expected that the sky would fall in.

---

4 A portrait of Barry D. Gibbons is said to have hung in the Art Union of Ireland but, unfortunately, could not be located.

One of the last buildings remaining from the Board of Public Works (Harbour Commissioners) complex at Dún Laoghaire – old Kingstown. Known as the Harbour Master's House, this was not the original harbour master's house and was designed and intended to be the dwelling of the Chief Superintendent of Kingstown Harbour, a position (not the house) held by William Campbell for ten years. The building was used, until quite recently, for administration by the Harbour Board. Author's collection.

Old diver's air pump still in the Harbour Superintendent's House at Dún Laoghaire Harbour (Kingstown). Author's collection.

The guardship, *HMS George* and the Royal Irish Yacht Club at Kingstown. Image is courtesy of the *Lawrence Collection* at the National Library of Ireland.

Storm at Kingstown in 1861, which devastated shipping in the region and kept the Campbells busy for some time afterwards. Author's collection.

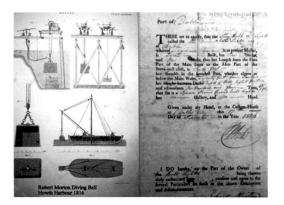

Drawing of diving-bell lighter and gantry, built by Morton's of Ringsend, Dublin and its registration certificate. The bell boat, *The Bell* was used in the construction of Howth and Kingstown harbours. Print is courtesy of Cormac Louth and the certificate was copied from Howth Harbour files in National Archives, Dublin.

This remarkable granite-stone lifeboat house was completed by William Campbell as Superintendent of Works, Kingstown Harbour in 1862. It houses the inshore lifeboat, which operates to this day.

Chapter 7

The American CivilWar Comes to Ireland, 1862-1865

A storm of quite a different nature had been brewing, for quite some time and exploded into conflict one year earlier, in April 1861. The north and south of America could not agree over the principal that one man shouldn't own another. The war between the North and the South would last four years and the blood of three quarters of a million of their citizens would be spilt. Whole families were divided, many of them wiped out and the country's future was squandered over the lack of respect for a justified advance of civilised society, in its attempt to prevent principles enshrined in property rights extending to humans.

Although most developing countries had expressed their objections to slavery, there was as always however, a buck to be made out of the conflict. Britain's declared policy of neutrality would not sanction any war advantage to be gained in the export of war material to either side, even though it did little to prevent exports of war material to both. It did, however, recognise the South as a belligerent and anywhere the empire had influence, Confederates sheltered under a protective British mantle.

A construct of rules was established for the conflict, designed to prevent any danger of engagement in neutral ports and allowed opposing naval vessels to resupply periodically – 'the twenty-four-hour rule'. However, the classic blind eye was often shown and the work of recruiting agents, suppliers of arms, ships and the establishment of complicated commercial supply networks of war material to the South, went largely unhindered for a time, while the other eye kept a sharp watch on financial opportunities.

HMS Himalaya

No different from others, the Irish business class were equally keen on confederate or yankee money, war or no war. A quite surprising number of merchants, factory and ship owners in Ireland actively supported the supply of the confederate army during the whole period of the war. Some were known to quip, "So what? It can't be stopped; it's a waste of time trying."

The counter to this was boycotts. Sanctions remained important diplomatic tools and are considered, rightly or wrongly, as being effective methods in preventing cruelty, oppression, the loss of freedoms, not to mention mass killings on the battlefields, to this day. Aspirational and often circumvented, the moral imperative represented a noble and peaceful intervention.

Union and confederate spies, recruiters, permeated British and Irish ports where opposing sides were permitted to dock their ships, re-coal and re-supply. They were not allowed to enter or leave together. Except, that in the case of the 'Grey ships', often weakly presented as being neutrally commercial, could come and go as they pleased. From a British port, ships that had only just been launched, laden with contraband and arms with obvious intent, were ignored. In cases of the 'Blue ships', re-coaling was sometimes made difficult in places that you might not have expected: not denying the coal outright but making a ship go offshore for it – 'out of sight, out of mind'. Legitimate shipping companies carried on a steady trade with both sides in items that were less warlike, such as uniforms, tools, leather goods and so on.

Kingstown Harbour was no exception and saw union and confederate ships seeking sanctuary within its walls. A sign of changing times and things to come, some of Kingstown's inhabitants began to detect unusual marine traffic in the harbour as early as 1859, when the *HMS Himalaya* made her first visit to Ireland. After the American Civil War erupted, the *Himalaya* was seen a number of times in Kingstown, sometimes relieving or topping up garrisoned troops in Ireland or, picking them up for overseas duty.[1] Before and after the Trent Affair, when US naval ships began to challenge British ones on the high seas, over blockade running and supplying confederate forces, the *Himalaya* was being used to bolster troop numbers and deliver military equipment to Canada and Mexico, in anticipation of conflict with the United States. The threat of union forces invading the British colonies in British North America was a very real one.[2]

This armed troop carrier was a ship with a perceivable difference. A magnificent looking passenger ship, built for the Peninsular and Orient Steam Navigation Company in 1853, it was heralded as the largest passenger ship in the world, with a displacement weight of 4,690 tons. With wars looming on several fronts, it was purchased by the Admiralty the following year, and *HMS* was added to her name. It was a handsome ship but its value as a naval vessel was criticised by the wooden-wall know-alls, who were busy proving that iron ships were more pervious to cannon

---

1 Some early photographs of the *Himalaya*, berthed in Kingstown, are on file in the National Library of Ireland.

2 The Trent Affair, as it was called, occurred in 1861 when two confederate diplomats were removed from the British ship, *RMS Trent* by US naval personnel from the, *USS San Jacinto*.

fire than wooden ones. An occupation, you might think that had little prospect of a pension. Despite criticism by the self-interested, it became one of the most successful troop carriers in the history of the Royal Navy, transporting thousands of troops, armaments and horses throughout the British Empire. She survived afloat until bombed during a German aerial raid in 1940.

Not only was it a modern and elegant looking vessel but, she was remarkably efficient and could also sail somewhat. Even though she cleaved some harbour furniture on the Victoria Wharf during her first visit to Kingstown, in 1859, she became a regular visitor to the harbour but remarkably shy of entering the harbour again. There had been an issue with the draught of the ship: the clearance between her keel and the bottom of the harbour. Ironically, even today, the depth of water in the harbour has proved challenging for large vessels and continues to frustrate plans for turning the harbour into a stopover for large cruise liners.

The Gunboat, Tuscarora

The appearance of confederate and union warships in British waters, such as the *Tuscarora*, caused the political temperature to rise. Unease was not only confined to the mainland but right around the coast of Ireland, the Irish Sea and in the office of the American Consul in Dublin. Cheered on by the public and the maritime fraternity as opposing flags sailed into Kingstown, higher authorities were not sorry to see the back of either belligerent as they sailed out. As in all cases of war, when nationalistic fervour or the sap of military adventure rises, men will respond and guaranteed – will line up in opposing ranks.

Despite the villas, marinas, mansions and prestigious yacht clubs that lined the shores between Blackrock and Kingstown, Ireland was not long out of the grip of the national catastrophe – Famine. Fifteen years earlier, William Campbell had travelled through the remotest parts of Ireland, building harbours and piers for the Department of Public Works and witnessed the worst ravages of the Famine in Ireland, *Black '47* being the latest cinematic adventure into that dark period.

Forward to 1862 and families were still striving to find miserly paid labour to survive, and cruel sentences were still being handed down for minor infractions of law, such as stealing bread. Charged as pirates, islanders and remote coastal villagers continued to board ships in desperation, in order to steal from their cargoes of grain. Very few cases of violence were ever reported during these episodes. Crews just threw their hands up and proceeded to the authorities to report the incident.

Starvation still prevailed in many counties and consequently, those who were fit and able ran from the land, in search of any kind of a better life – and even to war. Young men could see huge modern vessels enter their harbours on route to foreign lands of opportunity. Openly plied with grog by recruiters, with a promise of free passage and a bounty upon landing, they took flight. Vested interests supported or criticised recruitment for the civil war, by both sides. For different reasons, religious, anti-war, ship owners and commercial interests all espoused reasons why they should go or stay.

There have always been 'hurlers on the ditch' and Kingstown had no shortage of them. Many of the town's lords and ladies openly supported the South and encouraged others to do their bidding. Understanding that such might well be the case in Britain, officers of the Federal gunboat, *Tuscarora*, were surprised to detect such an open level of anti-Union bias amongst the "population of Ireland". Equally surprising is that union naval officers attempted to gauge the political temperature in Ireland based solely on the opinions of harbour populations. Instead, the manifestation of the conflict in Ireland, to some degree, would appear to have presented as Catholic Blue vs Protestant Grey. The British and spar-spangled flags fluttered over the harbour buildings and along the piers in Kingstown when the *USS Tuscarora* first arrived but, it was a visit that stirred mixed feelings.

Laid down at Pennsylvania in June 1861, she was "launched in 50 days" and there's that figure again. The furore surrounding *Tuscarora*'s visit to Britain and Ireland began in January, after she received orders to leave Spain and sail to England in pursuit of the confederate cruiser, *Nashville*, docked at Southampton. *Tuscarora* docked at Southampton but failed to capture the *Nashville* when she left in February. She was forbidden to leave and chase the confederate ship until 24 hours had passed.

In pursuit of confederate raiders once again, she anchored off Plymouth in July 1862, thus beginning one of the most publicised cat-and-mouse sea chases in the course of naval warfare. Remembered for her earlier visit, Joe Public's dander was beginning to rise in the face of brazen acts by Confederates, taking the war to British vessels during their lawful comings and goings in home waters – but this was to be no ordinary naval chase. It was even described as a, "Blockade of Ireland, Britain and France". A valuable lesson, perhaps, for when blockading became an effective weapon during World War I and, one that remains popular.

If there had been movies, it would have been reported in much the same way as the cat-and-mouse confrontation in the Battle of the River Plate during World War II. British cruisers lying in wait outside of the neutral port of Montevideo in South America, for the German battle cruiser, *Graf*

Spee, to come out, after resupply and repairs. If the British had entered, they may have been compelled to remain until the *Graf Spee* had left.

Instead, any entertainment that the public enjoyed during the *Tuscarora* incident in 1862, was confined to remarks in the press and some poetic commentary.

Portsmouth Times, July 1862

The Tuscarora at Southampton

V5/6

Lo, the Tuscarora
In Southampton Water!
People on the shore-a
Marvellin', what has brought her.
What again has brought her,
There, a fear and wonder,
Loomin' black and thunder,
Watchful Tuscarora,
In Southampton Water.

V6/6

Ready for the battle
Soon as the peace is broken,
When her guns will rattle
If the word is spoken.
Spoken, without quarter,
Ships and town to batter,
Slay, and smash, and scatter,
Lies the Tuscarora
In Southampton Water.

After the American Consul, Thomas Dudley, learned that Lairds were constructing a heavily armoured vessel for the South, he alerted his naval colleagues. Known only by its yard number, *290*, she was almost completed. Union spies in Liverpool warned that she would rendezvous with the *Merrimac*, also due to depart and suspected to be stuffed with armaments and munitions for the South.

At the end of July, the word was out that the *Merrimac* had sailed and the *Tuscarora* upped anchor in pursuit. Suspecting that she might sail for Queenstown, the most westward port for re-coaling before crossing the Atlantic, or heading for Madeira, the *Tuscarora* doglegged up the George's

Channel and then across for Queenstown. In her wake was the ship tasked with shadowing her, the *HMS Shannon*, a hefty, ironclad steam frigate.[3]

The *Tuscarora* entered Queenstown on 31 July and anchored. After a couple of days, visitors and the US consuls all safely back ashore, she set off again. The rumour was that *290* had left Liverpool.

Up the channel and back again, she couldn't find either the *Merrimac* or the powerful new warship, rumoured to be the equivalent of the powerful *HMS Warrior*. The rebel chaser was described as being "unfortunate". If the Confederates or the British navy were going to attack the *Tuscarora*, the pubic showed no sympathy. Words can be like daggers to the heart: poetry such as that which dogged the *Tuscarora*, might easily have been expected to sink her.

Tuscarora put out from Queenstown for a second time and headed directly to the heart of the problem – Holyhead. Reported to have met the *Merrimac* off Holyhead, there was still no sign of the *290*. After lingering off Liverpool Bay, the Admiralty ordered the *Tuscarora* to sail away.

The *Tuscarora* sailed north at first and, after taking on a pilot at Point Lynas, Captain Craven learned that the *290* had passed out of the North Channel at a rate of knots. The game was up – the 'bird had flown'.

Not giving up completely, as there were a number of vessels coming out of Liverpool and the Clyde at this time, all set for blockade running, Captain Craven set sail for Kingstown, with *HMS Shannon* still bringing up the rear. While in Kingstown, to the annoyance of Captain Secombe and the Union Consulate, it was put about that blockade runners, in the guise of neutral 'British ships', were being supported by some Irish interests, using islands off the west coast of Ireland for resupply. The accusation would seem to have had some merit, as such ships were seen off the west coast but a 'resupply station' and a strategy of repetitive landings – the accusation had shades of similar red herrings concerning German submarines during World War I and World War II.

The press, seemingly keen to rub it in, printed another broadside of verse.

The Daily Post, August 9

V1/5

Our friend, the Tuscarora,
Back again once more-a,

---

3 Strategically positioned, coaling at Queenstown meant that a steamer could sail west across the Atlantic or south to Madeira first, where it could pick up more coal and even rendezvous for transfers or arming. It was difficult for the captain of a pursuing vessel to determine which course his quarry might take, unless in sight.

A visit to Southampton pays, and then to Cork she goes,
Cat like, ever watching
What she would be catching
Almost all can guess, though no one exactly knows.

V4/5

Who was seen off Ireland's coast,
Running fourteen knots almost?
"Off to Charlston", as the song says, escaping as she ought!
Wasn't this a "floorer"
For the Tuscarora!
Wasn't it a triumph for the "Two-Nine-Nought"?

The *Tuscarora* entered Kingstown on 9 August and immediately became the source of intense curiosity. Thousands visited to see the yankee gunboat. Even more buntings and flags were strung all along the piers and buildings and from masts on boats moored in the harbour. Flower and winkle sellers pitched along the seafront and on the piers, after William Campbell had been instructed to erect some facilities for licensed traders. Local boats did a roaring trade, ferrying sightseers around the American warship. The age-old ways of card sharps and purveyors of illicit liquor all rankled with Captain Hutchison's sense of propriety and morals, and the proper manner in which a Royal Harbour should be run.

In time-honoured fashion, the committees of the Royal Saint George and Royal Irish yacht clubs bestowed honorary membership on the officers from the visiting ship, and everyone appeared to be happy and settled down to celebrations with the new visitors in the harbour. The love affair was short-lived, however. Criticism was growing in the press. How can an American warship be allowed to harass British maritime commerce on its very shores? All the niceties and formalities done with, except permission for the *Tuscarora* to re-coal being denied, she was once again asked to leave a British harbour.

The press announced the "Sudden Departure of the *Tuscarora* From Kingstown" and this occurred at 5 o'clock of Tuesday, 12 August 1862. "Destination unknown", "on a short cruise" the *Tuscarora* sailed north out of Dublin Bay but didn't go too far. She anchored, later, in Ramsay Bay and Douglas in the Isle of Man and only remained for a very short time. She returned once again to Kingstown, for "stores and repairs". No request for coaling was made but, as some observant "Trans-Atlantic cousins" were able to detect, the *Tuscarora* was actually lower in the water than when she had left.

This game of musical harbours had to come to an end. Tempers in Whitehall were fraying and Captain Craven was once again ordered to leave Kingstown – and did so on 19 August. Before she did and while still at anchor in Kingstown, it was claimed that thirty-six of her crew had been given permission to visit relatives ashore but never returned. It was also reported that the majority of *Tuscarora*'s crew were Irish, mainly from Donegal. Only temporarily short of crew, replacements were recruited from amongst an abundance of eager young Irishmen clambering on the quays in Kingstown, seeking adventure.

Some of the reports indicated that the *290*, known then as the *Enrica*, had rendezvoused with the *Merrimac* off the west coast of Ireland, where she took on her heavy calibre Blakely guns. She then proceeded to another fitting-out station in the Atlantic, also manned with 'blind eyes', the Azores, and was renamed, the *CSS Alabama*.[4]

The *Tuscarora* had missed the earlier *Nashville*; she had missed the *Merrimac* and had failed to catch the *290*. Not being able to confront and disable this particular vessel would play on Captain Craven's mind for the remainder of the war. The *Alabama* became a notorious raider and a terror of the seas, until put out of action in the English Channel in 1864. Her Captain, Semmes, was a superior adversary and had even eluded capture after his ship was sunk, rescued by the yacht, *Deerhound*. The story of the incident and the yacht's name have lived on under the yardarms of famous yacht clubs ever since.

The *Tuscarora* was never going to get the better of the British Navy, or wily politicians, on their own doorstep. Craven was at the mercy of a superior navy, an advanced armed coastguard service and the telegraph. Once he moved, his direction could be transmitted around the British Isles. At a distinct disadvantage, Craven had to rely on contact at sea or coming into port to communicate with his Consul, in order to gain any intelligence. Some British establishment newspapers seemed to be playing the game too, providing well out-of-date and confusing reports of movements.

Little could be done, in British waters, to prevent intending blockade runners leaving for America but, they were eventually prevented from reaching America when the Union's blockade measures improved and began to tighten. There was no way a poorly equipped Southern army or navy could ever have defeated a nation that could build warships in "50 days". Very similarly claimed mass production techniques defeated far greater adversaries, in the World Wars to follow – those rapidly built destroyers

---

4   A rendezvous to transfer arms to the *290* off the west coast of Ireland was never confirmed.

and Liberty ships. Quite ironically, that same figure, would appear again in the naval relations between America and the United Kingdom, when Churchill pleaded with Roosevelt for the "50 Ships that Saved the World", in order to prevent defeat during World War II.

HMS Ajax Out – CSN Ajax In

By the time the following incident had occurred. William Campbell had battled his way through terrible weather down the Atlantic in a 67-ton schooner. Not long after that event, he completed another leg of his voyage and rounded the Cape of Good Hope. Following a series of life-threatening adventures, he eventually landed at South Australia and never returned. Like many of the confederate sympathisers and blockade runners at the time, the schooner and its crew had left Liverpool on a course supposedly set for that strategic outpost, the Azores.

Campbell left Kingstown abruptly, almost secretly and to this day, those surviving members of his large extended family of descendants don't know why he departed in the way that he did, or even why he left at all. The *Ajax* incident occurred later but taken with previous accounts, will help demonstrate the different attitudes of citizens in the British Isles towards the opposing sides in the American Civil War, and how unfolding events at the time might have influenced decisions taken by the Campbells.

In February 1864, Commander of the Coastguards and captain of the huge 74 gunner, *HMS Ajax*, stationed in Kingstown Harbour, announced that a grand ball and supper would take place on board. The old Blackwall ship of the line was ending its tour of duty at Kingstown and was about to sail for England. Its larger replacement, the *Royal George*, was completing fitting out at Devonport. Local dignitaries, politicians, naval and officers of various uniforms were accompanied by guests from 'fashionable and influential circles' and a grand old time was had by one and all aboard the "handsomely decorated MOW", until well into the early hours.

To celebrate her departure, the population of Kingstown turned out in fine style and lined the piers as the *Ajax* took her leave in March 1864. She did not, as her masters in Whitehall had predicted, remain in Kingstown "until her bones dropped out". There was reciprocal cheering and waving with well-wishers, while the ship's naval band played them out between the piers and off she sailed.

Transferred to his new command, Captain De Courcy took up his post in the *Royal George* and, as was his want, the music and theatre evenings continued on the new Royal Navy guardship at Kingstown, just as before.

As the reader might imagine, when a rumour that the *Ajax* had attempted to put in to Kingstown after encountering bad weather circulated ten months later, in January 1865, and had ran up on to the harbour's east pier, it might have taken little wind for it to spread like wildfire around the town – and this is exactly what happened. Local people ran down to the harbour to see for themselves and were both disappointed and relieved, to discover a false alarm. The *Ajax* in question was the twin-screw steamer that was pulled off the east pier from the exact location where the unfortunate disaster had struck a couple of years earlier, when Captain Boyd and a number of crew from *HMS Ajax* had lost their lives during a shipwreck recue. One of twins, this particular *Ajax* had just been completed by Denny Brothers at Dumbarton and was a diminutive couple of hundred tons. Cleverly disguised, she was, in fact, a very stoutly built vessel, designed to punch well above her appearance as 'ordinary'.

Escaping bad weather and no sooner hauled off the pier by the tug, *Lightening* to a safe berth, another rumour ran around the town like lightening. "A mutiny in the harbour; the crew of the *Ajax* has mutinied" or, as the press cleverly put it, "A Serious Case of Emeute on Board the *Ajax.*"

Perhaps earlier mutinies were less dramatic but reports were adamant that nothing like it had ever been seen in Kingstown before. At first reading, the affair appeared not too dissimilar to other incidents of sailors 'jumping ship'. It seems that the crew were upset with the seaworthiness of the *Ajax* and refused to sail any further in her. The police magistrate was not happy and ordered a survey of the ship, which Captain Hutchison promptly completed. He reported that there was nothing wrong with the ship: she was seaworthy and "tight".

Apparently knowing more about what was going on in the bowels of the ship, the mutineers insisted that she should be hauled into dry dock for a thorough inspection. The magistrate was having none of it and ordered the mutineers to return to the ship. They refused and the magistrate confined them, threatening prison and hard labour.

Captain Adams of the *Ajax* began to hire replacement recruits, which supposedly included some boatmen from Kingstown. The fat hit the fire and another mutiny, with violence, took place in the harbour. Marines were called to quell the riot and marched the mutineers back to the Magistrate. Some of the crew were locked up for a short period and some were returned to the ship. Captain Adams fled Kingstown, as fast as the powerful twin-screw would take him.

At the heart of the story was *Ajax*'s true purpose. Ordered by the super spy, Commander James Bulloch, for blockade busting, her construction was supervised by CSN Lieutenant, John Low. Considered a confederate spy of significant abilities, Low had been apprehended more than once, only to be released. The *Ajax* was launched at Dumbarton in January as a tug – with no declared owner! She was later reported to have "escaped from the Clyde" with seven guns on board.

Partly due to the hearings before the magistrate at Kingstown being prolonged, revealing testimony by *Ajax*'s crew members began to appear in some newspapers. According to their testimony, to which all sides turned the familiar blind eye, the *Ajax* was a heavily built and armed blockade buster and was bound for the confederate forces at Wilmington. Not denied by Captain Adams, the whole world and its mother had discovered her mission but, she was allowed to proceed unhindered.

American consuls in Britain and Ireland had become aware of the *Ajax* and her mission but, were reported to have failed to reach Kingstown in time and were unable prevent her from sailing. The *Ajax* sailed, calling in at the familiar fuelling and intelligence gathering waypoint of Madeira in March 1865, eventually landing at Nassau.

Mentioned by the press, the "mysterious passenger" who hardly ever spoke and was "continually changing his clothes" the whole time while the *Ajax* was berthed in Kingstown, was none other than Bulloch's friend, naval lieutenant, John Low, of the confederate steamers, *Fingal*, *Tuscaloosa* and *Alabama*.

Low had supervised the completion of the ships at Denny's and sailed in the *Ajax*, with the intention of taking command when they reached Nassau. He did so, but between the flagging fortunes of the South and for the impounded, out-of-touch *Ajax* and her crew at Saint George's Harbour, the game was up. Denny's had constructed a valuable vessel for the South – only one in a long line of many more built around the Clyde and at Liverpool. It was growing late however and the blockaders were beginning to pile up in ports, due to the growing effectiveness of the Union's navy. The *Ajax* was sailed back across the Atlantic to Liverpool and was advertised for sale in June: "Only one voyage from new", failing to enlarge on whether or not it was by a 'lady owner'. It's true.

Sections of the British establishment had been openly in support of the southern cause, possibly due to commercial interests or, maybe still nursing the bloody nose from their own battles in the Americas, on more than one occasion. Some went further and took an active part in support of the Confederates, by running supply ships to the southern states, called blockade runners.

USS Sacramento at Kingstown

The very bloody and stubborn civil war came to an end after Richmond fell in April 1865 but, Kingstown was not finished with the yankee gunboats. US naval ships were still scattered across the oceans and two steam frigates, *Niagara* and *Sacramento* that had been tracking the Alabama, remained prowling on the coasts off Madeira, Spain, France and in the English Channel.

It was reported that they had received instructions to round up any armed confederate ships and old blockaders that had already returned to the UK, becoming bona fide commercial steamers. It was also reported that USN vessels had instructions to ignore adherence to the 'twenty-four-hour rule' and any national flag flown by ships that were suspected to have previously been blockade runners. This was, effectively, privateering against a country that it was not at war with.

The notorious commerce raider, *CSS Alabama* wasn't entertaining surrender and was sunk off Cherbourg in June, by the *USS Kearsgrange*. Old blockade runners were still returning from Bermuda and calling at Queenstown before continuing to England, tempting the two frigates to patrol off the south coast of Ireland. Two blockaders of some note – paddle steamers, *City of Petersburgh* and the *Old Dominion*, both built at Greenock – had made it back to Scotland and had been refitted by the time the two USN frigates steamed into Queenstown. A few days later, the *Sacramento* continued up the Irish Sea and headed for Kingstown, arriving between the piers, thronged with admiring onlookers, at the beginning of July 1865.

It was a convenient fact that these visiting American naval vessels always seem to arrive during the regatta season – not to miss a good party, so to speak. The Kingstown Regatta festivities were in full swing and the customary invitations were extended by the Royal yacht clubs to the visiting USN officers, the full list of whom were published in newspapers, with the intention of 'showing off' their strong Irish connections.

In the meantime, the two not so very old blockade runners, *Old Dominion* and *City of Petersburgh*, had been put into service by a syndicate of shipping investors on the cross-channel service between Liverpool and Kingstown was – the outfit was simply called the New Dublin Steamship Company. The ships were meant to capture some of the growing business being secured, at that time, by the popular City of Dublin Steam Packet Company (CDSPC), the latter company having snatched the contract for the delivery of mails, between Dublin and Holyhead, from the mitts of its competitors. The CDSPC fought a fierce war of competitive rivalry with the railway companies and their steamers until it finally succumbed, after losing two of its revolutionary design of twin-screw steamers during World War I.

It wasn't long before interested observers cottoned on to what they believed was the real reason for the American naval vessel's late visit to Irish shores. The papers had it that the *Sacramento* was after the old blockaders that were plying in and out of Kingstown on regular runs. One can imagine the looks and shouts that might have been exchanged as these blockade runners pulled away from the Victoria Wharf and puffed by the anchored *Sacramento*, still unable to apprehend them.

A very fine party was held in honour of the visiting Americans at the Mansion House in Dublin on the 6th. There was a long list of guests that included military, naval and political representatives from several countries. The health of Captain Walke of the *Sacramento* and many others was toasted heartily and celebrations continued into the wee hours. Still in the wee hours – Captain Walke and the *Sacramento* were nowhere to be seen in Kingstown when the staff at Kingstown began to appear for work.

There was some surprise when sailors attempted to desert from the *Sacramento* but, it was an even greater one when the *Sacramento* deserted twenty of her own sailors still ashore on leave, after she had hurriedly upped anchor and steamed out of the harbour, in a great rush, on 7 July. The reason given was that another paddle-wheel blockader from Greenock, the *Beatrice* (ex-*Rappahannock*) was believed to be in the channel. Said to have joined the *Beatrice* off Skerries and pursued her as far as the North Channel, there was no capture or engagement and the *Sacramento* returned to Kingstown the next day. It was an impressive chase, and at a dazzling turn of speed if reports were correct, the *Sacramento* was said to have returned to Kingstown, only barely missing lunch at 2.30pm.

The regatta and its festivities were not to be missed and realistically, there was probably little danger of any English steamers being seized or attacked by US naval vessels in this neck of the woods. There was more than ample protection afforded by British naval vessels sent to Kingstown and those present in the Irish Sea at the time.

Said to have been very surprised, the crew of the *Sacramento* enjoyed a remarkable level of hospitality for a couple of weeks and there was no trouble with coal on this occasion. Tedcastles[5] loaded her up with a couple of hundred tons to see the Yankees on their way. The two old blockade

---

5 An Irish company founded in 1800 by Tedcastle McCormick, operating mainly as a coal and shipping business. It continues to operate to this day, as a petrol, fuel and home heating supplier, trading under the name of Top Oil.

runners continued in and out of Kingstown and everyone went home happy.

The names of the two blockaders were changed to *Bridgewater* and *Sheffield* when they were inaugurated into another 'new service' in October, under the business name, the Liverpool and Dublin Steam Navigation Company.

Perhaps if the two frigates had hung around for another few months, they might have captured another prize, the *CSS Shenandoah*, before she surrendered to the Royal Navy at Liverpool in November.

Blockade Runners and Spies

Large numbers of businesses in Great Britain and Ireland (and in many other countries, no doubt) who had interests in the import-export trade with America, became embroiled in the civil war, one way or another. Some accepted trading restrictions imposed by the war and either suffered the loss of market share or sought alternative markets. Others, including many based in Ireland, exploited the situation and ran all kinds of materials to North and South.

Cotton continued to reach Great Britain and Ireland, albeit with increasing difficulties as the war wore on and remained untainted as it wove through the textile manufacturers. It arrived at the customer as a product. Large shipments of gold and silver were also travelling across the Atlantic to Britain, used to purchase ships and military equipment, at often grossly inflated prices.

It seemed that every right-thinking person agreed that slavery should end and, although trade between the South and supporters of slavery was still legal, albeit tenuous, it was also highly profitable if products could get through the union blockades. Reinforcing our flourishing growth of cynicism in all things politic, even merchants in the northern states of America were illicitly accepting southern cotton for the duration of the war.

Apart from the industries in Ireland that were supporting the South by continuing business as usual, Kingstown even had its own blockade runners and supporters. In 1863, amidst all the hype of blockade busting, new railroads being constructed across America and emigrants crowding the quaysides of Britain and Ireland, William Campbell might have begun to suspect that his son James could fall under the spell of foreign adventure. James became friendly with a man, well got around the harbour, who began to raise the subject of the civil war in America a bit too often for his father's liking.

Richard Brickley, mentioned earlier, was still residing in Kingstown but was away much of the time, cruising and racing yachts for and with his boss, George Powell Houghton. Considered a model landlord by many, he owned the large estate in County Wexford — Kilmannock. Despite his preoccupation with sailing yachts, Brickley was about to go into the yacht brokerage business for himself and would cross paths with the Campbells. This encounter was a piece of business that evolved directly between the two but, given the close proximity of their respective activities (both social and marine), it is almost certain that Captain Brickley was previously known to the Campbells: William senior, being head man for Public Works at the harbour, where all the fine yachts were constantly coming and going, requiring berthing and mooring facilities etc and Brickley, sailing some of the biggest yachts.

James' schooner, *Lively*, went off the scene around this time and was probably sold between the winter of 1862 and the spring of 1863. Whether or not the sale figured in any overall plan of the Campbells at the time is unclear but, they had been keeping a weather eye on the coastguard cutter, *Wellington*. A long-time favourite in Kingstown Harbour, it was rumoured that she was due to be condemned and taken out of service.

Like so many other aspects of this story, the recorded details of this coastguard vessel are but a few. It is believed she was built in 1816 and came into service on the Leith coastguard station, in 1817. She was sixty-six tons and armed with ten guns. Only presumption, it is believed she was constructed along the customary lines of a revenue cutter of its day and, there is little evidence that would confirm she had any individual detail.

The early years of the 19th century were worrying for the Crown, with so many smugglers seemingly having much their own way around Britain and Ireland. Particular concern was expressed with the remoteness of some parts of western Ireland, and an inability of the authorities to police them adequately. Whether it had more to do with complaints of the falling profits of legal distillers and a flourishing illegal but competitive trade or, the fact that armed smugglers were increasingly more brazenly hovering in greater numbers around the coast, either way, it meant something had to be done.

The Admiralty took over the running of coastguard vessels, built and fitted out a number of others and began to combat the threat presented by the smugglers' 'free trade'. Sweetening any prize, they also changed the law to allow the coastguards to share in the value of any vessel and cargo seized — a bit like privateering against your own. Efforts in this respect are still alive and ongoing.

The *Wellington* was active in service around Scotland and Ireland during subsequent years, chasing and apprehending smugglers. After a visit to Kingstown in 1836, she seems to have become permanently based there, where she competed well in the popular cutter races during regatta seasons. During her latter years of service with the coastguards, she could be seen decked out in flags and buntings during the summer and sometimes used as a committee boat, or as a rounding waypoint, during the regattas.[6]

If it ever came to the notice of the press, they never directly referred to Captain Brickley's spell of adventure for the Confederacy until long after events. Our inability to determine this correctly may also be due, in part, to the constant misspelling of his name.

Richard Brickley took up the cause in 1864 and became a blockade runner. His claim to fame seems to have been with just one vessel called *The Secret*. The steamer left the Clyde and sailed to Nassau, south about and, according to himself, "ran the blockade three times". Some reports claim, just one run, and an unsuccessful one at that.

Sister ship to the *Stag*, another Clyde blockade runner, the 800-ton paddle steamer, *The Secret*, with the Palmetto flag flying on her foremast, was launched from the yard of Bowdler Chaffer & Company two months after the former, in October 1864. Situated at Seacombe on the Clyde, cheers of, "Success to *The Secret*" rang out through the yards as she slid into the water.

The same yard built a series of ships for the company, Fraser and Trenholm. Closely associated with Fraser and Trenholm and *The Secret*'s owners, Beach Root & Company, they were all staunch and active supporters of the southern cause. They hired Captain Richard Brickley to deliver *The Secret* to Nassau in November 1864.

It's Never Just a Name

It takes some imagination to crack the reasons behind names that are given to some ships and boats. Our own two are called *Fourpence* and *Ouzel*. I mean, how is anyone, other than the owners, ever going to work out the reasons for such names? People do wonder though. The reasons are not obvious but, the ideas behind the names of some ships at the time did seem interesting – and this is almost always the case.

The lure of an idea or the name of one's favourite anything, becoming immortalised by way of naming their boat so, is perhaps irresistible

---

6 The period photographs of Kingstown, depicting the harbour and regattas, may very well have the *Wellington* in view.

to some. Something like writing the book that people are wont to say, 'everyone has in them'. You are wearing some part of your life on your sleeve and someone will ask. Thankfully, there will always be the curious amongst us.

The Clyde and the Confederates took the subject very seriously, continually changing the names of ships and their captains during construction and, after being launched.

The names given to ships and boats fall into almost endless categories, some more obvious than others. Warships usually have powerful or strong-meaning names: e.g. *Warrior*. Pleasure liners, *'... of the Seas'*, have their own style. Then there are those after monarchs, admirals of yore, and famous battles. Sailing ships, commercial and private, were likely to be compared to others that had a pedigree for swiftness and so on. These types of vessels are no longer being built and instead, today's craft are bestowed with names that seem almost delinquent by comparison: e.g. *Rubber Duck*, *Two Friends*, *Golden Monkey*, *Blonde*, and *Knot 2 Sirius*.

Nevertheless, there remains this thing that incubates in the mind of a boat-owner. It is his opportunity to make a quiet but nevertheless public statement about a part of himself, exploits or his good luck, perhaps: e.g. *Lotto*, *Freedom* or, his chance of adventure – *Great Escape*. It is a flag of some personal pride, perhaps, and a great topic for a bit of high-stool banter.

Forever popular and commendable, is to name your boat after a loved one, a wife, child, father, etc, the *'... Brothers ...'* being universally popular. My first boat, a clinker fishing boat, was called *Ann*, after my wife and in my case, it harboured a selfish appeal to vanity – hoping to diminish the reprimand for the dent in the family budget.

Some owners have even picked pop stars. Stars but not pop stars, popes too have had their names painted on bows. Similarly, names appear that have also been given to children, like *Elvis* and other stars of stage and screen and more recently, sports, like football. Biblical names and those of princes and emperors were also popular names given to ships down through the ages.

Interesting was how former day-ship owners, mostly commercial, chose Greek deities and these were prolific. The reasons for such popularity are not obvious but may have originated in classical aspects of their education – academic or religious. Mythical goddesses of 'plenty' were favourites. Maybe, they were just superstitious?

There is one name however, that gives no clue whatsoever to its meaning. Instead, it is firmly announcing that there is something about the vessel or its owners that is hidden. People will always wonder and even enquire about the total negativity of the name. It is a name that only became somewhat popular from the middle of the 19th century but, has remained a registered name from time to time, especially in the warm seas of 'tax havens'. It is, *The Secret*.

My good friend, a rock of sense in such matters, advises that money has a tendency to gravitate to where it is best looked after.

During the war years and for some time after, steamers making a transatlantic voyage quite often docked at Queenstown. It was the last or first port of call on a journey to or from America and a place to communicate with ships' owners: type and size of cargo loaded, taken off; crew or passengers on or off or, the topping up of bunkers with coal. There was a steady procession of steamers out of British shipyards, down the Irish Channel[7], sometimes stopping at Kingstown, then Queenstown, ostensibly vessels on ordinary trading voyages to America – if there was such a thing at the time but, every dog and its mother could pick out the blockade runners.

The Secret, with Brickley at the helm, put in to Queenstown for supplies and promptly set out again, after a short delay, to cross the Atlantic. Several days out, she hit a storm and suffered serious damage, forcing the paddle steamer to head back for Cork. Repairs to the steamer were completed (but not to the habit of misspelling Brickley's name) before she finally got away again and sailed to Nassau.

The Yankees were tightening their grip, the blockade runners were beginning to languish idle in southern ports and despite several attempts, *The Secret* does not appear to have made it through.

Getting upwards of 800-900 pounds sterling for a blockade run, Brickley may have pocketed a nice few bob to tide him through a period of recuperation, after his attempts to save black people from freedom and before returning to sail super yachts for their wealthy owners.

When the war ended, the British government was left with a hefty bill of compensation owing to the United States, for their 'blind eye' during the conflict.

The marine grandees of the Royal clubs continued to cruise the fjords, the west of Ireland and the Mediterranean. Brickley continued to captain for some of the big names and became entangled in a number of unsavoury

---

7   The author has chosen to describe the sea between Ireland and Great Britain as the Irish Channel. This includes the St George's Channel, Irish Sea and North Channel.

affairs. He eventually turned to regular commercial runs, on steamers for Cunard.

William Campbell had been bombed with correspondence ever since the death of his benefactor, Gibbons. Having travelled around Britain and Ireland most of his life, William did not now seem comfortable with the growing amounts of administration or with ledgers. His work as superintendent required exactly that and William was either not up to it or, didn't want to be up for it?

William's difficulties with clerical administration had persisted and by the end of 1862, there was still no respite in sight. Officials were having none of it, however. The correspondence just kept flooding in. Mundane it would appear, his work around the harbour continued. By this time, his son, James was only getting casual and financially small contracts from Public Works – times were changing.

The wheels of progress are relentless. The harbour was completed and was a big success. It had become a safe place for ships, with less incidents of loss or damage. The growth of steam and good communications was defeating bad weather and the incidence of shipwreck. The relentless drive of progress had removed any remaining mystery in the science of diving and the bravery of early divers was no longer required. Divers had become two a penny – almost.

Chapter 8

Their Last Regatta in Kingstown, 1863

It is hard to know – even their direct descendants are at a loss – as to whether or not the events of 1863 alone determined the Campbells' future and, whether their subsequent failure to return from a voyage to South Australia was planned or just fate.

In many respects, the building of Kingstown Harbour and the town of the same name, just six miles south of Dublin City, was unlike any other in the British Isles. During a fierce snowstorm, the *Prince of Wales* and the *Rochester*, packed with troops and volunteers bound for Liverpool, were wrecked off Dunleary in November 1807. Four hundred men, women and children died. Lifeless and mangled bodies were strewn all along the shoreline in full view, between The Rock (Blackrock) and the Point of Dunleary. Of those that were not visible on the shore, the majority of them were still in the two ships that were smashed in the surf. It was a surely a terrible sight and a terrible loss and, it was aggravated by the fact that the two wreckings took place in the surf, onshore and in plain view. To make matters even more shocking, the incident was accompanied by scandalous and cowardly behaviour by those clambering to escape, with little thought for so many trapped in the ship. An inquest on 31 bodies was convened nearby, at Merrion and found that they had been the victims of "casual death by shipwreck."

It had been the worst loss of life from shipwreck in Dublin Bay and its degree of infamy and loss has never been exceeded in the regions. And it was one which took place in plain view of everyone that lived from Ringsend, all along a fashionable sprawl of wealthy residences through Merrion, Monkstown and Blackrock, to Dunleary. This embarrassing catastrophe was probably the final straw, prompting right-thinking men to get up off their backsides and do something about establishing a decent harbour of refuge at Dublin, so that ships, growing rapidly in size, could seek refuge from easterly storms in the vicinity of Dublin Bay. The long talked about proposal for a large, all-weather deep harbour, to replace the inadequacies of Dublin Harbour, prompted quick thinking businessmen to row in behind the idea.

Big wheels can turn painfully slow and the first stone of the new harbour was not laid until 1817. By its generally agreed date of total completion, in 1859, a whole new town and harbour had been established. What had been considered, "at the time, an inconsiderable and dirty village, the abode of a few fishermen and the country between it (Dunlary) and Bullock to be a sterile tract, covered with furze and heath and traversed by a few footpaths", underwent a total transformation. Within a couple of decades, Dunlary had changed to Kingstown and was on its way to becoming one of the most fashionable towns in western Europe.

When the half million pounds was approved and the work commenced, the place was overrun with an influx of workers, animals, carts and steam machines. Thousands of squatting labourers and craftsmen lived in makeshift huts and continued to pile into the place to build the harbour and town. What emerged, when roads and the railway were extended to the harbour and beyond, was an attempt to mirror and even to surpass the port of Liverpool, one of the greatest maritime cities in the world.[1]

It is difficult to overestimate the scale of the attempt to model this enterprise against some of the finest coastal cities of Europe. We are fortunate that one contemporary journalist and his keen observations had a real sense of what was intended and had been achieved at Kingstown, capturing it in this article for the *Daily Express*, April 23, 1862.[2]

Kingstown Intelligence

(From our correspondent) Kingstown, Sunday Evening

Kingstown and Its Improvements – *Like a well-arranged stage, the scenery perfect, the lights duly set, Kingstown now awaits its tide of Summer visitors – as the theatre, taken as an illustration, awaits its fashionable admiring audience. Much, if not all, that once surprised the visitors, by the ill-assorted appearance of finished and unfinished works, is fast passing away. No longer can a Thackeray come within a caustic pen, and describe the caves of Salthill, and their miserable inhabitants. That dismal quarter, known of old as Dunleary, is daily becoming softened into pale picturesqueness. Ranges of stately terraces present their fronts*

---

1   The final bill for completion of Kingstown Harbour would amount to twice the original estimate. It was a sum and a project that became the subject of some considerable criticism and controversy, at a time when so much of rural Ireland was without the where with all to put one stone on top of another.

2   The names of individual journalists, correspondents or those that wrote the articles in newspapers were never given.

to the morning sunshine, as it streams across the glittering bay. Finished and convenient roads run along the sea face, like those in Brighton. The once rugged and uneven piers have become, under the judicious hand of improvements, broad and even causeways. Grassy embankments slope gently upward from road to road, like garden terraces; and one continued way for miles, leads the visitor from view to view of the spacious harbour and unequalled bay. Leaving the immediate seaside, where recent improvements are most conspicuous, terrace after terrace will be found in every stage of progress, from the first stone laying to the furnished house. Up at the summit of the gentle slope on which this fashionable town is built – facing the mountain views of vernal-clad beauty – these latter observations are most applicable. There, long ranges of fine and convenient houses command on every side prospects, whose variety is only equalled by their beauty.

The summer inducements of Kingstown can hardly be enumerated. Brilliant regattas, military bands, flower shows, bazaars, the daily arrival and departure of some of the finest steam-ships on the seas, a railway with luxurious carriages, offering for the outlay of a shilling or so, in every direction prospects of panoramic variety, are a few of the chief attractions of the place. Over all of this, is a body of Town Commissioners, chosen for their respectability, presides, and for the stake they hold in the well-being of the locality, overseeing, fostering, protecting and encouraging improvements, and carefully guarding against any cause, which might for a moment affect the well-being of residents and visitors; and who are perfectly competent to manage their own affairs.

There was lots of activity in Kingstown Harbour after the Great Storm of 1861 and William senior remained in or about the place and Dalkey, superintending for the Department of Public Works. Probably part of the problem, he had settled into routine, more or less but, he wasn't idle.

After William married Mary in 1851, the couple had six children in Ireland. Young William had been their first born and five more were born in Ireland: Charles in 1854, Elizabeth in 1857, Catherine in 1859, Albert in 1861 and Frederick in 1863. Little more is known about his eldest son, James, by his first marriage and his progress with contracting and diving activities up to that point. Since then it had been marine works and dispersing shipwrecks, and if he had in latter times lapsed from working shipwrecks and salvage, he was about to get busy again.

The perennial 'hurricane force' gales beset the Irish Channel once again from 19 January 1863. They were not referred to as 'extreme weather events' but, when severe, they were always the "worst that had ever visited these isles". The direction of the wind, this time, was predominantly from the NW and meant that Kingstown would have escaped the full force of this storm. The Lancashire coast, Liverpool and Anglesey were worst affected. By the time that the storm (reported to have had winds in excess of 60 mph with rain, sleet and snow) blew itself out, fifty-four shipwrecks were reported between 19-27 January and one hundred and seventy-seven since 1 January. We might think that the extreme weather events of today are unique but this "Great Storm at Liverpool" was also accompanied by some unusual weather phenomena.

For one, the height of the tide at Liverpool was reported a whopping six-feet higher than normal. A figure that we have good cause to rely on, due to the well-respected history of weather and tidal statistics collected at that port. A remarkable record of tide and weather observations was begun by the 18th century ex-privateer turned dock master of Liverpool, William Hutchinson. He set the bar high and it never lowered. Despite persistent downfalls, snow refused to 'stick' due to the temperature of the ground – and more pleasantly, the Northern Lights were "beautifully distinct".

Kingstown did not escape entirely but damage had been mainly confined to civil and private structures. The plummeting mercury had indicated the approach of the dangerous low and the telegraph warned of the effects that had begun to take place elsewhere. From the commanding structure, the offices of the Harbour Commissioners in the centre of the large depot, to the administrative centre for Public Works and across the yard to Campbell's own little office, the messages flew. And between the "hoppin and the throtin", the new wind speed indicator, the telegraph office, Fitzroy's drums and indicators, the moorings and wharfs of Kingstown were well attended to and proved their worth on this occasion.

Some indication of the pressure and the regime under which the mail boat service had to operate can be gauged by the fact that, despite the weather, the *RMS Leinster* sailed from Holyhead at the height of the storm and into the teeth of a ferocious gale, almost coming to grief. By the time she entered Kingstown, in a dangerous condition – a journey reported to have been five-and-a-half hours, some reporting seven hours, far more than twice her normal journey time – the mail boat's post room had become half filled with water, prevented from decanting into the rest of the ship by watertight compartments. There were no casualties.

Apart from damage to buildings, the only maritime casualty reported at Kingstown seems to have been the large fishing smack, *Sarah*, berthed in the old harbour, belonging to the "widow Cullen", more firmly reported as Mrs White. Some of the crew had remained aboard with the stove lit during the storm. Due to the fierce draught that developed in the fire, the stove pipe overheated and the boat burned to the waterline and was scuttled. It was later raised by the gunboat, *Rainbow* and cutter, *Wellington*. Apparently, the Campbells were not involved in the raising of the *Sarah* but completed by crew members from *HMS Ajax*, led by the "gallant Lieutenant Dyer, and assisted by Mr Blowfeld". The lieutenant obviously having learned a thing or two from the Campbells during their earlier experience with the *Badger*.

Two Weddings

As far as the Campbells were concerned, two weddings of note took place in 1863. One later in June, a scene altogether more reserved, meant an addition to the Campbell family. An earlier and unconnected one took place on 10 March. A marriage not approved of by his mother, Albert, Prince of Wales wed the Princess Alexandra of Denmark. There were celebrations and illuminations throughout Dublin City, which were only surpassed by those at the Wellington Monument in the Phoenix Park and around the towering edifice, Nelson's Pillar on Sackville Street (now O'Connell Street).

The buntings were strung out around Kingstown early that year: local yachts, visiting yachts, Admiralty vessels including the old cutter, *Wellington* (now *Lucy*) were all decorated and the small stallholders took up their customary positions at the junction of the east pier. There were fireworks and marine bands, banquets in the Royal yacht clubs lasting well into the nights and special trains were laid on for the late-night revellers. A mock sea battle was re-enacted around the harbour battery on the east pier and in Dublin Bay, with cannon fire, smoke and boarding parties hopping from one vessel to another.

SS Saint Andrew

The flow of vessels down the channel, from the Clyde and Liverpool, continued in support of the Confederates, some by-passing Kingstown and others, like the *Diamond*, stopping over to make repairs. The armada didn't always keep to the same route – England directly to the confederate south.

Orders were transmitted to the Public Works and to Harbour Master Hutchison at Kingstown, to keep the Carlisle clear on the afternoon and evening of 10 April. The telegraph, weaponised by then and proving to be a valuable method of communication, relayed advance notice that the screw steamer, *Saint Andrew* of the Montreal Line, would be leaving Glasgow and was expected to dock in Kingstown on the evening of the 10th.

Three hundred and fifty men, "steerage of the working class", had been recruited at offices in Dublin and were being despatched by rail to Kingstown, to board the *Saint Andrew* for New York. Controversy began to shroud the real purpose these men would serve. Some reports suggested they had been recruited for a one-year contract, to work on railways in Chicago. Others suggested they were recruited for the Federal army. The lack of women emigrants on board the *Saint Andrew* increased suspicion.

The operation went like clockwork and the ship was in on the evening of the 10th. Emigrants or enlisted men embarked and the *Saint Andrew* had sailed again before the following day. Newspaper notices that had run advertisements for viewing the "fine steamer" from aboard the "Kingstown Steamer", proved to be over-optimistic.

It was reported that agents were receiving 150 dollars per recruit reaching America, their passage was being paid and that thousands would be arriving. The fact was that thousands were migrating because of the lack of work and starvation, in Ireland and in Scotland and were signing up as combatants on both sides of the conflict. It just seems like some things don't ever change. Whilst the ignorant and innocent are recruited and enticed to fight each other on opposing sides (neither being their own) the recruiters, for both sides, just sail off into the sunset afterwards.

Sale of the Cutter, Wellington

Once a cutter of the Revenue Service and transferred to the later formed Coastguard Service, the *Wellington* was finally condemned out of service in the spring of 1863. Commander of the Coastguard, Captain De Courcy, based in Kingstown, decided that the sale of the *Wellington* from service would not proceed in the usual way – i.e. by putting her up for auction. His privilege, it was decided instead to sell her privately. There were no "For Sale" advertisements. The only news announced of the forthcoming sale of the Royal Navy cutter appeared in the press on 23 April.

> ... her majesty's cutter, Wellington, will be sold to the highest bidder shortly.

The next notification to appear informed the reader that "*Wellington*'s ballast was being removed and that she was being prepared for sale, on May 24" and that "... she is roughly valued at £130."

"Shipping Casualties at Kingstown", on May 21, reported that the *Wellington* had sustained damage to her stem and winch.

Despite Campbell's relatives' later claim that there was damage sustained by the cutter at Liverpool, when she lost her bowsprit in a collision, the two incidents may have been one in the same.

The next day, it was reported that "the cutter, *Wellington* had been purchased from the Admiralty at Kingstown and had gone to Dublin for repairs."

Those who had missed the *Evening Freeman* of 15 May 1863, might still be unsure just who had become the new owner of the *Wellington*. The following report appeared in next edition of the *Freeman* and does not seem to have been repeated elsewhere but, it was clear and on this rare occasion, Brickley's name was spelt correctly.

> *Naval Intelligence – Her majesty's cutter* Wellington *has been sold to Mr Kelly and Captain Brickley, of Kingstown, who have become joint owners; the purchase money was under £200.*

On 6 August, Public Works divers were re-establishing moorings in Kingstown Harbour – those that had been previously occupied by the *Wellington* – and, although it had been reported, in the meantime, that the Campbells were working on and converting the *Wellington* to a two-masted schooner in the harbour and, that young William fractured his hip, it was not until 27 August before details of the re-sale emerged, and the use for which its new owner intended.

> *Her Majesty's cutter* Wellington, *which was some months ago condemned as being unfit for the service, and sold by Captain De Courcy RN, for £120, was afterwards purchased for £239, by Mr Campbell of Kingstown. She is now being converted into a schooner and will be called* Lucy. *Her first trading voyage will be from Arklow to the French seaboard with a cargo of bivalves.*

One might assume that "Mr Campbell" meant William senior. I was wrong. The new registered owner of the ex-cutter, *Wellington*, converted to a schooner under a new name, was William's son, James with an address at Queenstown. Despite this fact, in later months, the schooner was consistently referred to as being owned by William Campbell senior.

A short time later, it was reported that she would be trading to the Azores and would be visiting Queenstown, with a view to contracting for the demolition of the Daunt Rock.[3]

Details of the sale are set out in detail here, in order to demonstrate the convoluted abnormality of the transfer. Brickley and Kelly had bought the cutter, had it repaired or not and then, sold it again in a very short space of time – possibly just a couple of weeks. Several questions regarding this

3 The Campbells are not known to have resided at Queenstown, Cork. They may have believed, at the time of the boat's registration that they and the *Lucy* might have been working there.

sale will come to the reader's mind and, I can assure you, they could not be answered satisfactorily.

"Condemned" as she was, after fifty years of service, the *Wellington*, might not have been suitable for the Royal Naval Coastguards but, she sailed on successfully in spite of storms, under fire from cannons, collisions and trading in the southern hemisphere for another ten years and, might have continued for a lot longer if it had not been for negligence. The hardy little schooner finally went up on rocks at the Solomon Islands during a typhoon and was abandoned in 1874.

How or why did Richard Brickley jump from mastering yachts to ship brokerage and then back again, quite so quickly? Was it just a temporary blip in his career? He had been out of a job since March, after George Powell Houghton had passed away and, although he would have been eminently suitable for hire to perform similar work for any number of wealthy yacht owners, he hung around for a while. There is no doubt that Richard Brickley had served Mr Houghton well, and could only have been genuinely upset by his passing. They had cruised the British Isles and beyond and, had raced and travelled to various regattas together. In memory of their relationship, George Powell's mother presented Captain Richard Brickley with an engraved silver telescope that read.

> *A memento of regret and sincere regard from Mrs Houghton to Richard Brickley, in grateful acknowledgement of his fidelity and affectionate devotion, to her dear son, who departed this life the 10th March, 1863.*

The presentation appears to have been made at the Royal Saint George Yacht Club, where Captain Brickley received hearty congratulations from the members. Just two months later, the "gallant Captain Brickley" was the centre of attention once again, when he was presented with a chronometer and sextant by members of the Houghton family. Everyone seemed to have been of the opinion that Brickley was indeed a worthy recipient of the gifts.

She was brand new and Brickley's last command for Houghton. It was the fabulous yacht, *Red Gauntlet* and it lay in the Custom House Dock, Dublin. Brickley was somehow involved in presenting the yacht for sale, along with another smaller vessel, which was in Scotland! This was the only other vessel that Brickley seems to have brokered and, for which a "for sale" advert appeared with his name. The Custom House Dock in Dublin was a common place for yachts of absent owners to be laid up and adverts for boats lying there were not uncommon. Almost a year to the day earlier, the cutter yacht, *Success* was offered for sale there.

Not far from Sackville Street, Dublin, Brickley ran some kind of sales or contact office for a short time, at Custom House Quay, aboard his employer, George Powell Houghton's famous yacht, *Red Gauntlet*. Also on the books, he advertised a "fast sea going cutter yacht of 25 tons", berthed in the Clyde. The notice regarding this "small yacht" appeared only once, in a single issue of *The Irish Times* on 24 April. Not a single advert for this yacht appeared in another newspaper throughout the whole of the British Isles.[4] It beggars belief that, if one were attempting to sell a yacht afloat in Scotland, from Dublin, that a single advertisement, placed in one edition of a local newspaper in Dublin, could be considered a road to success. It is almost as if some basic obligation was being met, or a particular reader of *The Irish Times* was being targeted.

Originally costing £3,750, the *Red Gauntlet* was sold in October to Mr O'Reilly for £2,550. Very large sums of money at the time. Captain Brickley's career with the yacht and the man was applauded once again and, true to form, his name was mistakenly recorded as Captain "Brinkley". It would appear that in any public association with Houghton, Brickley's name was reported with the misspelling, "Brinkley".[5]

The *Red Gauntlet* would achieve some notoriety after it was purchased by Edward Langtry of the Belfast shipping magnate family, who cruised in her with his second wife, the colourful, British-American socialite, Lillie Langtry.

Who was Brickley's co-owner in the *Wellington*? Mr Kelly? There was no shortage of Kellys in Kingstown – from town commissioners to coal merchants and it is difficult to be certain. The firm of Kelly & Son, of Sackville Street in Dublin, well-known hunting and sporting goods suppliers and dealers in gun powder of various qualities, had supplied blasting powder to William Campbell at Kingstown Harbour in the past. It may have been this Kelly, along with Brickley, who arranged for the purchase of the *Wellington* and its lightening re-sale to James Campbell.

---

4   It is worth noting that it is only with the aid of digitised and searchable newspaper collections, held by the British Library Newspaper Archives and others, that we have discovered this. The facts of the timing and extent of these adverts would have been nigh on impossible to discover otherwise.

5   Regarding the reference to the repeated misspelling of Brickley's name seeming strange, it is, nevertheless, just an observation. Similar unexplainable misspellings often occurred in the press over long periods. In the case of Kingstown's harbour master, William Hutchison, his name was continuously misspelt as Hutchinson. It is almost as if certain gentlemen, old school perhaps, held their own views on how a name should be spelt in the English language.

My own inclination is, as the newspaper reporting of the sale had indicated, and as they were both from Kingstown, then it may have been the Kingstown Town Commissioner named Kelly or the coal merchant by the same name. Either way, double your money in the space of a fortnight is a nice little earner. Was this a bona fide 'for profit' sale or, was it something else?

Brickley's excursion into ship brokerage was brief and he was off to sea again in early September. Reported with another misspelling, he docked at Belfast after cruising in the steam yacht, *Verina* from Stranraer. This particular spelling, "Verina", was a once off and any further mention of a yacht of that name could not be traced. However, reports of the steam yacht, *Varina* did appear. Newspapers described a visit by it to the Loch Ryan Regatta in Stranraer, on the west coast of Scotland, where the owner, Mr Preiolia, raced his new steamer and offered a challenged by his crew for a rowing match against some of the other yachts' crews.[6]

However, the steam yacht *Varina* (120 tons) was built by Messrs Jones Quiggin & Company Ltd in 1863 for, let's say, the reported owner, Mr Preiolia. Another reported owner was actually the shipbuilder, Mr J. Jones junior, who sold it to Sir Michael Robert Shaw Stewart MP before the next Loch Ryan Yacht Club Regatta in 1864. It was sold on again to James Duncan, who cruised the lochs for several years before she went to Germany at the turn of the century.

The confusion becomes clear – the spelling gremlins were at it again. Jones Quiggin & Company was a well-known shipbuilding firm at Liverpool, who completed a number of warships and blockade busters for Mr Prioleau (not Preiolia) of Fraser and Trenholm. With offices in Liverpool, they bankrolled the requirements of the confederate army. Mr George Trenholm became Secretary of the Confederate States Treasury.

Jones Quiggin & Company had so many orders on the books during the war that they expanded their yards and subcontracted out a lot of the work. These were the heady days for shipbuilding and design. The industrialists of war and yacht racing were alive and well in Liverpool, as well as in the competing yards of the Clyde. All the 'peculiar' ships were launched with the usual salute, "Success to ... (name of ship)".

As Jones Quiggin & Company were trailblazing the use of steel in the production of ships, the *Varina* (*Verina*) was, most likely the steel, steam screw schooner yacht that Brickley and Prioleau were trialling for some

---

6 *Varina* was the first name of Thomas Jefferson's wife, who was sometimes called Queen Varina. There is history of American yachts of that name however. A Mr Preiolia of that spelling, was not a name that could be traced anywhere either.

of the prospective winners in that "Peculiar Trade". When she lost the race to the steam yacht, *Valetta* at Stranraer, she returned to the reported ownership of Joshua Jones junior.

Mr Brickley seemed to be keeping his usual excellent company when we next hear of him and his employer, of a somewhat similar name as before. In command of his employer's yacht, *Ceres*, there was nothing in the least mysterious about their next 'grand entrance'. First mention of the handsome steam yacht, *Ceres* is when she was for fitting out before sale at Southampton, at the end of 1863. Her new owner took her on a cruise to Norway the following year, with Richard Brickley in command. On her return, she sailed into Kingstown Harbour with Captain Brickley at the helm and her owner, C.K. Prioleau, senior director and partner in Fraser Trenholm & Company, Liverpool, flying the new confederate palmetto flag. Fraser Trenholm & Company (essentially Southern cuckoos in a Liverpool nest) were major backers and suppliers of the building and acquisition of blockade runners and war materials for the South during the American Civil War. They were building a confederate navy.

James Campbell Marries Lucy Saunders

The second wedding: Lucy Saunders, daughter of a decorated military war veteran, Captain John Robert Saunders R.A. Dublin (deceased), married James John Campbell. The ceremony took place at Saint Peter's, Dublin on 3 June 1863.

James, by then a registered contractor in his own right, would appear to have previously lived, for a short time, at the cottage at 2 Margrette Place, Glasnevin. This was quite close to the Claremont Institution, Lucy's registered address at the time of her marriage to James and from where James may have contracted for construction work.

There were a number of Campbells living in this area at the time and it was also around the time that the Palm House was first constructed, of timber, at the Botanic Gardens. Campbell was a prominent name in horticulture at the time. Moving in different social circles, it might explain how James first made Lucy's acquaintance.

Converted by the family to schooner rig, James renamed the cutter *Wellington* to *Lucy*, after his wife. James had married Lucy at about the same time that he purchased, or became the registered owner of the old coastguard cutter.

When Lucy married James in 1863, her address was recorded as 'Claremont, Glasnevin'. Claremont House and Demesne was purchased in

1819 with charitable contributions. Converted into a residential school for deaf and dumb children, the project was widely supported and completed by a committee under the guidance of Dr Charles Orpen. It became a progressive and well-respected institution, where afflicted children could live-in and receive an education. Some benefited from work-life training, with aspirations and opportunities for adoption and further training in service or indenture.

The school also catered for a number of unaffected, fee-paying, live-in pupils. If Lucy entered Claremont when her father's estate was dispersed following his death, she would have been thirteen years old. Only a little in excess of the average enrolling age, we might assume that she was a pupil at that stage. If she spent the next eight years, until 1863, at the institution, we might also assume she became a governess or instructor.

After her marriage to James, it would appear that the pair then moved to 52 York Street (York Road) in Kingstown. Not long established, there was another similar charitable institution for young children nearby, the Bird's Nest. Almost consumed by a controversial incident that took place there at the time, it recovered and continued to do good work.

Other than some recorded contributions by a 'Mrs Campbell' (only a coincidence, possibly,) and after the surviving official records were checked, no official connection between Lucy and this institution could be found. It must also be added that no official record of Lucy was discovered in the scant records that survive from Claremont.

With an end to her work at Claremont, Lucy must have been anxious to make a fresh start and the couple settled down amongst their fashionable neighbours at Kingstown – short and all as their stay would prove to be.

Lucy and James' address at York Street was only a stone's throw from the Bird's Nest. It could not have escaped the couple's attention that this institution was the subject of an unfortunate and scandalous incident that occurred there some months earlier. Indeed it received considerable press coverage at the time.

Providing bed and board and an education for young children that had been orphaned or abandoned, this otherwise charitable and reputable institution fell foul of the law more than once – and in this case, it occurred when a lady, going by the name of Bessy Knox, overstepped the mark. The objectionable side to their charitable work, as seen by others, was that children at the Bird's Nest had to be reared in the Protestant faith and Bessy Knox was doing overtime in God's work. Married to Lord Templemore's land agent, her husband was M.W. Knox, mentioned earlier as residing at

Glendine, Arthurstown, Wexford. The pair, in cahoots or otherwise, were a double act.

A practise, sometimes highly contentious and leading to outbreaks of violence, it was claimed that Mr Knox had been the master of 'squaring' the acre. This notorious land agent and justice of the peace, representing the worst qualities of men described as 'middlemen', had been running tenants in and out of court and their property and became thoroughly disliked throughout the county. On the one hand, he was evicting tenants, and on the other, his wife, Bessy, was hoovering up the homeless children and feeding them to the Bird's Nest.

It all went south in 1862, when Bessy convinced Mary Fitzpatrick to travel to Dublin in the dead of night and to give her two children, a boy and a girl, up for care in the Bird's Nest. When things changed for Mary Fitzpatrick, she wanted her daughter returned but was refused. "Kidnapping" was cried and a storm blew up between the institution, the clergy and the legals, until sense prevailed and the child was returned. It was not a singular occurrence and the incidents did nothing to improve the otherwise good name of the institution and its charitable work.

Summers and Regattas at Kingstown

Early yacht races kicked off at Kingstown at the end of May, with the first heat for the Dublin Bay Subscription Cup – a race title that seems to have begun and ended in the same year. The Cup involved sailing from the harbour, out around the Kish Lightship and back to the harbour around the Bar Buoys.[7]

The Kingstown Regatta was scheduled to begin on 15 July and would run for three consecutive days. A number of matches warmed up before that week and then, it was just racing, racing, racing. Extra trains and omnibuses were laid on. Thousands travelled from Dublin each day and the yachts just kept arriving from all over the British Isles. Excursions on steamers from Kingstown and Dublin ran daily in pursuit of the competing yachts around the bay. There were races for rowing boats, lifeboats, fishing trawlers, greyhound yachts and the biggest and finest yachts ever to visit Kingstown. At the height of the marine extravaganza, it became impossible to get lodgings anywhere near Kingstown.

There was competition over a wide variety of 'aquatic' classes. Gentlemen rowed, lords and captains sailed. Some races were 'open', regulated by agreed committees and others were 'closed' for members of Royal yacht

7 The Bar Buoys are a series of buoys marking the safe, navigable passage through Dublin Bay, into the River Liffey and Dublin Port.

clubs only. Prizes were generous: from silver to guineas and sovereigns, pounds to shillings and even the competing lifeboats were rewarded.

The winner of the sailing-trawler race, *Commodore*, skippered by Mick Scanlan (Scallan?), received twelve pounds. First prize for the "First" race, was sponsored by the Royal Saint George, with "a piece of plate" valued at sixty guineas. The yacht, *Phryne*, fifty-five tons, owned and skippered by Mr T. Seddon of the Royal Thames Yacht Club, took this prize by two minutes.

It was the Victorians' 'hay day' and images of their magnificent yachts were captured by a number of professional photographers, who were beginning to emerge in Dublin and Kingstown. The surviving images in the National Library of Ireland can instil a sense of wonder to this day.

But it wasn't about the money. Obviously, the majority of the competitors weren't in it for the purse – it was all about competing in a Kingstown Regatta.

The brass bands played daily, and the fireworks lit up the sky each evening. The regatta rounded off with a large party aboard *HMS Ajax*. Her crew and Captain De Courcy wined and dined all the usual ball-goers, familiar with a good bottle of port, well into the early morning, some even retiring to ratings' bunks to sleep off excesses. Captain Hutchison was there but suffering from a deficit in the order of pecking; the superintendent of the harbour, William Campbell, was not.

The piers were lined with all the flags and buntings imaginable. The hawkers, many more than usual, were selling everything from liquor to binoculars. A blind eye was turned to the "three-card" and "shell" men. As well as the different bands playing their socks off, the piers had other entertainers. There were those with leather pianos, hurdy-gurdy machines, organs, flutes and bugles and mobile shows of Punch and Judy. The regatta of 1863 was probably the finest of the era and all agreed that they had "witnessed the finest gathering of yachting competitors ever, in Kingstown waters."

The military, police and institutional bands continued to strike up on the east pier and entertained strollers through the rest of the summer. Throngs of people still love to stroll on the piers today but sadly, appearances by brass bands are a lot more surprising now. The summers at Kingstown, watching all the "Flowers of the Sea" sailing across the "sparkling expanses of Dublin Bay and its villa dotted shores" were, by all accounts, divine.

Inequality has always been with us and behind the facade and promenade of splendour, there lurked a different Kingstown: squalid accommodation of the lanes and courts; water from a communal well and sewage in a bucket; disease was rife. Unfettered access to equality and fraternity are as elusive as a will-o'-the-wisp and we have learned to tolerate a less than acceptable measure of it. Institutionalised and neglectful treatment of citizens, based on some arbitrary boundaries of 'class', was and still remains intolerable. Understandably, public access was denied to certain working areas of the harbour but those who existed from hand to mouth in the squalid back lanes, could still walk on the piers – for free.

The Prince Consort Affair

Some of the world's finest yachts, steamers and naval vessels came and went during the Kingstown Regatta of 1863. The harbour was chock-a-block with sail and steam, and visiting yachts had to seek anchorage outside of the harbour in the adjoining Scotsman's Bay, between the east pier and Sandycove.

It was a summer to remember. The House of Commons resumed and continued to debate whether or not HM government should recognise the southern states of America. Many, only back from cruising and racing their yachts, had suddenly come face to face with the stark events that were unfolding in Liverpool and were forced to get some lard off the fence.

The Prince Consort, Albert, husband of Queen Victoria, had died in December 1861. Considered an active reformist, the nation mourned while the admirals prepared for the possibility of another war with France. Used to justify squandering huge amounts of taxpayers' money on arms, it was a familiar subterfuge, which meant the two could appear to remain arch enemies, with a prospect of battle at any moment. Warned that France had drifted ahead of England in the arms race for bigger and less sinkable battleships, British admirals came up with the plan for a new design – 'Ironclad'. Meaning exactly as it sounds, monstrous wooden ships were clad with iron armour to protect them from sinking when large bombs were hurled at them from their enemy's ironclads. Surprisingly, the innovation proved to be remarkably resilient to enemy fire but the combination of timber hulls with iron belting, timber bottoms with copper sheathing, enormous guns, steam and sail propulsion, up and down funnels, all lent to make the experiment and the ships cumbersome, and 'beasts to manage'.[8]

The production of this hybrid class proved to be a cauldron of disagreement between commercial and Admiralty ship designers, the press and the public. The least important consideration would seem to have been, how well was the taxpayer's money being spent? This class of ship sank under a wave of criticism and for a number of reasons, it was a relatively short-

8 Cannons were undergoing their own evolution and new designs would compel further resilience in the chicken-or-egg race in armaments.

lived concept. The experiment was soon replaced by the all-iron, then steel battleship.

The British naval response to the French lead had been to inaugurate a programme of capital shipbuilding, part of which was the production of the Prince Consort class, also known as Triumph and the Caledonian class of ironclad. Originally laid down in 1861 and named *HMS Triumph* in 1862, this ironclad was finally christened in memory of Albert – *Prince Consort*. The original design was for an all-timber vessel with three decks. One deck was removed, the ship was lengthened and the iron plating hung down all around the ship to just below the waterline, not quite from stem to stern.

By the summer of 1863, the American Civil War was in full blood lust and confederate spies were firmly imbedded in the shipyards of Liverpool, the Clyde and beyond. Their benefactors, shipping magnates and munitions barons in British port cities, had been buying and building ships and stuffing them with armaments to beat the band. It was a most 'peculiar' convenience that a ship could be built for a belligerent, armaments could be sold to a belligerent but, the two assembled together as a warship could not. The Confederates quite easily exploited the obvious loophole that was "as wide as a dock gate".[9]

Crews were being recruited and despatched in the blockade busters to the southern states at a time when it was said that, the number of confederate flags flying over Liverpool outnumbered British ones. Warships such as *Alabama*, *Florida* and *Shenandoah* (*Sea King*) followed and became synonymous with Liverpool and the scourge of commercial and naval shipping considered to be trading with the Union.

It should be made clear that, although there was constant criticism of Britain's apparent oversight or lack of, in the supply of armaments and ships to the South, little was said about similar oversight of supplies to the North.

What at first seemed like an incredible rumour, began to leak from that great maritime city, Liverpool, and permeated down through the corridors of Whitehall – then the fat hit the flames. After coming under severe pressure from the American Consular service in England and already suffering the embarrassment of appearing to be actively supporting the South and slavery, the British authorities began to tighten restrictions on the supply of British ships to the Confederates. This seemingly upset the cotton barons and the huge workforce at Liverpool, who were depending on trade with the South and more than just a rumour of a revolt erupted.

---

9 Strangely, the building, fitting out and arming of commercial vessels for combat or blockade busting by confederates was known as "that peculiar trade".

Elevated by the press to the "Siege of the Mersey", the perceived threat of rebels and confederate sympathiser seizing two of HM naval vessels nearing completion at Lairds, gained traction and spurred Whitehall into action. Two great ironclad rams had been 'secretly' ordered from Lairds for the confederate navy. Nearing completion, mounting pressure from the United States eventually spurred the British authorities into seizing the ships on the stocks. Gunboats were posted at the entrance to the dock gates and that was that. A deal between British government and Lairds for the purchase of the rams was hammered out and ownership was transferred – but that was not quite the end of the matter.

The rams, almost completed and ready for trials, the threat of revolt by shipyard workers and the presence of a significant number of confederate sailors in Liverpool, some of whom had travelled from the *CSS Florida* for wages that had docked in Brest, suggested a real danger of the ships being seized back again. The South had sympathisers in Whitehall and amongst the senior officer class in the Royal Navy. Despite this and some further successes at sea, this period marked a turning point in official attitude of HM government and a downturn in the naval fortunes of the South. The Confederates' attempt to establish a serious naval threat was doomed from this point.

Said not to have completed her trials and by some, not to have had any at all, the *Prince Consort* was suddenly despatched from Plymouth for Liverpool, in support of the HM blockading gunboats. The ship had not been assigned a full, permanent crew, and one was hurriedly cobbled together with ratings and officers from other ships. A large detachment of marines boarded and she set off in haste, under the command of Captain Charles De Vesey, previously in command of the *Adelaide*. It was Wednesday, 28 October 1863.

The *Consort* rounded Land's End and steamed up the George's Channel. South of Wales, a ferocious wind from the west and northwest began to pound the sea into the ship's port side. She managed to claw her way on up the Irish Sea but at a terrible cost. The pride of the Royal Navy was subsequently lambasted with criticism from the pen of some reporters. The ship was a 'log'. She rolled dangerously and was continually pounded by water that ran right over her. The water could not get away quick enough and permeated down through the decks, until it was head high in the bottom of the ship. The very idea that a brand-new ship of the line, costing a fortune to build – £360,000 – could be threatened by filling with water in the channel, during her maiden voyage, was incomprehensible.

Off Anglesey, things took a turn for the worse. Having reported later that no pilot came out, Captain De Vesey decided that his ship was in serious danger of being lost. He was afraid to risk going on to Liverpool or into Holyhead for much the same reasons. The situation had become so bad below decks, with more than seven feet of water in the bottom of the ship and already in the ash pans, inches away from the boilers, that something had to be done. The boilers were in danger of exploding and if the ship lost power, she might drift helplessly, ending up on the rocks of Anglesey. Her captain did the only thing he could. He battened down the leaky hatches and set into the teeth of the gale and the shelter of the Irish coast.

All hands were put to the pumps and were only barely able to prevent the water from extinguishing the boilers before they sighted the Bailey Light. Perched on the headland of Howth, on the north side of Dublin Bay, the light had been much improved since its unreliability had been blamed for the controversial loss of the packet steamer, *Queen Victoria*, ten years earlier. Unsure of how far he could safely proceed into the bay, De Vesey anchored the *Prince Consort* under the lee of Howth Head, late on Thursday night and rode out the storm.

Early the next morning in the fishing smack, *William and John*, Master William O'Rourke from Kingstown set off to fish near Howth. Failing to notice the large ship anchored off the Head, he proceeded to fish on the inside of the bay, just southwest of Howth Head. A few hours later, the weather threatened again and they hauled their pots and nets to make their return to Kingstown. The smack had been inside the Bailey and just off the two pinnacles that rose like stalagmites from the sea, known as The Candlesticks. As soon as he opened the point of the Bailey to the north, the huge battleship hove into view, apparently still anchored off the head. Not having seen it earlier, O'Rourke was gobsmacked, not least because this area was not considered a safe place for ships to anchor, never mind a whopping great battleship. Strong easterlies were not unknown on this coast, at this time of the year. In spite of the impending bad weather, O'Rourke proceeded to the big ship to investigate. 'Warning' the captain of a large British MOW was not a proposition that would have appealed to an Irish fisherman.

When the *William and John* finally got alongside the *Prince Consort*, it was dwarfed by the towering walls of iron. The captain hailed the smack and asked the surprised O'Rourke to come aboard. A boarding ladder was lowered. O'Rourke jumped from the smack onto the ladder and climbed up the lofty side of the battleship. Its crew were waiting for him and ushered him to Captain De Vesey's cabin. Few formalities were exchanged before the captain first wanted to know if O'Rourke was a pilot. O'Rourke replied that "he was not". When questioned further, he informed the captain that he knew the bay well and could guide the ship to a safe anchorage.

With the promise of a reward, O'Rourke's fishing boat was sent on ahead and the ironclad's anchor was hauled in. With steam still up, O'Rourke guided the *Prince Consort* to a safe anchorage in six fathoms, on the Kingstown side of the Man of War roads, about a mile and a half northeast of the point of Kingstown's west pier. Captain De Vesey and his crew, however, were not out of the woods just yet. Although a safer place to anchor, in the lee of Dalkey as she lay, the ship was nevertheless still exposed to winds from the north and east. It was curious, at first, why the ironclad did not proceed into the harbour of refuge, one that had cost so much money to build for just such an occasion.

No sooner had they dropped anchor and hauled up on it, the chain snapped. The Fitzroy storm signal over the Harbour Commissioners' offices were battering and clanging again, indicating "Drum with North cone", forecasting the approach of dangerous winds and in greatest probable violence from the northward. The second anchor was let go, and it held. O'Rourke was stranded on the ironclad, as no one was going anywhere until the weather abated.

The situation had been desperate and although still in danger of going to the bottom, which wasn't far beneath her, the day was saved. The decision not to proceed to Liverpool and to haul off the shore at Wales had proved to be a wise one, and the captain had surely saved the ship by his calculated action. However, it was a terrible day for the ironclads and extremely embarrassing to have been saved by the crew of an Irish fishing smack, no less.

I don't know who let it out first but, the scene that played out aboard the battleship during the bad weather was reported to have been dreadful. The ship was a terrible sailer, said to be the second worst roller in the fleet, the dubious honour of being top (or maybe bottom of the list) going to *HMS Lord Clyde*. Its crew said it just lunged through the water and "had no life".

The *Consort*'s decks were reported to be awash, with eight feet of water below. There were a number of sailors injured, as metal, big guns and rigging were flung around the decks while lunging up the Irish Channel. The detachment of marines must have been more than anxious to get off.

Proving to be a design fault in the arrangement of the scuppers, huge volumes of water had passed through the decks and filled the ship. Having no watertight compartments, the whole boat filled to a dangerous level throughout and was almost lost.

"Send for That Fellow, Campbell"

When the big ship hove into view and anchored off Kingstown, the harbour master, Lieutenant Hutchison, gathered his men and proceeded to the stricken vessel after the weather settled. Having been delayed, he thought to bring provisions and pumps and got the level of water under control as fast as possible.

The *Consort*'s crew were utterly exhausted and Hutchison replaced some of them with his own men. Others from *HMS Ajax*, the guardship at Kingstown, were also commandeered to help out. Injured and exhausted sailors were taken ashore and sent up to the Seaman's Hospital in Sussex Place, Kingstown.

Despite gaining on the water level, all the available pumps had to work continually to keep the level down – the ship was leaking, badly. Anchored in six fathoms, her keel must have been very close to the bottom. The fires were never let go out and steam was continually kept up in the boilers.

Once again, Hutchison sent for Campbell but it would be the last time 'that fellah' or any of the Campbells would be summoned to the harbour at Kingstown.

James was commissioned to complete two tasks. The first, seemingly the easier, was to recover *Prince Consort*'s lost anchor and chain, valued a bit richly at about £1,000. The second and more pressing task was to inspect the bottom of the ironclad, which many of the spectators that had journeyed by train to have a gawk at, believed was already resting on the seabed.

The *Consort*'s draught was reported to have been twenty-six to twenty-seven feet. If one allows for the little-contested figure of eight feet of water in the ship, it might add a conservative six feet to the draught of a leaky ship; the total amount of draught coming to 33 feet. The undisputed depth at her anchorage was reported as 6 fathoms, 36 feet. Was this at high or low water? The numbers were uncomfortably close.

High or low, James Campbell might have had to draw breath and stoop a little in order to get under her. Although James was getting little work directly from Public Works or Lieutenant Hutchison at the time, he remained a reliable professional diver, living locally and called upon, from time to time, by a number of other harbours.

By this time, James was employing a number of other divers and had been contracted to clean the bottoms of the Royal Mail steamers, one a week. He was paid eight shillings per ship and performed the work while they were berthed at the Carlisle Pier in Kingstown. This work meant that he was used to working under large vessels with little clearance. The work is physically demanding, and carried out in low visibility and, even conditions of almost total darkness. Under a six thousand ton plus battleship, subject to wind and tide, in open water and already in danger of grounding, was quite a different matter.

Until the contract was confirmed, Campbell took his schooner, *Lucy* and proceeded to 'creep' for the lost anchor. Between it and a skiff and with the help of some of the crewmen from the *Ajax*, they dragged in search of the huge anchor. Over the next few days and after several thousand square yards of seabed were 'creeped', they failed to locate the anchor.[10]

Even after a lot of water had been pumped out of the ironclad, the leak persisted and Campbell received confirmation to proceed with an inspection of the hull.

The *Consort*, along with others, had been lengthened: a twenty-three-foot piece had been inserted between the two halves after the ship was cut in two. The danger with the 'add on' was that poor reconstruction could give way to weakness. Not an uncommon design failure in such cases, it could often result in 'hogging' – sagging in the middle.

The ship was reported to have had naval divers on board but for some reason, the diving dress available at Kingstown was reported to have been unsuitable for their particular abilities or requirements. I am not sure what that meant or, if it was just another reflection of *Consort*'s unpreparedness.

Campbell sent to Howth Harbour for additional lengths of air hose and at considerable risk, completed the inspection of the muntz metal sheathed hull. It was reported that damage was detected by the divers and that a repair was made. It was never made clear exactly what damage Campbell had discovered. This, after all – a design faults in a new class of battleship – was information that should be kept secret.

The accolades flew across the channel. The wires signalled praise from the palace and the Admiralty. The crews of the *Prince Consort* and *HMS Ajax* were commended for their determined efforts in saving one of HM's great fighting ships. James Campbell's part in the affair (inspection of hull and his search for the anchor) were completely denied at first and no early mention was made of O'Rourke, the master of the fishing smack, *William and John* and his part in saving one of his majesty's battleships. After omission of the fishing smack's part in saving the battleship was noticed, an account eventually crept into *The Irish Times*. O'Rourke was summoned by Captain De Vesey and was offered half of the normal pilotage fee, which

---

10 Creeping was an old description of trawling a cable and weighted hook to catch a sunken target on the seabed.

he declined. The omission was again referred to in later print but there was no clarification as to how O'Rourke fared with any reward.

The *Lucy* returned to Kingstown, where James contracted additional emergency work on the brig, *Padre*. Loaded with coals, the foreign brig had been sailing from Troon for Naples, when she was struck by the same storm. After developing a serious leak, she made for Kingstown and berthed in the Inner Harbour, Old Dunleary. Campbell inspected the hull and performed temporary caulking, stemming the leak. Finishing up, he reported to *Padre*'s owners that the hull should be totally re caulked once again, exposing a need for dry dock facilities at Kingstown.

Excuse was offered by the Admiralty for *Consort*'s undue delay at Kingstown while Campbell was still searching for her anchor in Dublin Bay. Although the ship and crew had maintained that they were fully prepared to head for home, they were prevented from doing so until the anchor was retrieved. There was no mention of the real reason. The anchor was not retrieved in time and the less than proud ironclad eventually tidied up and made ready for sea once more. Reported that she was escorted and not escorted, the *Prince Consort* steamed away from Kingstown, on calm seas, on Thursday, November 5th.

The 'revolt' at Liverpool had petered out and the confederate navy never got the ironclads. However, the *Consort* was still not out of the woods and before she reached Plymouth, she burst a boiler in fog and almost went up on the rocks again. Despite all the praise for surviving the storm and her reported excellent sea keeping qualities, the new *Prince Consort* was hauled off into dry dock and the new ship was thoroughly overhauled, with an additional fortune. I'm sure that O'Rourke had something to say about that!

I'm also sure that the French had similar problems spending their own taxpayers' money on machines designed to sink other machines. With tongue firmly embedded in cheek, I still can't help wonder at the irony in how two major powers, France and England, at one another's throats for centuries, could manage to have so many French sounding names in command of ships on the English side? Seemingly a reflection of royal politics at the top tables of Europe.

The big ironclad's anchor was located by James Campbell, in the *Lucy*, almost immediately after the *Consort* had left the bay. Campbell sent down divers, buoyed it and made it ready for lifting. She was raised later by the

Lucy and the gunboat, *Rainbow* and brought in to the harbour. Did it ever get back on board the *Consort*?[11]

It was important that Britain's enemies should not discover that some of her battleships were unsuitable for the Atlantic and might not be capable of patrolling the channel without fear of sinking. So, through a friendly press, they just kept heaping praise on the wooden walls dressed up as iron battleships. Despite the praise, some of the great beasts were despatched to the more suitable waters of the Mediterranean and guardship duties around the kingdom. Kingstown later became home for the large ironclad guardship, *HMS Vanguard*. She was later lost off the Kish Bank, in 1876, when she was rammed by her sister ship, *HMS Warrior*, providing a salutary lesson as to just how effective their rams could be.

The Two Horse and Carts Incidents

Campbell dealt with horses his whole life. In fact, the majority of the population would have been totally familiar with horses, as these beasts of burden were everywhere. From the time he travelled around Ireland, building harbours during the Famine years, until he died in an outback settlement of South Australia, Campbell would have been in everyday contact with this working animal. Horses were used for everything: personal travel, pulling goods, lifting heavy loads, public transport and so on. Hundreds were used during the building of Kingstown Harbour. So it might be no surprise to learn that men struck up a relationship or affinity with an animal that was a constant companion and a valuable asset. In fact, it is quite common to read, in newspapers of the day, reports of fines being handed down by magistrates for cruelty to horses.

On a Saturday morning, 6 December 1863, a coal cart drawn by a stout horse had come down from Kelly's coal yard up in the town. It was a regular operation, drawing coal from the recently landed piles of it in the Coal Harbour at Kingstown and returning with it up to depots in the town. Later that evening, an unusually bright light shone in the sky for about a minute and lit up the whole harbour. Not another party, it proved to be a meteorite, part of a shower that fell across the British Isles and northern Europe and led to a certain amount of superstitious foreboding around the place.

The story of this coal cart incident is not significant in itself, if it had not been for how it upset the harbour superintendent, William Campbell and

---

11   An accompanying photograph (see page 165) shows a large bower anchor discovered in the bay many years ago. Remarkably similar to other ironclad anchors of the period, it was airlifted by helicopter to a plinth at the new marina in Malahide, on the north side of Howth, in 1992, where it has remained.

his recall of a similar incident earlier. The accident and its occurrence at this time was significant, in that his son, James had recently travelled to Liverpool, in search of a professional crew for a deep-sea voyage on the schooner, *Lucy*. Family life was about to change and an important decision had to be made by William Campbell.

The road that ran immediately adjacent to the water frontage of the harbour was called Quay Road. It might be hard to envisage now but, consider the amount of activity taking place along a quay that was thronged with sightseers in carriages. Join with that, the fact that almost everything of consequence that moved was by horse. Commercial traffic to the harbour complex, to and from passenger boats, passengers to and from steam trains, the fishing boats, the mail boats, the Admiralty boats – this was a lot of horses and carts. The result was a prolific amount of horse manure, constant hustle and bustle and 'accidents' for those not too deft of foot or, not paying attention. Now the rub was this; this particular road and the harbour ways were all in the charge of Public Works and it was their job to clean up all the 'shit'.

Court appearances for transgressions of bye laws and collisions were regular and the problem was an ongoing item on the agendas of the town commissioners. In other words, they shouted, "foul Quay Road" and God knows they had been kept focused due to the sheer number of horses. William Hutchison received some of their angry correspondence, transmitted it to Public Works and poor old Campbell jumped.

Harbours are well known for their loud and sudden noises, such as the blast of a steam whistle. Mr Kelly's horse and cart stumbled backwards, went over the side of the old pier and into the sea and, fortunately for the poor horse in this case, the tide was high at the time. A number of men jumped into boats, grabbed the horse by its reigns and still attached to the cart, the horse and cart were led into the nearby shallows, where they were recovered to safety.

There was very little about the incident in the newspapers and passed over with little observation. Occurring on Campbell's patch, it gave him mind to recall an earlier similar incident and the bollocking he got for the manner that he chose to report it. That incident occurred two years earlier and was described as being similar to the "Portobello Lock Tragedy".

It was early on Friday morning, 19 July 1861, at the Carlisle Pier when a horse and cart owned by Mr Beahan, a fishmonger merchant from Moore Street in Dublin, was delivering hampers of fish for export aboard the steamer, *Scotia*. Beahan was a well-known fishmonger, with premises in

Moore Street, Dublin City. And was not just any old street trader with a temporary trading licence, for which Moore Street has become famous.

One of the oldest trading streets in the capital, it was an exciting day when your mother brought you there on a Saturday. Both sides of Moore Street were lined with small wooden stalls, erected in the early hours on carts or on infant's prams. Piled up in pyramids on top of the carts, the colourful displays of fruit and vegetables seemed to test gravity. Throngs of customers passed up and down the stalls, gawking and smelling the produce, in pursuit of a bargain.

The produce would have been purchased at public auction in the fruit and vegetable market, as were the fish from the fish markets in Dublin. Some fish were brought directly from the fishing boats in the harbours at Howth, Ringsend or Dún Laoghaire and carted to Dublin. As you walked along, the sellers, almost exclusively women, clad with their good Catholic head scarves and large coats covering a wide apron with a deep front pocket for the cash, would cry, "Get your cheap bananas, the ripe tomatoes, 2/6d a pound."

"Get some fresh fruit for the little one missus", attempting to appeal to the mother's sense of responsible child rearing … and so on

The fish was never that popular and was often displayed on a three iron-wheeled wicker cart or on a breadboard atop a perambulator with the hood lowered. Surrounded by rich fishing grounds, strangely, the Irish were not known to be great fish eaters.

The prices were indeed lower than the shops but, whether or not you got a bargain, was something else. Some traders performed a sleight of hand, something similar to the notorious shell game. The fruit looked great but you couldn't pick your own from the display. The displayed fruit was in beautiful condition but for display only.

"How many do you want, mam?" and the trader would quickly take your fruit from a pile below and have it into a paper bag in a flash. It was not until you got home, or further up the street, eating it on the hoof, did you realise that some of the fruit was slightly off or bruised. The dealers had sold it cheap because they got it cheaper. Returning it was not on the cards – these were a race that could reduce you to Lilliputian proportions with a few choice words.

The same trading families were often engaged in selling during other festive periods, such as Christmas or Halloween. Not all having their licences in order, they only had their cry out, "Get your Cheeky Charlie", when the coppers would come running the down street.[12]

At Halloween, fireworks, although illegal, were in feverish demand. Being illegal, they were often hidden in clothing where the coppers wouldn't dare venture and when not around, the traders could be heard to cry, "Get your starlights and bangers."

Back to the hampers of fish and the *Scotia*, a paddle steamer, owned by London and North West Railway Company (LNWR), it carried passengers and freight across the Irish Channel. It was, as it happened, to be one of her last journeys for the LNWR, as she was sold to Cunard soon after, who fairly successfully ran her as a blockade runner for the Confederates.

The shipping companies were getting great prices for their aging-but-useful shallow-draught paddle steamers, which were eminently suitable for blockade running. These favourable market conditions prevailed at a time when shipping companies were moving to screw and steel steamers. A double-whammy or win-win you might say.

Anyway, the "Portobello Lock" incident was still fresh in the minds of the public, having occurred only the previous April. The terrible accident involved a horse-drawn omnibus of the Favourite omnibus company, which backed into the Grand Canal lock at Portobello, adjacent to La Touche bridge. Six persons and two horses were drowned in the half-full chamber, which quickly filled when the wrong sluice gate was opened.

At Kingstown, Mr Beahan was attempting to turn the horse cart on the pier when the wheel slipped over the edge. The cart and horse (fish and all) ended up on the bottom of the harbour, after falling from a considerable height, due to the tide being low on this occasion. The hampers of fish were the only items that came back to the surface and were retrieved. Harbour staff were summoned and, under the supervision of Mr Campbell, the dead horse and cart were fished out of the harbour.

This horse and cart story ran in a number of papers. Not only as a result of Mr Beahan's own contribution but, it also presented criticism of the harbour authorities, for not taking proper precautions to prevent an accident that might have resulted in the loss of a "human" life and not just one of a horse, as in this case. As it happens, similar and more regrettable accidents have occurred in the harbour ever since, involving the loss of humans, RIP.

Mr Beahan threatened to sue the Harbour Board for the loss of his horse and cart. The commissioners agreed to pay, subject to arbitration. The

---

12 "Cheeky Charlie" was a wind-up, mechanical toy that looked like a monkey and clashed its cymbals as it jerked around after a wind up.

ink had no time to dry before word got out. Other previous and similarly injured claimants began knocking on the door.

Mr J. Beahan's fish shop was not just any old fish shop. The family sold a wide variety of fish, some exotic, such as the 180lb, seven-foot sturgeon caught off Skerries fishing village in north County Dublin. Beahan was also a wholesaler of ice and provided fish products to the rich and famous on both sides of the Channel. The shop at 24/25 Moore Street, which is still standing, also played a significant role in Dublin's Easter Rising of 1916 and is being considered for National Monument status.

Campbell was a forthright man, an honest man, a man of action and clarity. It is unclear if he gave an interview to the press on this occasion, as he did on others but his report did make it to 'head office', the Commissioners for Public Works, where his mentor, Gibbons was headquartered. He had, in effect, bypassed his harbour master and his local officials. The pecking order and the chain of superiority across departments in public establishments at Kingstown was continuing to come under pressure.

Following Campbell's report, and the harbour commissioner having received the memo of enquiry from Public Works regarding the incident, who were none too pleased – Lieutenant Hutchison being particularly upset. The upshot of it was, William was reprimanded both verbally and in writing, instructing him that any future reports concerning the harbour should be made through local officials. It was probably correctly assumed that it was Campbell who gave details of the incident to the press. This threesome was falling out.

A few weeks later, there was a royal visit, landing at the same pier. A lot of money was discovered in the kitty and spent making the place comfortable and weatherproof for the welcoming ticket holders and invited guests, only.

Campbell had travelled for years, going from county to county, plying his trade, diving and building harbours and blowing up wrecks. He married a second time, accepted a plum job in Kingstown and began a quieter life as a family man, in a fashionable suburb of Dublin. One could only describe his position as, 'comfortable'.

It was cumulative. The ignominious embarrassment of the outstanding debt at Bunowen – the reprimand over the repair of his diving boots at Kilmore, and all of the little tasks that had to be tended to around the harbour. The constant letter writing to and from clerks, with endless address to the necessity for financial propriety. Applying for permission to redecorate his dwelling, the Board's house that came with his position.

Applying for a new fire grate, etc, etc. There was just no end to it: Campbell was drowning in a sea of regulations.

The flag staff and the big clock perched over the offices of the Harbour Commissioners, peering over the whole complex of the Royal Harbour below, were marching time. A man who previously had no regard for time, only tide, now had to regularly tend to the maintenance of a giant clock and then, the second cart, Kelly's, went into the drink. William bottomed when his old friend, Gibbons died suddenly the previous year and the mood of his superiors promptly took a turn for the worst – his 'IN' tray filled quite smartly, literally, and it all just got to him in the end.

His son, James, was preparing the *Wellington/Lucy* for a journey that his father may not have approved of at first. As the time passed and while James was making the final arrangements at Liverpool for his departure, William began to wrestle with thoughts of his own future.

Chapter 9

Campbell 'Absconds' and the Lucy Sails, 1863-1864

Their minds concentrated on travel adventures and, it being one of most religious and festive periods of the year, 25 December, time for the Campbells must have slipped by in blur. Unlike today, it was straight back to work after the Christmas feast day. Boxing Day, a religious celebration and a day of good will but not yet a holiday with pay, the Campbells sat around the fire grate completing their travel arrangements.

A fad that came a little later, there was no need to peek under a Christmas tree. The idea of Christmas presents from your employer, one of the largest employers in the British Empire – Public Works – hadn't arrived. Habits of a lifetime broken; you might say. Social welfare recipients now enjoy a double up of their allowance, as a Christmas box, during the festive period.

The Board of Works' official correspondence leading up to this period is copious and revealing and even somewhat overwhelming. The only other person to receive nearly as much correspondence as William Campbell, in December 1863, was the harbour master, William Hutchison. It had been a build-up of what amounted to and would have been classified today as, harassment. The memos consisted of regular questioning on all manner of working procedures and finances, admonishment for failing to make returns, authorisation or failure to obtain it for purchases, etc. How Hutchison saw his own 'IN' box, I couldn't tell you.

December's crescendo also included requests to explain labour costs for the preparation of estimates and a reprimand for hiring casual labour and for making purchases without any prior authorisation, which, as Campbell said himself, was just how he operated when Mr Gibbons was alive.

After James purchased the *Wellington* and the family converted her to a schooner rig in the old harbour at Kingstown, her name was changed to *Lucy*, after his wife. She was registered at Dublin, on 19 August 1863 and he began to trial her with short runs and trips across the Irish Sea.

Manager of harbour works at one of the finest harbours in Europe, William Campbell wrote to his employer, the Commissioners of Public Works on 29 December, applying for seven days' leave. He requested his leave period to begin from the following day, the 30th. By the time the application was received and authorised on the 30th, Mr Campbell had already left, on a late steamer for Liverpool, with his two other sons: William (12) and Charles (10).

James was already at Liverpool, reportedly having departed in the *Lucy* from Kingstown on the previous Sunday, the 27th. Reported incorrectly on two fronts, it was to be his first voyage in the coasting trade, proceeding to Cork and then on to the Azores for fruit and wine. James and the *Lucy* did not set out on this announced journey but delayed in Liverpool.

"William Campbell Has Absconded"

The Kingstown Harbour superintendent did not return on 6 January after seven days' leave. On 16 January 1864, the cashier with Public Works, Edward Powell, was in no doubt when he reported, "William Campbell, collector of harbour dues, has absconded leaving harbour dues of £39.6.5 & halfpenny unaccounted for."

A serious sum and by then, William Campbell and his three sons were long gone and no longer in the British Isles.

On 18 January things were looking more serious after contact was made with Campbell's wife, Mary, who was still residing on harbour property. Mr Powell reported, "Mrs Campbell sent £10 to her husband at Liverpool on the 5th inst., has seen £3 & a few shillings to her possession. States that she told him[1] that she would sell her furniture to repay the sum due to the Board."

On 20 January, the Board wrote to the two men who had sponsored and guaranteed surety for William Campbell in the post of Collector of Harbour Dues. Rochford Battley and James Twamley, both reported to be members of the Royal Saint George Yacht Club, lived locally but the letter appears to have been sent to the yacht club, just across the road:

> With reference to your joint bond of June 1861, as security for Mr William Campbell as Collector of Tolls at Kingstown Harbour. I am directed to inform you that he has absconded, and that as far as the Board have been enabled to ascertain from the accounts, he is a defaulter to a sum of about £40, of which it is considered right to fine you. As one of his sureties the earliest intimation.
> Yours & E.H. (Secretary, BOPW, Edward Hornsby.)

The intervention of Hornsby, a senior figure in Public Works, was ominous.

On 13 February, Mr Hornsby wrote a second letter to the two men:

---

1   It is not clear if this refers to Powell or Campbell.

Gentlemen,
I am directed by the Commissioners of Public Works to state that
William Campbell, late collector of harbour dues at Kingstown
for whom you are sureties, has become a defaulter in the sum
of £11.6.7. Against which £5.13.8 for salary due at the time his
ceasing to perform duty has been audited [to the] *correct amount*
£5.12.11, and which sum, I am to request you will have the
goodness to repay into this office.
Hon Sec.

To be called out at the Royal Saint George Yacht Club as an 'absconder' and 'defaulter' was strong stuff – shutting the door tight. There was very little chance of re-entering the fold, whether he intended to or not. The amount first stated had been trimmed to the halfpenny and got the issue off the steps of the court before William's post was filled – by no less than two men. Mr Berry, a surveyor, became superintendent and Mr Walshe who became collector of the dues.

A lot of mud was thrown over the Revenue post that paid £25 per annum (a day's pay a week), a post of great trust but small remuneration. The position fell under the control of the Revenue Commissioners but was managed by the harbour staff employed by the Board of Public Works. The harbour master, William Hutchison, was keen to keep it in the family, so to speak, and applied for retention of its management. His request being a throwback to the original entitlements that went with the position of harbour master.

While officials and the harbour master were making cases for increased pay for increased workloads, Berry got the same pay as Campbell when he got the job in 1856.

I have no doubt that Campbell, although disappearing from duty, had not what we might now describe as 'absconded'. There is a connotation of fraud in the use of the term and I don't think the missing £5, then or now, cuts the mustard. The entries for December, in the ledger of cash received by way of harbour dues and ancillary charges at Kingstown harbour for 1863, makes no mention of a shortfall. The final entry for 1863, made in a different hand to those entries in the remainder of the ledger, refers to a retrospective payment of four pounds and change, submitted on behalf of the ship, *Dred*, which had been in Kingstown during November.

There appears to have been a rush to condemnation. He hadn't been liked by some previously and, having thumbed his nose at a comfortable position and the establishment, they seemed keen to make an example of him.

In April 1864, while the Campbells were making their way from Trinidad to Cape Town, James had become a father when his wife, Lucy, gave birth to their first child, Hannah Mary Simpson Campbell. The birth was assisted by William's wife, Mary and took place at the Campbells' cottage in Kingstown Harbour Commissioners' Yard. The baptism was performed by Reverend Henry George Carroll at Glasnevin, where he tended the flock at Claremont. Presumably, Lucy still had some ties with the place, emotional or otherwise.[2]

Richard Brickley separated from his wife in Kingstown and remarried in Liverpool, in 1869. His two children, Anastasia and Richard, lived with their father and stepmother over their public house, *Crystal Palace*, renamed *My House*, on the quays at 53 Waterloo Road. They also owned or leased the Dock Hotel at 18 Waterloo Road. Richard and Ellen's marriage was a stormy one and after a failed attempt at divorce, his only daughter, Anastasia, died in 1872. His wife, Ellen, died aged 33 in 1880. Richard Brickley died in 1894 and was buried, after a splendid ceremony, at the Catholic graveyard of Saint Albans, Liscard, Wallasey, Merseyside, remembered by many of his friends from Cunard and from those "peculiar times".

The boatman and lifeboat coxswain, Richard Brinkley, died in 1872 and was buried in Carrickbrennan Cemetery, Monkstown, County Dublin.

Lieutenant William Hutchison, who may have retired as captain, died a widower at 87 years of age, in 1881. Press record and obituary reporting was surprisingly slim for a man with such a long-standing service to the king and country. Just like William Campbell, he fathered ten children.

William Campbell disappeared from a prominent position in public service overnight – a career that had begun just before we first encountered him at Portpatrick, in 1838.

The Board of Public Works, as we know it today, began in 1831 when it combined a number of other public administrative agencies into a single new government department. It was a monolith when Campbell left and although it has continued growing until recent times, it now relies more heavily on external contractors. The number of construction projects it completed in Ireland, up to Campbell's departure, was phenomenal. The list of government buildings, military and naval establishments and, a

---

2   There was a strong representation of Campbells in the Glasnevin area and seem to have had a significant interest in horticulture. It is perhaps no coincidence then, that the National Botanic Gardens are in Glasnevin. It remains to be explained why Mary would travel to Glasnevin in order have her son baptised, when there was a fine large Anglican Church, the first in Kingstown, only a couple of hundred yards away. It was called and still is the Mariners' Church and is now a maritime museum.

plethora of civic buildings is endless. An extraordinary number of small piers and larger harbour and marine projects, housing for various staff of the service, drainage and water supply and a multiplicity of undertakings so vast that contemplation of a fraction would be baulked at today.

Almost entirely by outside contract now, we do manage motorways, bridges and quays but the likes of the Royal Harbour at Kingstown, or Dublin's underground sewage network would have difficulty getting out of the Dáil Éireann. More and more now, government relies on a partnership with private investors, who make a lot of capital from public projects, such as roads and bridges and, dare I say, hospitals.

By its present title, the Office of Public Works (OPW) as it came to be known, continued to employ teams of permanent divers at different establishments around Ireland. As the 19th century ended, the practice was beginning to wind down, with only a few divers remaining. The Board was returning to the older custom in Campbell's time, of hiring diving contractors for the tenure of the job only. The photographs from the archives of the Department of Marine, in the National Archives, show some of the last OPW hard-hat divers in Cahore, County Wexford and the Donahies in County Donegal, just after the turn of the 19th century.

Painting of *Regatta at Kingstown* (circa 1860s) by Richard Beechey. The figure depicted in the black harbour-master's uniform, on jetty in foreground, is presumed to be Kingstown's harbour master, Lieutenant William Hutchison. Carlisle or Gibbons' Pier is on the right. Reproduced by kind permission of the Royal Saint George Yacht Club.

Regatta Week at Kingstown, circa late 1860s. Extremely popular civic events, with some seating being a little better in places. Courtesy of the *Lawrence Collection* at the National Library of Ireland.

SHIPPING INTELLIGENCE.—The condemned preventive cutter Wellington, now the Lucy, the property of Mr. James Campbell of Kingstown, and recently converted into a schooner, proceeded on her first voyage in the coasting trade on Sunday for Liverpool, and thence to Cork, where it is said Mr. Campbell has been invited to have a look at the Daunt Rock, having taken his diving gear and apparatus with him. We understand the Lucy will afterwards proceed to the Azores for a cargo of fruit and wine.

Notice announcing the Campbells' schooner, *Lucy* (ex-cutter, *Wellington*) departure in December 1863, on her first trading voyage. The Campbell family never returned. Dublin newspapers.

Ships at Kingstown

USN Sacramento at Kingstown in 1865

HMS Prince Consort. James Campbell, son of Kingstown Harbour superintendent, William, made underwater repairs to the *Consort*'s hull in 1863.

Courtesy of *Southampton Archives*

Bower anchor that was lifted, by helicopter, from Dublin Bay and erected on plinth in Malahide Marina in 1992. Author's collection.

Chapter 10

Voyage of the Lucy or, "England to Australia in Nine Months" and the Campbells' Adventure, 1864

"The soft balmy morning air seemed to be all a-quiver with radiant sunbeams, which flashed and sparkled on the racing wave tops, before which the schooner dipped and curtseyed as the long green seas ran in steady procession under her keel." – Bully Hayes by Basil Lubbock

'Seeking fortune' or just plain emigration, are the only suggestions offered by surviving members of the Campbell clan for their ancestors' sudden departure from Kingstown. Mary Campbell in 1925, and William junior in 1933, both admitted that "like many others at the time, they pictured Australia as a veritable gold mine."

By-lines like, "Extraordinary Irish Exodus to the Western Continent" decried a hypocritical amnesia of all those who had been starved from the land, and to compound the ignorance, it also suggested that "if it continued, sufficient labour couldn't be had either in England or Ireland for harvest operations, and that inducements will be held out for foreign labour to come to this country."

The repetitive irony in life's saga of forced emigration is inescapable.

It may have been that the Campbells' purpose for their more than eight-thousand-mile voyage, to the other side of the world, was emigration or fortune seeking but the timing and manner of their departure was, by no means, just ordinary or impulsive. The *Lucy* was bought by the Campbells in the summer of 1863 and it was reported that the fifty-year-old, condemned, ex-Royal Navy revenue cutter was going into the coastal trade. Was it a planned purchase – one of opportunity? Did William or James Campbell intend, at that point in time, to emigrate in a tired old vessel, lock, stock and barrel or, was it something else?

Observed loading their diving gear and apparatus, the Campbells (This was only James and some crew, at that point.) were reported to have been considering a contract that involved the removal of the top of the Daunt Rock, a dangerous cluster of rocks situated just outside Queenstown, County Cork, in the south-west of Ireland. It is a possibility that is very plausible, as the submerged rock, badly situated near the entrance to the busy port of Queenstown (now Cobh), County Cork was said to have been the cause of shipwrecks in the past and remedial measures were being actively considered by the Board of Trade and the Cork Harbour Commissioners.

However, the *Lucy* was still sitting in Liverpool while a hullabaloo was being raised in Kingstown. Balmy days are hard to come by in Liverpool during January and, when the *Lucy* finally departed in January 1864, it was reported in Dublin that she was heading for New Zealand. All these remarks were confusing and all proved to be incorrect.

The Saga of the Daunt Rock

The anxiety concerning the Daunt Rock required attention but James Campbell never got the job and there is no indication that a competitive diver had better luck, or that that the Campbells ever stopped over in Queenstown in the *Lucy*, to take a look at the offending rock that needed blowing up. Being much further south, in sunnier climes at the time, it is likely that news of the "finest ship of the Inman Line", having run up on the same rock just a few weeks after they had sailed from Liverpool, had escaped their attention.

The argument over insufficient navigational warnings at the Daunt Rock had rattled on in the marine boardrooms of Britain and Ireland through 1863 and into 1864. Could we "blow it off the map"? What light should be placed on what headland, on what rock, and so on? The Board of Trade wanted to put a lightship there. Trinity House and their elder brethren were nervous of the financial repercussions, and the estimated annual running costs of £1,300 was a showstopper for the Cork Harbour Board – until March arrived.

In March, the large American mail and passenger steamer, *City of New York* (2,360 tons) was totally wrecked after striking and getting stuck on the rock. Pressure from Inman and American authorities moved things along somewhat more urgently, producing an embarrassing but swift climbdown by the battling sides. Except for those who wanted to turn the wreck of the big steamer into a lighthouse! Truth is sometimes stranger than fiction, I hasten to add. A lightship was eventually placed near the Daunt Rock. It figured prominently in another more infamous but unrelated tragedy that occurred there many years later – The Daunt Rock Incident.

Excursions on the steamer, *Lee* ran out from Queenstown to the wreck of the American steamer for two shillings return, dropping to one shilling just before the big ship defied efforts at re-floating and broken up in April. Its remains still draws visitors, however. Local scuba divers still manage to find small mementos from the once beautiful ship, amongst the piles of iron scrap scattered around seabed at the Rock.

Despite later news reports, it is believed that James had sailed from Dublin for Liverpool around 17 December 1863 and began to arrange for the hire of a professional crew. The *Lucy* was not going coasting but deep sea: a foreign voyage. The registered crew agreement that was drawn up and dated 4 January 1864, covered the Atlantic and Pacific Oceans. It also stipulated the return of the *Lucy* and or her crew to Liverpool within one year.

Some of the crew that James hired were, indeed, professional: the skipper, William Myers, having particular deep-sea experience in the Atlantic and Pacific oceans. At first glance, you might say he was overqualified for the little schooner. However, the Campbells were not hiring a crew just to sail a cargo of molluscs to France or, to Madeira for wine, as was reported. A plan was being acted upon, the ducks were being set up in a row but no one told the Harbour Commissioners, the Board of Public Works in Kingstown or, the weather gods. Judging by the makeup up of the two families in question – William's and James', their respective young wives, children and a pregnancy on James side, his wife Lucy expecting their first child – it is unlikely that they were not all aware of what was intended. Mary's urgency to settle the outstanding debt after the "absconding" was discovered is understandable in any event, as the Empire had a long reach when it came to its law arm and anything, even pursuit, might have ensued.

Liverpool was the centre of the universe as far as ships and shipping were concerned and probably the best place to muster up a crew. At first and including the experienced skipper, William Myers, James registered a total of seven hired crew members at Liverpool. The registered crew agreement of the *Lucy*, a 'foreign-going ship', states that her voyage was "Liverpool to Tenerife" with permission to travel and trade to places in the "Atlantic, Pacific and Indian Oceans", returning to port of discharge, Liverpool, after no later than twelve months. Obviously, the press had not got hold of everything.

James initially hired and signed up the following crew:[1]

---

1 On the ship's agreement, William Myers' address was written as "Whitehaven". There is evidence that an earlier attempt was made to disguise (the alteration was initialled) Myers' or the clerk's initial attempt at recording his address, which began with the number, "8". A William Myers lived at 8 Strickland Street in Liverpool at the time. Involved in the case of "maliciously casting away the ship Earl of Derby", due to his support for the accused, he was recorded as an engineer.

William Myers, (Cumberland), 38, master. No wages quoted.
George Holden (Holdin or Holder), (Dublin) 35, carpenter, (bos'n).
£4 per month.
Thomas Anderson (Kingstown), 20, seaman. £2 p.m.
Charles Henry Saunders, (Dublin) 18, 'first voyage. £1-5 shillings p.m.
Thomas Kilberry, (London) 22, ordinary seaman. £2 p.m.
William Tapson, (Liverpool), 17, ordinary seaman. £1-15 shillings p.m.
Alexander Wilson, (Cape Breton) 23, seaman. £2-10 shillings p.m.

Crew members, Thomas Kilberry and William Tapson cried off, by agreement, before the voyage commenced.

Charles Henry Saunders, 18 years of age, was the brother of James' wife, Lucy, and was registered as crew.

The agreement was dated 4 January 1864.

Two crewmen had cried off at the last minute and three passengers joined James aboard the *Lucy*: his father, William and his two sons, William junior, and Charles. There were now four immediate members of the Campbell family and one from James' wife side, all setting out on an adventure, trading (as the crew agreement had it) to the other side of the world. An interesting balance of five hired crew and four members of the same family.

In total, there were nine persons aboard the schooner, *Lucy* when she left Liverpool. The eight-month voyage that followed would surpass all expectations of adventure, with a significant measure of trepidation.

Departing Liverpool

Statistically, December through to February were the most dangerous months for sailing vessels travelling around the coasts of Ireland and England. A combination of violent gales and bitterly cold temperatures produced dreadful conditions for men before the mast, and thousands were lost over time. December 1863 did not fail the statistics and, I am sure that the Campbells must have been watching, in horror, as the reported numbers of lost and damaged ships continued to pile up in the shipping offices, through one of the worst months for loss and damage to ships.

This Strickland Street Myers was employed at the Vauxhall foundry, where Blakely guns and steam engines were being manufactured for the Confederates.

Amongst other colourful and similar employers, Richard Brickley, short-time owner and seller of the *Lucy* (ex-*Wellington*), mastered the yacht, *Ceres* for Captain Blakely of the same firm. This may be no more than a coincidence but the yacht, *Ceres* was the same one owned by Prioleau of Fraser and Trenholm, also doing business with Blakely and was skippered by Brickley.

Enough to keep hopes high, it is a feature of geography and weather that if a ship can get away from northern Europe at this time, it can expect to enjoy more kindly weather further south, in the Atlantic trade winds. Plagued with repeated hurricane weather from the Atlantic to the North Sea, a long list of vessels were destroyed or damaged during the month but, the Campbells hung on. 'Cruachan', their banner, the Campbells were stoic, William senior in particular, as they waited it out for their moment to depart Liverpool.

Planning a passage in a small sailing ship, weather is everything but you can't wait it out forever. The winds dropped off from westerly and swung around through the north to east and blew ice across the North Sea. The temperature plummeted but the wind strength eased. It became even hazy and foggy at times, with below-freezing temperatures and ice began to form on many rivers and estuaries.

The two-thousand-ton steamer, *Louisiana*, had taken on her cargo and passengers and was belching out black smoke as she powered out of the Mersey for New York, at about the same time that Myers was delivering his papers to the harbour office. As a result of the two crewmen signing off, the compulsory alterations to the *Lucy*'s crew agreement were made, copied and resubmitted. *Lucy* took on a cargo of quality coal and waited.

The weather continued to moderate towards the end of December and vessels arriving from the Atlantic and West Indies were reporting fair passage. A window opened and the Campbells were reported out of Liverpool on 8 January 1864. They were not to know that the weather window would blow shut again when they were halfway down the Bay of Biscay. The quick change, not an uncommon feint by the weather around the British Isles at that time of year, caught many an unwary vessel and crew sorrowfully unprepared.[2]

The *Lucy* sailed at first light on a Friday and the wind saw them nicely into the Bay of Liverpool. It was their intention to be positioned off Anglesey, in order to catch the falling tide, at 10.30pm. The temperature was still below freezing and they would catch their wind from that notorious quarter, southeast by east. When accompanied by snow, with reduced visibility,

---

2   The schooner, *Lucy* and the Campbells left Liverpool on 8 January. Departure from Liverpool was reported as the 9th, when she reached Table Bay. With no documentary evidence, other than the reported statement by Mary Campbell about settling William's debt, one can only assume that there was no direct contact between the Board of Public Works and William Campbell after he applied for leave and left. If any at all, it must have been through his wife, Mary. It is easy to understand that officials at Kingstown might have presumed that Campbell was absent without leave and had possibly even deserted the rest of his family.

these conditions had been the cause of a whole plethora of emigrant ships being lost, missing or mistaking another for the critical way point, Tuskar Rock, off the south-east coast of Ireland. During these 'middle years', ship after ship was driven up on the shallow sandbanks off the east coast of Ireland, with hopeless regularity and disastrous loss of life at times.[3]

According to Lucy's documentation, the Campbells were not heading to the other side of the Atlantic but for Tenerife. This meant that they did not need to steer so close to Ireland whilst proceeding down the Irish Channel but, kept closer to the coast of England, until they reached The Smalls, off Wales. After rounding Anglesey, the estimated route, SSW, was a lengthy first leg of their intended voyage to their first port of call, Tenerife, a distance of 1,700 miles approximately, in a straight line – on a good day. The actual distance travelled could be considerably longer.

Built beside the 290, the yard number of the CSS Alabama, another covert build had been completed in Liverpool, in March 1862. Ostensibly destined for the Italians, the Oreto was launched without any armament and was recorded out for Palermo. Instead, she would proceed to Bermuda. After some hand wringing, seizure and a flurry of diplomatic wrangling, she became, the CSS Florida. The talk of Kingstown at the time, Campbell would have recalled the controversial Liverpool launches and the famous cat and mouse chase of the 290 and Merrimac by the Federal cruiser, Tuscarora, when she visited Kingstown Harbour.

After several cruises, the Florida came back across the Atlantic and had laid up in Brest. After being holed up there for several weeks, she was due to leave around the same time as the Campbells left Liverpool in the Lucy and their paths would cross.

The Florida's commander, the 'Prince of Privateers', Captain Maffitt returned home ill and Lieutenant Commander Charles Morris assumed command. After experiencing some difficulties with the crew, Morris finally sailed the Florida out of Brest, about a month after Campbell left Liverpool, making for the same island – but they would not make first landfall at Tenerife. The crew consisted of confederate officers and ratings from various countries, including some from Ireland.

---

3 The 'middle years' are considered to be those when steam vessels reached such a degree of reliability and efficiency that they were outdoing and superseding sailing ships. At the same time, there were remarkably large flows of emigrants travelling from Europe to the new worlds. Many of these were lost on sailing ships that were skimping on maintenance in order to compete with the new steamers.

Madeira – A Portuguese 'Pearl in the Atlantic'

During the height of empirical adventures in the 19th century, aided by a rapid development in ship design and steam propulsion, the geographical and political disposition of maritime fuelling stations, such as Madeira, became tremendously important. Design and armament weighed heavily against how long and how far a steamer's supply of coal might carry it. Improvement in engine design would eventually mean that some stations were eventually bypassed altogether. The critical period was a short one.

Previously only famous for their sugar and wine (and less so, bananas) Madeira has more recently become another island where some quiet money has discovered diminished responsibility to the avaricious taxman. Previously, its position at the crossroads of international shipping, along with the Canary Islands and often mistaken as the Azores, became strategically important as a re-coaling and supply station. Their importance was increased even further with the onset of the American Civil War.

Considered neutral, Portugal, just like others, allowed the civil war belligerents to refuel and resupply at the island, under certain provisos. Rules covered amounts of coal that could be legitimately purchased, when they could proceed to sea and when they could return. Those who were profiteering and even sympathising with one side or another, discovered flexibility. This form of expedient flexibility might take the form of a belligerent legitimately obtaining what it required by way of provisions and fuel from the authorities while in port. And later, with the assistance of more malleable profiteers, sympathisers with smaller vessels would establish a rendezvous at sea for the transfer of additional goods or fuel, or even just behind some nearby island. The intimidation presented by the sight of a large gunboat outside your harbour could also prove persuasive.

The main supplier of coal at Madeira was the Blandy family. More famous for their wines that have swirled on the palates of emperors and kings throughout the world (and still fetch astronomical prices at auction today) they were pressed into alternative businesses when the vine began to fail. An opportunity presented by the island's geography was seized with the advent of steam and they diversified into trading coal. The American Civil War provided some welcome icing on the cake.

Not having its own coal, supplies were delivered to Madeira and a wide cross section of vessels stopped to supply and refuel there: commercial steamers, mail steamers, naval vessels, and even small schooners. The Blandys were considered to be sympathetic to the southern cause during the civil war. Although illegal, slave trading to the Indies and some southern states was still brisk. Growing numbers of commercial interests were divesting their interests in slaving, in favour of the new 'black gold'. Unfortunately, that dark side of human nature, slavery of many kinds, still remains with us.

On 13 January, five days out, the Campbells were no more than about halfway to Madeira. Two days earlier, on the 11th, the steamer, *Louisiana*, mentioned earlier, had left her last port of call on the eastern side of the Atlantic, Queenstown and set out to cross the Atlantic to America. Disaster struck when hurricanes from the northwest returned. Vessels all around the United Kingdom hugged the wharfs and jetties and those just out fled back to ports. The decimation caused earlier by the terrible winds during December remained fresh in every sailor's mind. The large steamer, *Louisiana* hit the hurricane on the 13th and her main deck house was washed clean off the ship – fifteen lives were lost. She did an about turn and fled back to Queenstown.

Family lore has it that William Myers took to the grog on this leg of the journey and had to be relieved by William Campbell senior – not James, her declared owner, funnily enough. Campbell's wife, Mary and her own memory differed and maintained that this did not occur until after Cape Town and that William Campbell remained in charge of the schooner thereafter, until they reached Australia. So, if William's wife, Mary was correct, this is where Myers earned his money. Turning back or running for the coast of Spain or Portugal, for refuge, had its risks. Lesser navigators might have flinched at the thought of entering through the 'Mouth of Hell', but Myers chose to face the weather and the open sea, and to sail on. He probably calculated that if he could just get another day or two further south the weather might moderate and the kindlier southern climes would embrace them.

The *Lucy* sailed on but was badly damaged. Even so, we believe that she did not put in but continued to sail south. Her sails were torn, a top mast and bowsprit were broken and the main boom was also smashed. Some of her bulwarks were washed away or damaged. The schooner had taken in a lot of water but was kept manageable by constant pumping. Despite her age, the grand old lady was still tight. There were no reported injuries but poor young William must have felt delicate, as he was still only mending with the broken hip he had sustained during the summer, when he fell from the crosstrees during the dismasting of the *Wellington* in Old Dunleary.

The *Lucy*, reported as a yacht and also as a sloop, arrived at Funchal, Madeira twenty-three days after leaving Liverpool on 31 January. She arrived in a poor state of repair, probably jury rigged, with a cargo of coal that was reported to have been consigned for the Blandys Brothers. It was undoubtedly a welcome relief for the crew when the *Lucy* finally gained the shelter of the volcanic island, on the east side and slowly made her way round to enjoy the pleasant disposition of Funchal Bay.

Anchoring well into the Bay of Funchal is not only possible but necessary, as Madeira is essentially the top of an underwater mountain and it is far too deep to anchor any distance from the shore. There was a small harbour in Funchal, overlooked by a fort and *Lucy* made for it.

Young William, telling his story to the press in 1933, reported that *Lucy*'s cargo of coal was forty tons. It was also reported as 60 tons. There is another obscure reference of 73 tons in some official records, which might have been a reference to a cargo of sugar that was taken on later. The cargo of coal was loaded at Liverpool as 'ballast'.

William also recalled that failing to fly a flag when the *Lucy* approached the harbour, the small boat was unexpectedly fired on from guns mounted in the fort. The authorities later claimed that as the schooner was not flying a flag, they were unaware of her identity or nationality and, as that there was a war on, a 'warning' to the approaching schooner was required. Three shots landed 'under her stern', which proved to be the warning. If perhaps, the schooner had any remaining semblance of the gun ports for the small cannon she carried during her earlier days as a revenue cutter, there might have been some excuse for the unwarranted aggression but this is extremely unlikely.

The coal was a clever cargo, ballast or not. It was, by then, an international currency and could be sold almost anywhere. You could buy a ton of pretty awful stuff for as little as five shillings. Good steam coal in England was fetching around one pound a ton. Campbell would have been carrying the latter if it had been consigned to the Blandy Brothers or, it may have even been smokeless anthracite, favoured by the Confederates.

By accident or design, to choose a cutter converted to schooner as a means of travel to the southern hemisphere, Australia or New Zealand, was another useful choice. The inhabitants of that part of the world were using small schooners as an everyday means of transport. The populations were distributed around the coasts, where travel inland across unpopulated arid regions was difficult. A schooner of good quality, ex-HMS, British made, would sell well.

Campbell reportedly bought the coal in Liverpool at the higher end – three pounds per ton. It was good stuff and was certain to do well. He might have done even better than expected after they reached Madeira but, as young

William remembered, although his father was offered forty pounds per ton, from a confederate gun boat, the small fortune may have temporarily eluded him. The Governor of Madeira would not allow the sale. One has to wonder how the offer was made. Was there contact between the crew of the schooner and those on the *Florida*?

Not only did the quick turnover elude William at first but, the governor also put the tin hat on it. The authorities were challenging every ship that entered Funchal at the time and the *Lucy* had not been flying any colours. Her nationality undeclared, warning shots were fired from the fort, which led to another form of harbour dues being levied. The Campbells got the bill for the warning shots: three guineas each. A painful price to pay for a bit of gunnery practice. It was poor treatment meted out to a small schooner and its crew that had sailed through a bad storm, badly damaged and unavoidably dishevelled, having to seek shelter in a neutral commercial harbour. Maybe the bad treatment had something to do with fact that Campbell wouldn't play ball with the cargo of coal. Flag or no flag, coal or no coal, I strongly suspect the Governor wasn't minded firing any warning shots at gunboats.

Small and all as the harbour was, with considerable repairs to complete, the *Lucy* remained there for several weeks. Many ships would come and go while the *Lucy* was at Funchal. Among them was the British naval vessel *HMS Lyra* and three 'blockade runners', sporting the same 'lead grey' hull colour – *Greyhound*, *North Heath* and *Julia* – on route to Bermuda. Among them also was the Royal Mail ship, *Armenian*.

If there was ever any doubt about the future of steamships, there was none amongst the Campbells and the crew of the *Lucy*. Having earlier set out from Africa, the *Armenian* had docked at Madeira and then left for Liverpool while the *Lucy* was travelling south from Liverpool, in the opposite direction. The *Lucy* had passed to westward of the *Armenian* coming through the storm of the 13th. The *Armenian* offloaded in Liverpool, turned around again for Africa and put in again at Madeira before the *Lucy* arrived. Another West African steamer, the *Athenia*, a sister of the *Armenian*, also put in at the time that *Lucy* was docked in Funchal.

The *Armenian* was a new steamer, with the latest, advanced propulsion but alas, suffered the same fate as many before and after her. Captain Leamon and the *Armenian* fell foul of the familiar compass error – the southeast by east winds in the Irish Channel – poor lights, and the notorious banks off the east coast of Ireland, when she ran up on the Arklow Bank a year later and was totally lost. In almost all cases of this type of disaster and in particular, the loss of large vessels on the notorious banks off the east coast of Ireland, "compass error" was one of the first reasons offered as cause.

Repairs to the *Lucy* took a number of weeks and when complete, Campbell ordered the old schooner away immediately. During the time they were repairing the boat, William and James might have had a 'double take' when the most prestigious yacht club in the world, the Royal Yacht Squadron, cruised some of its big yachts into the bay. Some, familiar with the waters at Kingstown and its summer regattas, would probably not have recognised the badly battered old flag boat, *Wellington*, dressed up as a badly battered schooner.

It may have been an oversight in repairs, another bout of bad weather, a short trading voyage to Tenerife or, something quite different but soon after the *Lucy* left Funchal in February, she returned to the island. She was reported to have 'put back' on 28 February.

Approaching the island for the second time, they could see there had been a new arrival. The Federal naval ship, *Saint Louis* had been anchored about a mile from the harbour. Her commander had already delivered diplomatic despatches to the Governor of Madeira, containing instructions to refuse any kind of war material to confederate vessels. The instructions would be put to the test sooner than anyone realised. The same night, at about 10.30pm on 27 February, the confederate *Florida* dropped anchor between the anchored *Saint Louis* and Funchal Harbour. When the sun rose the next morning, the temperature had increased by a noticeable few degrees above the normal.

Sporting a huge confederate flag on her bows, the *Florida* was looking for coal. The governor refused it; the *Saint Louis* wanted to prevent her from getting it and to "cut her out", as it was put. Meanwhile, the *Lucy* still had hers – £40 a ton!

The standoff got heated. A noticeable blink and the Blandy's got the business. The confrontation was nursed along by consistent press reports, stating that the *Saint Louis* might attack the *Florida* in a neutral port. Rumour of the ruse freed the Portuguese to save the Confederates and themselves by providing the coal and preventing conflict on their watch. Details of the incident received sparse and minor reporting by and large, with the exception of *The New York Times*. It described the interesting standoff in some detail, including some of the political machinations that were got up to.

The *Saint Louis* was already at anchor, outside of Funchal Harbour, when the *Florida* dropped her anchor about a thousand yards from the shore, between the harbour and the *Saint Louis*, effectively, thumbing her nose at the enemy. Commander Morris of the *Florida* and the Federal consul were in and out of the Governor's office, arguing for and against coal for the *Florida*. Despite the earlier despatches, Blandys were instructed to give her 20 tons. Much to the annoyance of the Federal consul and the crew of the *Saint Louis*, a likely understated twenty tons was delivered in six lighters! The *Saint Louis* then gave the appearance there was action in the offing but the *Florida* steamed away unhindered on the evening of the 29th. Unfortunately, there had been no wind, and not being a steamship, the *Saint Louis* had to delay for wind, until 1 March. They never saw the *Florida* again until they reached Santa Cruz in the Bahamas.

There were a number of aspects to the stand-off: the significant difference steam propulsion was making over sail; the ever-present motive of profit was another and the sympathy that prevailed in some strategic areas for the Confederates. Sympathy alone, however, would not win the war. Only coincidental maybe, the infamous confederate marauder, *Alabama*, was refuelling in Table Bay at the same time.

There was also the question of the coal. It is believed, from subsequent reports, that William Campbell offloaded the coal at Madeira – to whom? Well that's another question. The £40 pounds a ton must have appeared irresistible. We will discover, from later reports, that the *Lucy* arrived "in ballast" at Table Bay and that William Campbell was carrying quite a large amount of cash. After a number of weeks, they left Table Bay for Mauritius, with a large consignment of fish. There had been no mention of coal, in or out.

With the Campbells' arrival in Madeira, an extraordinary coincidence occurred. Whether William Campbell was aware of it or not at the time, we may never be sure, and from the following events, the reader will have to decide for his or herself.

During November-December 1863, it was announced, in a very brief and singular press statement, that the well-known civil engineer, Arthur Ussher Roberts, living at County Wexford, Ireland, was travelling to Madeira. Roberts had replaced Lord Templemore's previous land agent at Dunbrody, the notorious Mr M.W. Knox from Northern Ireland and moved into the estate's property, Glendine House.

A.U. Roberts was a member of a gifted family of architects, engineers, designers and draughtsmen and amongst other projects, he himself designed Waterford's first public People's Park. Being a Quaker, there may be little wonder that he was also considered a progressive agricultural innovator and had been well respected for his "fair valuing" during the sale of lands under the Encumbered Estates Act. He was also involved in what was probably the first building society – a form of lottery designed to help less affluent but aspiring landowners to acquire property and build homes in County Waterford. Sitting on a number of local committees and boards, he was routinely contracted and consulted by the Waterford Harbour Commissioners, at the same time as William Campbell and even his son, James had been active in the county and, at times, in the harbour at Arthurstown, just below Robert's house, *Glendine*. It seems highly improbable that the two never met.

If the foregoing is not enough to raise a curious eyebrow, then let me take you back to the incident at Errislannan Harbour works, in 1848/1849, when the Board of Works District Engineer, Roberts, was sent to investigate allegations made by Colonel John Lambert against the site foreman, George Gregory, accusing him of being fond of drink and being missing from his post. Roberts interviewed a number of men on the site while William Campbell was working there and found George Gregory to be innocent of all charges levelled against him. The engineer was Samuel Ussher Roberts, brother of Arthur. It could be said, being the district engineer for Galway, S.U. Roberts was Campbell's boss while he was working in the county. Campbell also worked to Roberts on other projects requiring a diver in Galway.[4]

Having lost his first wife, Arthur Ussher Roberts, along with his young, second wife, Emily Fraser and infant son, Edward were reported to have left their house, *Glendine*, Arthurstown in November 1863 and travelled to Funchal, Madeira. Roberts was said to have been in bad health and was going to the island to recuperate. Given its moderate climate, Madeira had become popular with those suffering from tuberculosis. It was announced, in some Irish newspapers, that he died there on 25 March 1864, aged forty. I wonder if the Campbells and Roberts became aware of the others' presence on the same small island in the Atlantic, while they were both there and, did they pay their respects?

Not unique but unusual, nevertheless, there is no certified record of A.U. Roberts' death in Madeira, United Kingdom, Portugal or Ireland, just a newspaper report of his death that was released by the family to the press. Neither is there is record of Mr Roberts, his wife or child having landed or left Madeira. A.U. Roberts' will was seemingly changed and certified shortly after his death, apparently to write out some family interest in his

---

4 Samuel Ussher Roberts became a Commissioner in the Board of Works and among many other notable works, designed the nearby famous tourist attraction, Kylemore Abbey.

estate, which was left to Emily and his son Edward, with provision for his daughter by his earlier marriage.

On the present-day website of the property, Glendine House, Arthurstown where A.U. Roberts resided with his second wife, Emily for a short period, there is an intriguing description of the residence. Now a tastefully preserved, old world, boutique hotel, the description contains a remark which may cause the reader to wonder, as did I:

> *It was first occupied by the Chichester family and later by land*
> *agents until one of them absconded with a nursery maid, causing a*
> *great scandal.*

Not written on the website, there are some further interesting details to this story, related to me by the present owners, for which I am most grateful. They are as follows. It was said that the land agent in question travelled to Dublin with his wife, their young child and the nursery maid, in order to deposit money in a bank for the landlord (Lord Templemore). They stayed the night in a Dublin hotel and, when the wife came down to breakfast the next morning, it was discovered that the husband had absconded to Australia with the nursery maid. It's only a story, but like you, I regret that there are no more details!

With tensions rising between the two belligerents in Funchal Bay, Myers and Campbell may have thought better of delaying any further at Funchal. With two additional passengers, there were now eleven on board the schooner when they left Madeira, and the Canary Islands, on 28 February.

Part of any log entry that might have existed for the schooner, *Lucy* would have been a record of their journey to date and may have read:

> *February 28, 1864. Sailed, Liverpool – Madeira – Tenerife –*
> *Madeira, 1710 miles. Proceeding south for Cape Town, South*
> *Africa.*

Without precise and factual account, a diary or a ship's log or even correspondence, the next leg of the Campbells' voyage was initially difficult to understand. Young William stated many years later that after they left Madeira, the next place they arrived at was Trinidad. This was confusing: why they would have decided to head westward, to the West Indies if their intention had been to sail for Australia? No diary or log was kept or, at least, none survived and the only record of this leg of the journey was provided in William Campbell junior's interviews with the South Australian press in 1932 and 1933.[5] This newspaper article included an interview given to a travelling reporter from the *West Coast Sentinel*, based in Campbell's hometown, Streaky Bay. Being one of the earliest young settlers in a remote part of southern Australia in 1864, William junior's series of brief recollections are a remarkable tale. They were considered, by collectors of local history and lore, to be important enough to record in the publication, *Streaky Bay*.[6]

Included in William's recollections is his strange account of an incident involving a bear: one that escaped and created havoc aboard a schooner that was berthed in Cape Town at the same time that the Campbells were berthed there, in June 1864. The story is somewhat reminiscent of the *Phantom Ship; or, The Flying Dutchman* by Captain Frederick Marryat (1839), with similar occurrences described on board the ship, *Ter Schilling* in Table Bay. In that instance, the bear's name was Johannes. In 1864, Campbell's account described a bear on a neighbouring schooner, which supposedly escaped on deck and killed the captain's daughter. Having searched a number of contemporary South African newspapers in an attempt to verify this tale, no similarity could be found. Young William's story would seem to stretch credibility and, one wonders if he was having a leg pull. On the other hand, so many details of his recollections have been verified and I still wonder.

Also in his recollections, William referred to a "couple" (The "couple" were a man and a wife. Some references state, "husband and wife" and some add a child.) who boarded with them at Madeira, seeking passage to Australia, and these proved to be correct. His memory was in working order. The couple were Richard and Mary White, a strong County Wexford name and were documented by Portuguese authorities as "commercial", aged 48 and 28 respectively and British. They were officially signed off by Captain Myers as passengers on board the *Lucy*, bound for Cape Town – which appears to have been the same intended passage that might have continued to Australia. Nothing more precise is known about these two mysterious passengers and they were not heard of again but later immigration records do mention a Richard and Mary White reaching Auckland, New Zealand.

We do not have any reports of the schooner, *Lucy* again until an entry appeared in *Lloyds List* and South African newspapers. During the intervening months, there were no family letters, no shipping intelligence

---

5   William Myers, a certified deep-sea captain, almost certainly would have adhered to the legal requirement of keeping a log of the voyage.

6   Photographs of buildings erected by the Campbells in Streaky Bay appear locally. Others are on file in the National Archives of Australia. Some appear in this publication.

reports, no mention in *Lloyds List*, no newspaper reports, just young William's account seventy years later. His recollections seemed suspect at first but were investigated word for word. His account proved to be accurate for almost all of his report – except for the 'Bear' story. No corroborating report could be found.

The *Lucy* was reported to have left Kingstown with all of the Campbells' diving equipment, suits pump, hoses, etc. There is no mention of the equipment being sold at Liverpool or, anywhere else for that matter. However, the gear was not on board the schooner when it reached South Australia. The naval vessels belonging to both the American North and South during the conflict were a mixture of sail and steam. Taken literally, in the case of the *Florida* and many others, this meant that they could sail and conserve coal when the wind was favourable. In the case of the *Florida* and many others, extra speed was achieved by disengaging the propeller from its shaft and raising it out of the water and into the stern of the ship. An interesting feature but an awkward operation to perform, as the mechanical operations with these heavy parts of the drive could be problematic, especially if the ship had a large deposit of barnacles and growth on its hull. Neither navy employed permanent naval diver ratings aboard their vessels at the time and had to rely on contractors. Campbell's diving gear would have been of considerable value to any naval ship at the time and a tempting offer for his equipment might explain its disappearance during the voyage.

The Uninhabited Island of Trinidade

The schooner, *Lucy*, five crew, four passenger owners and two fare paying passengers left Madeira for Cape Town and, although young William's memory was fine, the devil was in the detail and the lack of it in newspapers. The anomalous journey to Trinidad was only cleared up in recent years by a great-great-grandson, Trevor Dowling. After checking with some other members of the family, they were emphatic that the island was not Trinidad in the West Indies but Trinidade, in the South Atlantic.

Up to this point, my belief was that the Campbells had never intended to sail any further south and would trade westwards and back to Liverpool on the Gulf Stream. If young William had not mentioned the two passengers, who had boarded at Madeira seeking passage to Australia in his interviews with the press, researchers who were commissioned might never have checked emigration archives in Madeira. The couple's identity was discovered and their recorded destination was Cape Town. Young William's story was confirmed and it became obvious that Cape Town was indeed intended to have been the next port of call. Leaving the island of Madeira, their heading would have been similar to her first leg but a little more SSW until they passed the Cape Verde Islands, then back SSE, passing through the equator for South Africa.

If Myers had ever been 'hitting the grog', then he must have recovered and taken the helm once again, as the voyage almost certainly required a cool head and some knowledge of the south Atlantic, in order to get the little schooner through the next few weeks of dangerous adventure, which bordered on disaster at times. What cargo they carried, if any, is difficult to be certain about but just like the coal, Blandys' wines were popular everywhere. Although young William's memory has proved reliable, we are not absolutely certain whether or not they had sold the coal, despite the persuasive attempts of Blandys and the Governor of Madeira.

William's press interview describes how the *Lucy* and her crew had to overcome fresh tribulations thrown at it during the next few weeks. For a number of days during strong winds, they were blown off course and found themselves with damaged sails once more and without water, in the middle of the south Atlantic. After pushing through more bad weather, they were blown too far westerly and well off course. Further damage was sustained to the rigging and the boat had shipped more seawater. The mood on the schooner became anxious when they discovered that their fresh water supply, stored in barrels, had gone off, and couldn't be drunk. Seemingly the result of an excessive ingress of seawater and barrels that had opened, young William described how his father went about constructing a still and distilled some seawater, filtering it through some sand and charcoal to survive.[7]

Lucy's crew managed like that, until they reached the remote and deserted island of Trinidade. Southwest of Ascension Island, it is not to be confused with the West Indies' island of a similar name. This Trinidad(e) is situated about 600 miles east of Espirito Santo, Brazil. It is one of five small islands in an archipelago known as Trinidade and Martin Vaz. Discovered by Portuguese explorer Estevao de Gamo, they were occupied and also claimed by several other countries. It is inhabited today by a small detachment of Brazilian naval personnel and some research scientists from time to time.

---

7   An apparatus known as a filter jar was often carried aboard deep-sea vessels for such emergencies. It is likely that both Myers and Campbell were familiar with the workings of the apparatus. Campbell would have been familiar with the construction and operation of a 'still', as he almost certainly would have seen a number of them in Scotland and, during his travels throughout the west of Ireland. The operation of distilling the water, through the application of both or either methods, would have worked fine but keeping a fire going on board might have been difficult.

The clipper routes rounding the capes Horn and Good Hope from Europe passed through this region. Keeping more easterly was the older Brouwer route to Good Hope, South Africa. Ships rarely stopped at Trinidade.

Short of water and far more west than they should be, when the island was first sighted, it probably seemed like a vision from heaven. However, the small island that loomed on the horizon could not provide any comfort or assistance by inhabitants. Situated over six hundred miles east of the coast of Brazil, in the south Atlantic, the island that *Lucy* was approaching was Trinidade: a small, uninhabited, volcanic island of rock with some lush vegetation and a few small islets to the south. Importantly, it had some fruits and large colonies of birds. Even more importantly, it had fresh water. Soon to be discovered by the crew of the *Lucy*, it was also known by sailors to be very difficult to land on, with frequent high surf and almost totally surrounded by high cliffs and a rocky foreshore.

When they reached the steep volcanic shoulder of the island, they sailed along the shore for several hours, before finally choosing a landing place that looked promising. William Campbell, along with two of the crew, volunteered to row ashore in search of some badly needed fresh water. During their final approach to the shore, the boat was toppled in the breaking surf and was damaged. Considering that Campbell senior could not swim, it was a brave effort and he did well to save himself, being first to scramble ashore.

Somewhat unusual, young William mentioned that they had a second small boat and luckily, were able to stand off the shore and haul the casks of fresh water out through the surf. In the short time they stayed at the small island, they rested, cleaned, and replenished their casks with fresh water. They also managed to explore the island for a few hours but made no attempt to get out of the boat again. William said that they rowed around a small adjoining island, sightseeing for about a half day, all the while managing to stay clear of the "fourteen sharks" that followed them continuously.

The journey from England to Australia, in such relatively small schooners, was not unheard of. In 1861, the well-known schooner yacht, *Chance*, a similar size to *Lucy*, had made the journey in 142 days. Campbell may well have been aware of the *Chance* and the story of her voyage down under, as she had visited Ireland and Kingstown on a number of occasions to compete in regattas and races. In her case, she was cruising, not trading and completed the voyage in a far shorter time than *Lucy*'s. She too had brushed with sharks when her trailing log was taken as bait by a large one.

The twenty-five-ton schooner, *Vivid ex. Scourge* completed the same journey, in 1864, in 108 days. Interestingly, the *Chance* was a converted cutter, as was the *Lucy* and both made the voyage to Australia within a short time of each other. The *Lucy Chance*, in the undated photograph held in the State Library of Australia, is also of a cutter, converted to a schooner of similar proportions, presenting a good representation of what Campbell's *Lucy* would have been like.

Once again, I am sure that it must have been Myers who came up with a new course. He was an experienced skipper and a trained navigator with considerable experience of that part of the world. Given his professional navigational skills he would likely have had some idea of where they were and how they should proceed. Not quite in the middle of the south Atlantic (Brazil being much closer to the west than Africa, many times that distance to the east) they set off once again. The schooner repaired, plenty of fresh water and still carrying the two strange passengers, they left Trinidade behind and headed eastward.

The *Lucy*'s log, at this point, might have contained the following:

> *After repairs to the boat and taking on fresh water, we departed the island of Trinidade situated in the SW Atlantic and set a course ESE for Cape Town, South Africa. 5330 travelled miles since departing Liverpool.*

It must surely have been the confidence and ability of Myers, who was able to decide to push on eastward, in line with their original plan, and the motley lot were soon on their way again. Heading southeast, the next leg of their voyage was threatened by more bad weather, after young William recalled that they had seen and spoken with a small steamer heading for Madeira. After they parted, there was another anxious period during which they avoided "four waterspouts and had seen a large ship go down in a whirlpool."

Beginning to ship water again, there was a sigh of relief when they eventually reached Table Bay, Cape Town, South Africa. The schooner was reported in *Lloyds List*, dated 20 May, as having reached there on 9 May. Young William, who was a much older William when he recounted his story to the *Sentinel*'s reporter, gave no further details of the unscheduled adventures on the island of Trinidade in the south Atlantic. We are only left to wonder what other adventures the seven men, two boys and two passengers might have experienced in the ninety-foot, condemned, fifty-year-old schooner before they reached the Cape, and sailed into Table Bay. The schooner, *Lucy*, her passengers and crew had not been heard of since they left Madeira over two months earlier. It would have been a worry at first, for the remainder of the family in Ireland, if they had read the reports that did not appear until late February and again in March, that the schooner, *Lucy* was lost near Table Bay. This vessel was also reported as British brig and a two-masted snow and she was lost on 12 February, on her way to London from Cape Town. Fortunately, it was not the Campbells' *Lucy*.

Table Bay

Situated on the north-western side of the 'Cape', on the Atlantic side, is the harbour, more a bay than a harbour, then called Table Bay. Overlooked by the impressive Table Mountain, it is, by all accounts, a beautiful place. Despite its popularity and beauty, it was or could be a very bad harbour for sailing vessels. Totally exposed, as it is, to any dirty weather from the west to north, this broad bay had very few places where a sailing vessel could shelter from all weathers and had seen a large number of shipwrecks take place in the bay. Indeed, Campbell referred to three large sailing vessels that had previously been driven onto the shore and were still high and dry when they arrived. Nevertheless, it did provide refuge from the extreme weather that could come from the remaining quarters. It was also an ideally situated station for resupply and, for to enjoy some respite, before or after rounding the Cape.

The construction of a huge breakwater at Table Bay had not long begun and the railway had just reached the coast when the *Lucy*, carrying what might have been coal, but described only as "ballast" by the authorities, berthed in Table Bay. According to additional reports, dated 20 May, she had indeed arrived at Cape Town on 9 May. After their second argument with the Atlantic and seemingly happy to be alive, they remained in Table Bay for a number of weeks.[8] Further repairs to the schooner were necessary but, not so urgent that they couldn't enjoy some time to relax and take in the exotic sights.

After escaping the clutches of no less than four waterspouts, one whirlpool, into which a 'large ship disappeared', the 30 June edition of Gore's *Liverpool Advertiser* reported under "Shipping":

> *Arrived Wednesday June 29. Lucy Meyer from Liverpool at Table Bay for Australia.*

---

8 The Campbells recall that the *Lucy* remained in Table Bay for six weeks. Their stories also recall that they spent six weeks in Madeira. The sum, twelve weeks, seems too long. Port authorities describe the *Lucy* as being "in ballast". The thing about ballast is, it does not attract tax.

Shipping reports and their ultra-economy with words can sometimes lead to confusion. The report above was either an indication that the *Lucy* had arrived on or before 29 June or, there is inaccuracy in an earlier report by Lloyds. There is little doubt in the South African newspapers, *Cape Argus* and *South Africa Advertiser and Mail* that the *Lucy* arrived there on 9 May. William junior's recollection was that they had delayed six weeks at the Cape of Good Hope, waiting out the weather again.

While repairing and seeking out a cargo for delivery, two significant incidents occurred at the Cape. The first concerned the 327-ton English bark, *Grahamstown*. After loading a cargo of wool at Algoa Bay for London, she got into trouble several days out and off Table Bay. A fire spontaneously ignited in the cargo of wool and, despite efforts by Captain Wade to quench the fire by closing all ports and hatches, it continued to burn. The *Grahamstown* made a dash for Table Bay on 26 June.[9]

The tall ship remained anchored offshore in the bay and a municipal fire tender was sent out in a small tug, to help put out the fire. After attempts failed, a number of other boats also came alongside and helped to remove all the valuables they could, before she was allowed to drift on to a nearby beach. Despite further attempts to quench the smouldering wreck by putting holes in it, cannon fire and so on, it eventually just burned down to the waterline.

The wreck was sold and to everyone's surprise, including the Campbells, the whole ship, cargo and rigging only fetched slightly more than £500: a new ship, with a cargo that also consisted of hides and horn valued at twenty-one thousand pounds – it had to be a steal. At least young William thought so and seemed to remember it well. The Campbells had apparently bid for the wreck, "over £500" young William said but William senior got cold feet and opted out of the bidding before the end. After the wreck auction, William, probably more than James, was said to have been disappointed, as it was discovered that a considerable amount of wool had not suffered any damage and the ship's timber alone would have fetched more than the auction price. There were supposedly three layers of undamaged wool remaining in the ship. The gentleman who outbid William was reported to have profited by two to three thousand pounds.

Young William later complained that "his father had lost a fortune by not increasing his bid."

---

9   The reader will notice that date is more than 6 weeks after Lloyds reported that the *Lucy* had reached Cape Town. The two reports remain irreconcilable.

Old William had, of course, not lost a fortune but he hadn't made one either. Like all good Scots though, he did hold on to his money – but only for a while longer.[10]

It is obvious that the Campbells were 'carrying' and apparently intent on picking up a deal or a cargo wherever they could. It is unlikely that they ran out of Kingstown with empty pockets but, there was no record or suggestion that they had resumed diving anywhere. Peculiarly, there was never a mention of their diving gear and no indication that the family were ever involved in diving again. A valuable expertise to have built up in the family and what became of all their diving gear? Did they get an offer for that too?[11]

Talk of the Kaffir wars reigniting was spreading around the Cape and the United Kingdom began to marshal troops and warships into a state of readiness, in order to confront the natives once again. Diamond and coal mines were still being discovered, land seized and redistributed "on a military basis" in some cases. Sensing an appropriate moment for departure once again, the Campbells decided to push on. *Lucy*'s log at Cape Town would have recorded an additional 3,040 miles sailed from Trinidade.

The Whites reached Cape Town with the Campbells but may have thought better of proceeding any further with them or the *Lucy*. New Zealand immigration records reveal that Richard and Mary White boarded the emigrant vessel, *Eveline* at Cape Town on 2 December 1864 and reached Auckland on 22 January 1865. Unlike the majority of the other emigrant passengers that boarded earlier, the White's passage was not 'assisted', paying their own fare. Despite one getting a bit younger and the other a little older since Madeira – Richard now 36 and Mary 30 – it is, nevertheless, believed that they were the same passengers and that they landed in Auckland, New Zealand. What became of them may be of some interest. Their arrival was at a time when the New Zealand government was giving land grants to immigrants.

---

10   William Campbell must have had a lot of cash with him. £500 pounds was an awful lot of money and one is tempted to assume that he had sold the coal, for a good price at Madeira, to someone.

11   A design feature of these iron or ironclad gunboats was that they could be propelled by steam through a propeller or by sail. The propeller arrangement was somewhat novel and complicated, being able to retract up into the hull so as not to impede sailing ability. All the ups and downs of the propeller, barnacles and damage, annoyed the process, and as a result the machinery frequently needed to be attended to in dry dock or with temporary repairs by a diver.

Mauritius

The schooner, *Lucy* was listed having sailed from Table Bay on 2 June, bound for the island of Mauritius. She was carrying a cargo of 1,419 bundles of dried snook (fish) for shippers, Philips and King and shipping agent, Borradaile & Company.

Two passengers down, a cargo of fish up and bound for another coaling station, Mauritius, the Campbells sailed their schooner out of Table Bay. And despite the recollections of William's wife, Mary, Captain William Myers was still registered at the helm – in early July. Whether Mary (who outlived her husband by a considerable number of years) was correct or not, she had recalled that it was on this leg of the voyage that the crew of the *Lucy* had to relieve Myers, due to intoxication.[12]

Reports and memory have it that there were no further stops before the *Lucy* reached Mauritius and she sailed into the "small harbour" of Port Louis on a day prior to 14 July. The island is not so big either that it can't be easily missed. The hand of Myers and his knowledge of deep-sea navigation would still seem to be guiding *Lucy*. This does not mean that Mr Campbell was not an intelligent man, or a quick learner.

Once again, scant details exist about another leg of this voyage. Nevertheless, some important details have been uncovered. The *Lucy* exchanged (or at least took on) a new cargo in Mauritius – 90 tons of sugar. The deal was negotiated with Younghusband & Company (as reported), shipping agents and traders who were based in Port Adelaide and in several other countries.[13]

Not a native plant, sugar became a common enough export, with fairly stable prices but producing unremarkable profit, at this time. Invaded and colonised a number of times, Mauritius has a regrettable history of slaving, before and even after it was abolished and large numbers of slaveholders were compensated. Young William's story may have been contextualised

---

12   For the purpose of this account, we have accepted that William Myers was in command of the *Lucy* for the whole of the voyage, from Liverpool to Australia. This is based on the fact that when a vessel docks in port, the captain must register the ship's arrival, crew, passengers, freight and so on. It is a similar procedure when leaving. If either of the Campbells had assumed command of the *Lucy* at any time, and registered her "in" at any of the ports they visited, she and her crew would have been liable for arrest, until a hearing and adjudication had been completed. Mutiny was a very serious offence, and no matter how justified it may have seemed at the time, the law rarely sided with mutineers. All marine reports, made on behalf of the *Lucy*, were accompanied by Captain Myers name.

13   It is unclear if Campbell purchased the whole or any part of the cargo from Younghusband or, contracted for transport and delivery only.

poorly when he mentioned that Madeira was a "great place for growing sugarcane", recounting that "the cane was brought in open boats to the town and when buyers saw the boats coming, they got to the beach and waited till the occupants got out of the boats, with the sugar on their heads. There was always a white boss, with an ugly looking whip in his hand, to keep them going."

The account could just as easily described the same activity on the island of Mauritius, as young William's account mentioned that it appeared to be a "rich island and that all the work was done by coolies and coloured men."

On the other hand, it was probably happening everywhere that sugar cane was grown. The only record of their stay on the island was William's reference to the sugar cargo and "horse racing".

Another strategically located island, Mauritius was home to a large British military establishment at the time. After seizing it from the French, they took the unusual step of creating the horse racing track in 1812, appearing to placate the settled French. Champ de Mars is the second oldest thoroughbred racetrack in the world. I suppose, a lot of the military had to be kept entertained. When the crew of the *Lucy* visited the famous racetrack, William senior said that it was the "best racing track he had ever seen."

William and the Campbells would have seen some racecourses in their day, as many of the towns and harbours they had worked around in Ireland had one located nearby. As well as coursing, horse racing was a favourite sport and a summertime recreation of the Irish and British. Racing on tracks in the sand dunes, murroughs or on the beaches drew huge crowds every year during the summer. A time to forget grey times and damp winters, and when the work was completed, for a week of betting and merry making.

The Champ de Mars was built when the British took it from the French (who took it from the Dutch, who took it from the Arabs) in order to provide polite gaming for gentlemen. Nestling at the foot of large mountains, just above the capital, Port Louis, it is not visible until you are upon it, after a short walk from the city. It remains a world-famous racetrack.

I can't help thinking that William senior left Mauritius with hopes high. He managed to dispose of his cargo of coal for a handsome profit, to take on and deliver a cargo of fish and to reinvest in another safe bet – sugar. With the bags of sugar all stowed and two passengers less to care for, the *Lucy* pushed on, eastwards for Australia, having recorded another 2,800 miles sailed.

Eastward and South Australia

The *Lucy*, her crew and the Campbells had some narrow escapes during their long voyage but now, in sight of their destination, a very near-fatal incident occurred that almost sank all of them and their dreams.

Given their departure date, 14 July, out of Mauritius, the *Lucy* hadn't dallied too long and began to make good progress. She was nearing the end of her long voyage when she had set sail on the last leg from Cape Town to Australia. We say Australia even though the family had it that their original destination was said to have been New Zealand, although they never got there. The British were putting down another tribal revolt in New Zealand at the time and, once more, maybe the familiar fortunes of war influenced the course of events for the Campbells.

Once again, we are ignorant of the reasons why Campbell chose to travel to South Australia, apparently ignoring any temptation to land on the west coast of the continent. The fact that they did not put in until Port Adelaide, South Australia fifteen-hundred miles further on might suggest that, either they had been heading there or, did intend to sail on to New Zealand, or just that the cargo of sugar was consigned there. Since they remained and settled in South Australia – albeit in a most unusual place and manner – seems to suggest that this was their intended destination all along, except for a few not insignificant details.

Having sailed over five thousand miles from Mauritius, the *Lucy* sailed into the Investigator Straits and shaped a course northeast for Port Adelaide, on the evening of 27 August 1864. They were close to but just west of the Cape Borda lighthouse, on the south-western tip of Kangaroo Island, with the Yorke Peninsula on their port side. This was a common approach for commercial deep-sea passage into Port Adelaide. Not a bustling or congested waterway, it has more than adequate sea room.[14]

The South Australian mail steamer, *Rangatira*, bound for King George Sound in the west, put out from Glenelg anchorage, Adelaide at around three o'clock in the afternoon. It proceeded south down the strait with mail and passengers. Weather conditions deteriorated during the passage and it became unusually dark. The *Rangatira*'s bell was rung twice when Cape Borda's light was sighted on their port side, at about nine o'clock in the evening. The *Rangatira* was going out and the *Lucy* was coming in.

Almost immediately after sighting the Borda lighthouse, the bell rang again – once. The officer on the deck had seen a light to starboard, close to. It

---

14   Investigator Straits was discovered and named by the explorer, Captain Mathew Flinders, in *HMS Investigator* in 1802. Flinders' exploits in South Australia will figure further in the Campbells' choice of a place to settle in.

was later stated that the *Rangatira*'s navigation lights were all working but that the small boat close by had no navigational sidelights and that her sailing direction could not be determined. To make matters worse, the dark skies had already forewarned of a further deterioration in the weather and it arrived just then, with strong squalls of wind and rain.

As is often the case at sea, when the direction that another ship is travelling remains unclear from lack of lights or communication, uncertainty arises on both sides – and delays reaction. Seemingly so in this case: both vessels failed to alter course until the worst possible moment and then, in the worst possible direction, leading to collision. The *Rangatira*'s engine was disengaged, which reduced the force of the impact but it was initially thought that the *Lucy* had been sunk. Along with the crew, Captain Paddle of the *Rangatira* ran to the rails and saw that the schooner's mainsail was all torn. He also heard the harrowing screams, "We are going down; we are settling fast" emanating from the *Lucy*.

The two vessels parted and Captain Paddle gave the order to his chief officer, Mr Simpson, to lower a boat with crew and to pursue the schooner. They did so but just then, the squalls grew stronger and they could not catch the schooner, which seemed to be 'sailing' for Adelaide. The rescue boat returned to the steamer and they continued on their journey for King George Sound. Maybe Mary's memory was not so bad after all![15]

With the condition of the occupants in the rammed vessel weighing on his mind, Captain Paddle nevertheless resumed his course and steamed westward. He hadn't travelled far however, before he was informed of a startling discovery. The *Rangatira* had acquired an additional passenger! The seaman, Thomas Anderson from the *Lucy*, had quite literally 'jumped ship' and boarded the steamer unscathed when the two vessels had touched. Dumbfounded by the unobserved agility of the stowaway, Captain Paddle ordered Anderson to his cabin and questioned him. The seaman described the schooner, *Lucy*: out of Mauritius with sugar for Adelaide and admitted that they had no sidelights.

The event was an extraordinary one and all the more extraordinary from the deck of the schooner. Anderson had been at the wheel when the collision took place, cleaving six feet off the schooner's stern. Self-preservation kicked in and Anderson jumped onto some part of the steamer's rigging,

---

15 The above account was extracted from the reporting of the subsequent hearing into the collision by the Marine Board. It has been shortened from the original, with a modicum of paraphrasing but nothing added. It can be deduced that certain aspects of the incident are unclear. This was frequently the case with the reporting on maritime incidents, when key elements are either left out because they are not understood or, not reported accurately.

abandoning his shipmates. What went through Anderson's mind when he discovered the *Lucy* had not sunk?[16]

Anything like a straight stern and the *Lucy* would have been a lot luckier … or a gonner. As it was, in circumstances such as those on the night, she was very lucky and the old cutter had done well to hold together after her tail was shaved off.

Lucy limped into Port Adelaide on Sunday, 28 August with ninety tons, 2,327 bags of sugar bound for Younghusband & Company. More than had been thought, the size of the cargo its customer had reported in *Shipping News*.

A function of Captain Myers' authority as captain, he toddled up to the marine office and reported the collision in the strait, along with the loss of their helmsman, Thomas Anderson. Officials arrived at the dock to inspect the *Lucy* and, although young William declared later that the sugar had been destroyed, the officials were astonished at the sight of the damaged schooner, wondering how the schooner made it into port at all. The description of the damage was reported as follows:

> The main boom was carried away; the mainsail and the entire taffrail, ripping open the counter and laying the stern completely open. William had described the length of the missing piece of the boat as being, six feet. An emergency tri-sail was set on the aft mast, enabling them to reach port.

In any man's language, this was serious damage to a relatively small sailing schooner. To a condemned, fifty-year-old cutter, it should have been fatal. They were, indeed, fortunate to have had some sound men in the company.

A coasting steamer, the *Rangatira* eventually returned to Port Adelaide and at the sight of the lucky *Lucy* and Anderson's survival, words proved inadequate for a short while. It would seem that this should have been a joyous reunion but, it might equally have been an embarrassing one.

The hearing before the Marine Board kicked off fairly smartly and adjudicated on witness statements concerning the circumstances of the collision. They found that the *Rangatira* and her crew were to be congratulated for their prompt action in stopping and avoiding a far more serious collision and, for their attempt to locate the schooner. Also that the owner and skipper of the *Lucy* should be reprimanded and severely punished for having no sidelights. Unfortunately, Anderson had already

---

16   The stern of some of these old cutters, described as a "counter stern", often had a long overhang. The style was accentuated in the beautiful large cutter yachts one sees in very early photographs of yacht races from this period.

admitted that the *Lucy* had no sidelights and they were unable to purchase any at Mauritius. Unaware that Anderson was going to 'turn up', Myers had claimed they had lost them in bad weather after leaving Mauritius. The two separately reported accounts were at odds.

There was no reason given as to why the steamer didn't go after the damaged schooner. There is no evidence that anyone was "severely reprimanded". Young William's memory is challenged once again, as the cargo of "finest white crystals" – all of it – was successfully auctioned later, in an undamaged condition. Or was it? Another story by William junior describes how the sugar was sold for two pence less per pound than what was paid for it! If William had owned the cargo, he held on to most of his money but, through no fault of his own, he had almost lost *Lucy* and a significant amount on the sugar.

The log of the *Lucy* would have shown an additional 3,700 miles sailed from Mauritius to Adelaide. According to Google, the total voyage amounted to almost 15,000 miles.

The Land of Fortune – So Far and No Further

The port authorities in Adelaide reported that the *Lucy*'s owners had called there "for orders", meaning that it had been their intention to offload the sugar and to take on another cargo, for another port. And what did that mean? Were the Campbells going to continue on to New Zealand, as was later believed or, were they just going to trade in Australian waters? Or were they going to return to Liverpool, as stipulated in the crew agreement? And what about the crew: the five men who had signed on for a twelve-month voyage that was due to terminate in Liverpool?

Despite reports that a man and woman boarded at Madeira and the Campbell family's own story, that William Myers left Liverpool with his wife and daughter, those who were registered ashore from aboard the *Lucy* at Adelaide, were the same names that were registered leaving Liverpool the previous January:

> *William Myers, master. George Holden, carpenter, bosun, (35).*
> *Alexander Wilson, seaman, (23). Thomas Anderson, seaman, (20).*
> *Charles Saunders, ordinary seaman, (18). James John Campbell,*
> *owner. William Campbell, junior, (12). Charles Campbell, (10).*
> *William Campbell, Engineer. Harbour Superintendent, (51).*

Whatever was going through their minds at that juncture, the *Lucy* and the Campbells sailed on but they never left Australian shores. The Campbells' own record, newspaper and official reporting has never addressed what became of Lucy Campbell's brother, Charles Saunders or the crewmen, Thomas Anderson, Alexander Wilson and George Holden (Holder?).

The carpenter, George Holden(r), sued William and James Campbell for wages in September 1864 but William wriggled out of it, claiming that the sailor had not been discharged, as they had not yet returned to Liverpool, the port where his contract terminated. The case was thrown out. Holden was ordered to return to the *Lucy*. There is no evidence that he ever did.

William Myers sailed on with the Campbells until October 1864, before moving to another, similar vessel for a short time and then to another ship in 1867. William Myers' certificate shows that he was captain in charge of the Australian ship, *Aggie M*, during the years 1867/8, before returning to London, putting an end to the entries against his official record in the captain's registers.

16th January 1864.

Colonel McKerlie - Mr Le Fanu.

Read report of Mr E. Powell. of this days date informing Board that Mr W. Campbell, acctnt of Tolls at Kingstown had absconded - leaving a deficit in his accounts of £39. 6. 5½.

Referred to Solicitor to instruct what measures be taken for Recovering balance due.

The Board of Commissioners are informed that William Campbell has absconded, leaving a deficit in the accounts of the harbour's (Kingstown) tolls. The amount was a mistake; the actual was later relegated to less than £5. Image of entry in Board of Public Works letter book, 1864, with permission of the National Archives, Dublin.

Table Bay, late 19th century. At the time that the Campbells and the schooner, *Lucy* arrived in Table Bay in 1864, the huge breakwater needed to protect shipping in the "Bay of Storms" had just commenced. The parameters of the construction have been reached in the photograph but completion work continues. Permission for reproduction was given by the Transnet Heritage Library.

Uninhabited island of Trinidade, off the coast of Brazil in the south-west Atlantic. The Campbells and crew were stranded on the island for several days, in search of water and effecting repairs to the *Lucy*. Image by Simone Marinho.

Image of 19th century Funchal, Madeira. Permission to reproduce by www.madeira.com

Lucy Chance. Converted cutter to schooner rig. This undated photograph is contained in the Edwarde's Collection (Adelaide), held in the State Library of Australia. The vessel represents a fair representation of the Campbells' schooner, *Lucy*.

Chapter 11

The Shores of South Australia 1864-1925

The *Lucy* continued in coastal trading in Australia for the shipping merchant and trader, Younghusband & Company[1], immediately after repairs. She carried all kinds of supplies to the new stations west of Port Adelaide and returned with wool. A transport service that was often irregular, these coastal schooners also carried passengers to and from a number of the early settlements. Apart from long overland and dangerous travel by horse or ox-drawn wagons, there was no other form of travel or communication at the time. The lack of water and even, attacks by natives were a real threat.

We'll never know, it seems, if the *Lucy* and the Campbells were compelled, in some way, to remain there: such as working off their losses and the cost of repairs to the *Lucy* or, a jaundiced view of the native unrest in New Zealand but, they never left and they never returned to Ireland or Scotland. Perhaps, this was the place where they had intended to make their fortune. The story of the Campbells and their schooner thus far, had been, without doubt, a real adventure, an almost unbelievable tale at times. The next part of their journey, the Campbells' "second bite of life's cherry", has baffled their descendants to the present day.

The *Lucy* had not long arrived in Australia when she came to the notice of the Marine Board and Port Adelaide Harbour Commissioners once again. Officially reported but not so serious an incident, she was in a collision for a second time entering Port Adelaide, already having stranded twice earlier. Whether or not her incident-prone sailing record had anything to do with it, the Campbells' tender to the Port of Adelaide for work at part of their old game – putting down moorings – was not successful. They also offered to contract the little schooner as a light vessel but, this too seems to have attracted little interest. Not surprising perhaps but a tender was

---

1 A company by the name of W. Younghusband Junior & Company, with offices at Gilbert Street, Adelaide was founded in 1845 by William Younghusband and George Young, as a woolbroking and shipping business, said to have been wound up in 1867. In documents consulted during the course of compiling this volume, it is variously referred to as 'Younghusband & Company', 'Younghusband & Son', 'Younghusband & Sons'. For the sake of consistency and to avoid confusion, the variant 'Younghusband & Company' has been chosen here and throughout.

accepted in a very different quarter, after the Campbells settled in Port Blanche – Streaky Bay. Their building skills soon came to the attention of settlers and the religious authorities of the Protestant faith, and building works began.

If, at any time, there had been doubt in the minds of the Campbells concerning their decision to have set out on such a voyage and emigrated to Australia, it must surely have occurred at this point. Australia was, in many respects, a raw country at that time. Vast tracts of land lay undiscovered and much of it, only barely mapped, was uninhabited except for aborigines. The outlying stations and settlements were founded mainly around livestock, sheep and wool. Prospecting for precious stones and metals was alive and well but townships, the growth of culture and homesteading, was slow to take hold and develop. Maintaining law and order fell on the shoulders of one or two policemen, who were sent to these settlements and a policeman and his wife had to live and survive amongst the settlers. Whether they were there to maintain law and order amongst the settlers or to protect them from the aborigines was a moot point.

When Campbell arrived on the coast of South Australia, he began trading the coast between Eyre Peninsula and an area with obscure connotation, Israelite Bay. He put in along the coast at intervening bays, with just a few having anything resembling a rickety old jetty and with names landed on places since they were discovered by Captain Mathew Flinders, in the early 1800s. Streaky Bay, Venus Bay, Fowler and Baird bays, all situated in the Great Australian Bight, that great geographical shape in its southern coastline that corresponds to a missing bite by a set of spiritual jaws. Early 19th century settlers believed that the coast had been settled even earlier, by whalers, in a repetitive migratory fashion.

Streaky and adjacent bays were described scathingly by early explorers and even at the time that Campbell arrived, as "… a hideous anomaly, a blot on the face of nature, the sort of place one gets into in bad dreams. For several hundred miles there is no harbour fit to shelter a mere boat from the furious south wind which rushes up from the Antarctic ice to supply the vacuum caused by the heated waterless continent."

The name Streaky Bay was bestowed by Captain Flinders, who observed 'streaks' across the bay, caused by the reflection of sunlight on a particular species of seaweed. Water at Streaky was almost non-existent and is still a problem. Its absence, extending over vast plains of featureless wilderness, was described, in 1862, as follows:

There are vast stretches of coast unbroken by a single stream and without a single harbour. From Cape Arid (west of Streaky Bay) to Streaky Bay not a drop of fresh water fills into the ocean. In 1865 it was no better; from Mount Arden (east of Streaky Bay) a distance of 800 miles in a direct line, no water, no stream was found on the surface, except a small solitary spring, sunk in rock at Streaky.

Nevertheless, there were three waterholes in the vicinity of Streaky Bay: a small hole in limestone at a place called Acraman Creek; another, further out, called Perlubie Soak and, nearer to Streaky, Cooeyanna, also known as Eyre's Waterhole. The quality of water in these holes was frequently poor and even unfit for drinking at times. The one at Cooeyanna was of a superior quality and small and all as it was, it became the main water source that allowed Port Blanche to develop.

An example of the doubt harboured about the place was included by the committee of history collectors, who wrote the book, *The Streaky Bay* in 1988. This is a remembrance by William's wife, Mary, spoken many years later:

I arrived at Streaky Bay when there was just a police station in charge of TPR (trooper) – John Mudge and Mr Cotton had a sheep farm about two miles out. I remember one day sitting down and crying bitterly because I did not know how to make bread in the big camp oven. Mrs John Mudge came along and baked it for me, saying that my hands were much too white and delicate for such work, but I soon got over that.

The new life seems to have been a disappointing surprise for Mary. The climate presented harsh extremes and she took time to adjust. There were some aspects to the place that she never got used to though.

And now, its sun-kissed, deserted beaches and islands are of "outstanding and breath-taking beauty"; rare lagoons and conserved areas with protected wildlife being all too numerous to mention. It is now a place amongst the world class tourist attractions, where you can 'catch a wave' like no other.

William Campbell had worked throughout Scotland and Ireland during a period, if not the worst, then a close runner up, in their respective histories. He had seen, lived, and worked amidst squalid deprivation and starvation of unspeakable horror, until he eventually elevated himself to living and working amongst some of the richest people in the British Isles, in one of its most fashionable cities, Kingstown, County Dublin. The Campbells left a place we would rate today as, progressive – first world. It was as modern as you could get in the western world at the time. There was famine (or forced starvation) for some in places but the Campbells had had it good in Kingstown: fine clothes, summer regattas, education, all kinds of societies and clubs, telegraph communication, public gas lighting and running water in places, well paid jobs with accommodation and prospects.

Relying entirely on their own abilities and wit, they were about settle in a place where you could die of thirst and about which, a kind word could not be found, unless you were a journeyman sheep shearer. Were the Campbells some kind of evangelists? It is believed, by descendants, that they were devout and, at that time, William's wife, Mary, "unmistakably" was.

In the comfort of an armchair now, fingering the keys, the cursor bouncing along, attempting to assess the structure and elements of peoples' lives from records, newspaper and genealogical databases, it remains so difficult to understand – why? These are glimpses, nothing more and no matter how hard one tries, it remains impossible to imagine what it is in a man that makes him so determined, even to the point of self-destruction, to look over the hill. The continuing and fascinating story of this Campbell family is so much more and the whole will be told by a Campbell at some future date. William senior is our concern, and *Lucy*, and an adventure that has carried his family to this place, is a story we will finish here.

At the time, shipping companies were being sponsored by the governments of Australia and New Zealand to provide free passage for emigrants from Liverpool and elsewhere. The remainder of the Campbell family, Mary, Lucy and their respective children, sailed on 16 July 1865 from Liverpool, aboard the 'old favourite', *SS Great Britain* and anchored in Hobsons Bay, Melbourne 59 days later. Whether or not the remainder of the family fully approved, or even knew, Campbell had settled his eye on Streaky Bay.

The family were reunited at Adelaide, and the schooner, *Lucy* headed off for Streaky Bay with her new batch of settlers. The five hundred miles westward took three further weeks, before they were carried ashore through the surf at their new home. Their surroundings, a rude awaking one might guess, contrasting in the extreme from the height of respectability and fashion they had left, with a remote outpost that had not even got a landing place. When they arrived at Port Blanche, passengers had to be transferred to a small boat and rowed ashore, where they either hopped into the water or, were carried ashore. Their immediate source of life and sustenance was that "little hole in the ground", fish, sheep and, religion. Despite its remoteness, there was no shortage of the latter.

There is no mention of the Campbells ever having dived again. There is no mention that they sold their gear. There are no mementoes or photographs of their equipment or, from their days diving and underwater construction. This is a fact that has remained impossible to fathom, if one can pardon the pun.

After settling into life's routine, all seemed to go well for about two years. The trading voyages back and forward along the coast remained constant, not diverging or adventuring any further afield. The *Lucy*, as well as being skippered by the family, traded under a number of different masters for the Campbells, including Myers for a short while, Monroe, Crocker and Freebridge, along with some others.

When William Campbell arrived at Streaky, he began to set up the first 'store' there. The construction was unorthodox: the Campbells excavated a 'room' out of the limestone cliff on the shoreline and covered its top with metal sheeting. He also constructed the first stone landing place for small boats – not a royal slip, but "Campbell's Jetty". During building works, William senior fell off a ladder and knocked himself out. Believed to be dead at first, he recovered from a fractured shoulder and built a proper store, on an area designated for a street. He obtained a licence to trade there in 1866 and also lived in the store.

The same year, the Campbells either ran into trouble with mounting debts or, just simply decided that they were getting out of the schooner and trading business. The previous year, they had a déjà vu moment off Kangaroo Island and, I suspect that the authorities may have begun to examine any certificates of competency the Campbells might have had – or the lack of them.

It was reported that the *Lucy*, in passage from Streaky to Adelaide on 9 November 1865, narrowly avoided another collision with a steamer in the dark early hours, in pretty much the same area as before. This time, all lights were reported to have burned and a collision was avoided. However, the unfortunate repetition was logged by the harbour master.

Whether or not, with the assistance of Younghusband & Company, Campbell had secured a mortgage on the *Lucy*, in order to meet the cost of repeated repairs, William had failed to keep up payments and sale of the *Lucy* was forced. Younghusband passed away in or around the same time and *Lucy* was sold to Captain Tulloch, in May 1867, and her trading continued as before, albeit for a new owner. From the Northern Isles in Scotland, Captain Tulloch already owned at least one other schooner at the time and was well liked, even at Streaky, where the *Lucy* overnighted on many occasions, in full view of her previous owner's new dwelling. Captain Tulloch owned a number of vessels and continued in shipping and trading for many years afterwards.

A new ship, the 800-ton barque, *Aggie M* left Mauritius in 1866 for Melbourne. During the passage, off South Australia, she was struck by lightning. The masts and rigging were all severely damaged and a number of crew were injured. The competent Captain Boyd managed to get her into Port Adelaide, with the help of a tow, where she underwent extensive repairs. In May 1867, she set sail for England and, it is believed that William Myers travelled as her mate or second mate during the passage. This was the last ship mentioned against Myers in the captain's registers, and his sailing career seems to have ended thereafter. Possibly seeing 'the light', a Captain Myers, in a religious context though, continues, with some notoriety, in the press.

Campbell had his own store and, as well as running supplies to the place, his family also turned their hand to a number of other projects. Along with just a small number of settlers, they continued to trade and got on with establishing a town at Streaky Bay. Just as most of the immigrants in the outback at that time took to sheep farming, at one level or another, so did the Campbells but only in the shape of William junior. It would be the senior William's older hat of builder however, that would make William & Sons legendry in South Australia.

Apart from his career of building and diving in Scotland and Ireland, William and his family became known for a number of 'firsts' at Streaky, and they have never been forgotten. I am sure that the Campbells were the first divers in Streaky Bay albeit, not active, as far as we can discern. Nevertheless, this did not prevent him from getting into the sea again.

William and his family were the first to harvest oysters, on a commercial scale, in the bay. Young William manufactured the cans and they went into the canned oysters business.

They built and established the first store in Streaky, built and operated a post office in 1868, and later provided a contractual postal service by horseback, with neighbouring townships. And Campbell, true to form, built the first stone jetty, probably for his own convenience with the *Lucy*.[2]

---

2   The post office-store property was later owned and occupied by the *West Coast Sentinel*. It was one of their reporters who later interviewed young William and printed the story of his emigration voyage from Liverpool to Australia in the schooner, *Lucy*.

Ironically, the replacement extension of Campbell's Jetty was the scene of another incident with a horse, in 1913. A ship was offloading and its cargo was being loaded on to the jetty when a horse backed over the side, fell into the sea and drowned. The inadequate jetty was blamed.

One of Campbell's tins of oysters was discovered in Melbourne, in 1933 and when opened, its contents were said to have been "as sweet as the day they were canned". It is true, however that there were other Campbells in the oyster business at the time and that the quality was often suspect. It was reported from the Royal Agricultural and Horticultural Society's show in South Australia, in 1875, that William Campbell's preserved oysters were 'not worthy'.

The Campbells built two other buildings of some distinction at Streaky Bay: the Institution Hall and the first church. The want for a church at Streaky and its surrounds seemed to have welled up amongst its pastor and immigrants at an early stage. The settlers banded together to construct the first Anglican Church there, dedicating it to Saint Augustine. The land was donated and the construction commenced, based on an inflow of subscriptions. William Campbell was one of the organisers of the project and builder of the church.

On 15 March 1869, the missionary chaplain, Reverend R.B. Webb, laid a stone into the foundation, which had a time capsule – "a tin safe" – inserted into a cavity cut in the stone. The capsule contained the following inscription.

> *In the name of the blessed Trinity, the foundation stone of this building, erected to the worship of God, and dedicated to St Augustine, Bishop, was blessed and inserted by the Reverend Robert Bennet Webb BA, of Pembroke College, Oxford, Missionary Chaplain to the Lord Bishop of Adelaide* [... followed by a host of names of people who had probably never been to Streaky, the building committee and ...] *Messrs Campbell & Sons, architects and builders.*

The church was completed a few weeks later and its inauguration was officially celebrated with a service on 16 May. The service was conducted by the licensed magistrate, Mr O.K. Richardson, who cast his net wide with the help of scripture from *Luke XIV.22*. His niece accompanied hymns on the harmonium. The reader brought the congregation's attention to the fact that the church was erected solely on subscriptions but needed additional support in order to complete it and, for the purchase of their own harmonium – all by way of further collections. The building was described as a "substantial edifice of stone, with iron roof, in the pointed Gothic style of architecture."

I thought the report continued a little begrudgingly though:

> *It is small and plain, to suit the numbers, requirements, and means of the place, but neat and comfortable.*

Perhaps poor old Campbell was just unlucky or, perhaps his 'celebrated' days were well and truly over. He had, amongst other fine works, completed two beautiful buildings, the lifeboat house at Kingstown and the not too dissimilar styled church on the other side of the world, in Streaky Bay, along with several others to his credit. Given the times that they were in, praise seemed a little thin on the ground!

Further reports from the synod stated that "Saint Augustine's was a struggling church out in the Wilderness" and highlighted some financial disagreement, suggesting that Saint Augustine's might have been on a sticky wicket at Streaky. The congregation was thought to be too poor to support the synod and too few to be grant aided. Something had to be done – and it was. After some procrastination, a grant was finally approved to finish the works. The congregation, outgrowing the "small plain church" of Saint Augustine's, has a fine new church at Streaky today, although it's a bit hard to make contact these days.

Unfortunately, the whereabouts of the time capsule, the "tin safe", cannot be ascertained now. Campbell and Saint Augustine's original church was demolished after completion of the new one. Mrs William Campbell senior, Mary, was presented with a silver trowel to lay the foundation stone of the present Anglican Church in 1912. Along with the first white woman to live in Streaky Bay, the policeman's wife, Mrs John Mudge, they both placed some coins and a history of the church at Streaky under the stone. So, maybe everything is still in the little "tin safe".

Nevertheless, they are remembered. There is a painting of William and Mary hanging in the new church, which has the pews constructed from driftwood, a ceremonial chair and a water font. These were all constructed by William for the first church.

The Campbells constructed a number of other buildings in Streaky and in the surrounding area. Some buildings of note were the very large shearing shed at Maryville, the first post office and the Institute in 1887. These buildings and the huge shearing shed (in use at Maryville until recently) with cut stone two feet thick, are singled out, as they demonstrate some style, with pleasant proportions in fine stonework.

Streaky emerged in this remote region at a time when life's finer details were not a first priority and seldom required in order for things to get done. The Campbells had grown used to these 'fine things' at an earlier time and, at times, must have missed them. They intended to stay for the long haul and a road through the centre of the town was laid in their honour.

The property that William Campbell junior eventually settled, was about twenty miles away, at Piednippie. A reported 1800 acres, he named it Wexford and clearing it was a mammoth task. He and six other men built the school there in 1898.

James continued in the building trade after he moved with Lucy to Adelaide. He never returned to diving or the sea. An impression remains that James and Lucy somehow became estranged from the remainder of the Campbells. Being an only child from his father's first wife, Mary Simpson, his birth mother, may partly explain. James died in Adelaide in 1916 and his wife, Lucy died there in 1933.[3]

After a spot of gold prospecting at Darwin with the *Lucy*, Captain Tulloch sold her on and she was sold once more before a new owner emerged in Sydney. Obviously trading on reputation, in each of the subsequent "For Sale" notices, it was declared that *Lucy* had been, the "ex. British revenue cutter, *Wellington*".

As it has been throughout this story, the name of her new owner, John Campbell, the "Honourable John Campbell" or, Campbell & Company, was another spanner in the works when first discovered. Adding to the confusion, it appeared that there were Campbells everywhere. The *Lucy*'s details were registered after this sale in Sydney, in 1873 and were updated again after she was eventually lost and read as follows.

> *LUCY. Wooden 2-mast fore and aft schooner 66 tons. ON45839.*
> *Formerly the British Revenue cutter Wellington, Lbd.71.5 x 22.4 x*
> *9.8 ft. Private ownership 1863, renamed Lucy, reg. Dublin. After*
> *refitting in Liverpool, came to Australia under Captain William*
> *Myers, with owner William Campbell, and some of his family,*
> *leaving 8 January 1864, arriving eight months later after a 'leisurely*
> *trip', arriving Port Adelaide 28 August 1864. Collided with the*
> *steamer Rangatira on entry to Port Adelaide, considerable damage*

---

3   Just to explain, Maryville was the name of the 'station', one of the earliest and largest grazing farms in the area. The port or landing place on the shore was called Port Blanche or Blanche Port and the bay, to seaward, was known as Streaky Bay. The whole of this area was known as the Township of Flinders and was changed to Streaky Bay in 1940.

to the schooner's stern. Family became settlers at Streaky Bay. Reg Sydney 25/1873, John Campbell. From Sydney on 25 October 1874, to Solomon Islands, struck Indispensable Reefs, 11 November 1874. Crew picked up by vessel Lytonna (Lyttona?[4]), landed at Mackay, December 1874.

The above states that William was the owner of the *Lucy* – senior or junior? It was not James, however. Mystery remains about the real ownership of the *Lucy* – whether it had been purchased by William senior or by his son, James – and if it belonged to William senior, why did he not have his own name recorded on the ship's papers?

Possibly tempting the first born, James, it had been a time when a prevalence of an adventuring spirit existed amongst prospectors of precious metals and stones in Australia, and the less admirable activities of the likes of Bully Hayes and their practices of blackbirding: not quite slavery but an exploitation of native and island labour, similarly disgusting and equally slow in being outlawed.

Was the trip to Australia a "leisurely" one? These Campbells still populate Southern Australia and this is a question that may be answered by them in the fullness of time. How 'full' it has to get, I don't know!

It is strangely coincidental, despite Campbell being a very popular name amongst Australian pioneering lore, that a John Campbell (William's father's name, and his son's second name) purchased the *Lucy* at the time. Were they unconnected? The answer is no. There is no connection that we know of between the two Campbells. The Honourable John Campbell of Messrs Campbell & Company, Campbell Wharf, Sydney, was a prominent Anglican politician – some putting him in the vacancy of Australian royalty.

Her timbers may have been shivering and her decks creaking but the Honourable Mr Campbell sailed the *Lucy* straight into a sea of controversy. Violent clashes, during a period when there were rising numbers of reported cases in which natives were being captured for forced labour on sugar plantations in the waters off north Australia, had come to a head. British cruisers had threatened to seize and destroy any boats that were found transporting coloured native labour. Pearl fishing, a native speciality, was being used as a loophole to avoid the enforcement of the Kidnapping Laws, by pretending that these schooners were transporting natives from one island to another, in order to participate in activities such as pearl fishing – earn a crust, if you will. Civil administration and law in the South Sea Islands were hard to enforce and prosecute and the number of ruses that were used to transport male and female natives are legendary.

---

4 The names 'Lytonna' and 'Lyttona' are both reported in this account.

The Honourable John Campbell, also a talented artist, was forthright in the Australian House in condemning British interference in Australian affairs. He cited the activities of his own vessel – the schooner, *Lucy* – being one that could have been seized and he was having none of it. Support was not thin on the ground.

The *Lucy* traded and pearl fished throughout the South Seas for Campbell & Company during the 1870s and came to the notice of the authorities once again, in September 1873 and then finally, in December 1874. Whether or not the *Lucy*, under Captain Brodie for Campbell & Company, had been engaged thus at the time she rescued crewmen from the brig, *Iserbrook* in September 1873, is not clear. *Iserbrook*'s crew had been stranded on Duke of York Island for two months. Earlier, the crew and the brig had established a couple of 'stations' at New Britain Island in the South Seas and after they were attacked by natives, they fled in a small boat.

Captained by Brodie of the brig, *Iserbrook* and late of the labour schooner, *Lavina* (both vessels with long and colourful trading service) was working out for the famous trading company, Godeffroy Brothers & Company. Originally French Huguenots, they settled in Hamburg and created a shipping and trading company that was known from India to America. Known almost everywhere but said to have been little liked anywhere.[5]

Following a continuous bout of pearl fishing in the South Sea Islands, the *Lucy* came to grief and wrecked on Indispensable Reefs, on the southern end of the Solomon Islands in December 1874. She was under the command of Captain Nicholas, for the Honourable John Campbell of Campbell & Company and said to have been trading at the time. The crew of the *Lucy* were rescued by Captain Rosengren of the schooner, *Lyttona*, reported lost in December 1875.

The ordeal began four days after Henry Nicholas passed *Lucy* out of Sydney on 24 October. She reached Lord Howe Island on the 31st and the weather broke. Heavy winds, rain and lightning struck and it was heavy going from then on. On 11 November, the wind altered but the going was still heavy, with all hands on deck. On 12 November, *Lucy* struck on the southern end of the Solomon Islands. She became fast on rocks but did not sink. The crew put in to a skiff and stood by the schooner. The weather continued heavy and they were washed over the reef, away from the schooner.

---

5   It had not been the first time the schooner, *Lucy* was associated with the brig, *Iserbrook*. Both vessels were alongside each other when the *Lucy* was berthed in Table Bay in May 1863, while on her voyage to Australia. The *Iserbrook* was destroyed by fire and dispersed at Sydney, in 1878. Was it the *Iserbrook* that had the bear? The *Lavinia* was attacked by natives twice in 1873, again in 1883 and wrecked in 1896.

The crew drifted for several days and landed on Kennels (Rennell) Island on 18 November. No water could be found on the island and they set off for Matura Bay, San Cristobal. They drifted off their intended course and finally landed at Cape Henslow, the southern end of Guadalcanal, on 20 November. The exhausted crew were picked up there by Captain Rosengren of the schooner, *Lyttona* and returned to Mackay on mainland Australia, were news of their ordeal unfolded. The *Lyttona* met a similar fate in 1875.[6]

The thing of it is this – the subsequent enquiry revealed that the crew "stood by" the *Lucy*, in the ship's boat, until they were blown away. They did not see her go under. Many a vessel has turned up again, after they were believed to have been lost! Ask Bully Hayes and the Ouzel Galley Society. For now, we must presume that this was the end of a remarkable vessel, a credit to British shipwrights and subsequent owners with similar talent.

It was also the end of an era in many other respects and the end of an association between the Campbells and the schooner, *Lucy*. The Campbells never won a regatta race with a cutter at a fashionable seaside town but, they and their schooner have never been forgotten and they have left their mark in blood and stone.

---

6   Captain Rosengren had replaced Captain Coath. With somewhat of an unsavoury reputation, Coath had been attacked and wounded by natives, with bows and arrows on the previous voyage (RIP 1874). On the current voyage, Captain Rosengren had his own problems when he lost the government agent, Obbard and his mate, Haskills to an attack by natives in the Torres Strait.

Roughly marking the spot where the *Lucy* landed. Trevor Dowling, great-great-grandson of William Campbell at Streaky Bay. Image by Trevor Dowling.

Route of the Campbells' voyage in the schooner, *Lucy* in 1864 and the area, off north Australia, where she was abandoned. Author's collection.

Old photograph of Streaky Bay, showing some of the buildings that were constructed by William Campbell & Sons. Old Augustine Church in the very left of photograph and the stylistic Streaky Bay Institute, right of centre behind General Store. Image courtesy of Streaky Bay National Trust Museum.

Their name is carved on a board that still hangs beneath the stonework that they were so good at. Not glamorous but not forgotten. Photograph by Trevor Dowling.

Old shearing shed at Maryville, built by Campbell & Sons. Photograph courtesy of Streaky Bay National Trust Museum.

Church of England, Saint Augustine's, the first church in Streaky Bay, South Australia. Built by William Campbell & Sons in 1868/9. Reproduction courtesy of Streaky Bay National Trust Museum.

A number of items (such as seats, water font) fabricated by the Campbells were removed from the old and into to this later Church of Saint Augustine, Streaky Bay. Photograph by Trevor Dowling.

One of the seats with a plaque dedicated to William Campbell & Sons. The inscription reads, "These two sanctuary chairs were made and presented by W. Campbell & Sons, builder and people's warden of original Church of St. Augustine, Streaky Bay. Built 1869." Photograph by Trevor Dowling.

Portrait of Mary Campbell (née Charles) at Adelaide, South Australia. Courtesy of Trevor Dowling.

Painting of William and Mary Campbell hanging in Saint Augustine's Church, Streaky Bay. Photograph courtesy of Trevor Dowling.

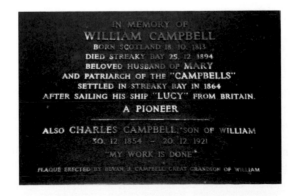

Plaque erected in memory of William Campbell and his son, Charles by Bevan J. Campbell, great-grandson of William Campbell.

Epilogue

There is so much to be told but, regretfully and within the space and time that modern story telling is allowed, it has proved difficult to choose just what to tell and what must remain untold. What has been omitted, I hope will be taken up by a Campbell one day and the full story concluded. Albeit reluctantly, we must, nevertheless, summarise and offer good grounds as to why it is believed that there is much more to this story.

Even in what is told here for the first time, there are several aspects that remain unsatisfactory. For one, those missing seven years, 1838-1846. We have no idea what William Campbell got up to during those seven to eight years. The number of years might suggest a term of some kind of service. Son of a farmer, pronounced to have been educated in engineering, such a record could not be located. This in itself is not unusual, as many of the qualified civil engineers of the time obtained their profession, not by a degree course but, by serving under another recognised engineer.

Campbell was described as a "carpenter diver" while working in a diving bell on the construction of a pier in Portpatrick, Scotland in 1838. We know nothing more about his career until he was next caught in the limelight, after being "almost" declared a bankrupt in Dublin, in 1846. During those earlier years, he married for the first time and they had a son named James.

No details of William's father and mother, his brother, James or his sister, Margaret have emerged. There was a James Campbell, an Inspector of Works for the Kingstown Town Commissioners at the same time that William was superintendent for the Board of Public Works and a John Campbell, listed as Superintendent of Works (not on record) for a short time just before our William took up the post. No connection between them was discovered.

William Campbell is believed to have married Mary Simpson in 1838 and their son, James was born the same year. William Campbell was married once again, in 1851 but we do not know for how long he had been a widower before his second marriage or, if James ever knew his mother. Unfortunately and even surprisingly, neither James nor his father, William, for more than half a century, ever informed any members of their very large family of any details regarding Mary Simpson. No memory of Mary Simpson or her fate exists in the Campbell family.

William's record in contracting and public service is well documented, albeit in dusty files but it is the things that are not recorded, mainly because they were private and personal matters, which remain puzzling.

The passengers, Richard and Mary White who boarded *Lucy* in Madeira present a fascinating curiosity of coincidence. Coupled with the fact that Arthur Ussher Roberts from Wexford, almost certainly acquainted with William Campbell, was in Madeira and died in Funchal while Campbell was there, is intriguing. Researchers were not able to find a death certificate or a burial record for Roberts. Given the history of a certain land agent that also resided at *Glendine*, Arthur's residence, it is a great pity we were not able to separate out and make sense of the various strands of this part of our story.

It has also proved disappointing not to have been able to get any further details regarding William's second, very young and beautiful wife, Mary Charles. There is a suggested connection with a family of Charles at Annestown, near Duncannon, County Wexford. Born in 1833, the mother's name is also Mary. There were very few Charles surnames recorded in Dublin City in the early 1800s. There was one at Mary Street, at Abbey Street, at 4 Mercer Street, at Golden Lane and one more at Ship Street – all in the centre of Dublin City and very close together. Some of these were connected with book binding and publishing. The photograph taken in Australia, with Mary holding a book, is interesting then in that regard.

From farming, diving, harbour and pier building to managing works at the Royal Harbour, Kingstown, William eventually became a settler and returned to the land, albeit on the other side of the world. His life seems to have been typical of the era: exploring and conquering the outback and its challenges, or a life on the sea, travelling and continuous interaction with other similar-minded adventurers. Or is that just all storybook stuff – essentially just being hard graft? What guided men like Campbell? We might remember that Campbell always travelled and adventured near, on, or in the sea.

For Mary it was quite different. She herself has already been described as being ill-equipped for a life of discovery in the wild. Mary's sensibilities were said to have been more delicate and refined but still, she stuck the course. Her obituary, in November 1928, is revealing. Already mentioned, her cooking skills were not up to the most basic facilities of the outback. What was not often mentioned, until her death, was how she "… could never get used to the Blacks. They were horrible and so fierce looking."

The obituary revealed some other important details about Mary:

"She was a great church worker, ... she laid the foundation stone of the old Augustine Church at Streaky Bay, ... librarian at the Institute, ...she was intellectual, ... musical and of great business ability. Above all, she had a disposition that endeared her to everyone."

It so easy to cite a statement out of context, like calling the "... Blacks horrible ..." giving the impression that Mary was racist and had remained so. However, in an earlier sit down with the press, she explained that during the early days, when they just arrived from the 'old country' and lived behind the store in Streaky, 'the Blacks' would come round, put their faces to the glass and stare in the windows. Being able to see through the store, she was frightened at their unfamiliar features and unabashed curiosity. An understandable reaction for a young woman from a place such as Kingstown, perhaps?

Having to surmount the crests and troughs of a settler's life, in such places required stamina and a strong spirit. To her eternal credit, she endured. She became known as "The Grand Old Lady of the West Coast" and was survived by 109 descendants at the time of her death.

The Campbells arrived in Australia not to make their fortune. In relative terms, they had left very well-to-do lives behind them, in one of the most fashionable towns in the British Isles, for a remote outback, in a land not long colonised. Their journey had to have been one of intention, to create a new and a different life and we are left with just a few descriptions that might fit. Was it missionary or seeking fortune? The headstone on William Campbell senior's grave describes him as a "pioneer".

Trevor Dowling and I pulled the strands of William Campbell's life together, mainly from records in public service, newspaper reports and his family's remembrances. Archives in Dublin, London, Madeira, Australia and Africa were also researched. All these enquiries, at first, seemed to have been adequate but when examined in total, they reveal only snippets of Campbell's life – a view from the outside looking in. They tell us little of the real substance of the man and we are left only to wonder just who he really was. For that answer, I believe a lot more may be required. As the mother used to say, "If you want to know me, come and live with me."

GLOSSARY and ABBREVIATIONS

BOPW   Board of Public Works

CDSPCo   City of Dublin Steam Packet Company

CSN   Confederate States Navy

CSS   Confederate States Ship

Dúchas   Ireland's Heritage Service. An executive agency of the Department of Arts, Heritage, Gaeltacht and the Islands of the Government of Ireland, responsible for heritage management including natural and built heritage.

ESE   East Southeast (see *Points of a Compass* on page 217)

HM   Her/His Majesty

HMS   Her/His Majesty's Ship

INFOMAR   A joint programme between the Geological Survey Ireland and the Marine Institute, surveying Ireland's unmapped marine territory and creating a range of integrated mapping products of the physical, chemical and biological features of the seabed. See website for further information – www.infomar.ie

LNWR   London and North West Railway Company

MOW   Man-of-War (warship)

NW   Northwest (see *Points of a Compass* on page 217)

RMS   Royal Mail Ship or Royal Mail Steamer

RN   Royal Navy

RNLI   Royal National Lifeboat Institution

SSE   South Southeast (see *Points of a Compass* on page 217)

SSW   South Southwest (see *Points of a Compass* on page 217)

SW   Southwest (see *Points of a Compass* on page 217)

TPR   Trooper (denotes a rank of Private in army regiments with a cavalry tradition

USN   United States Navy

USS   United States Ship

WAW   Wild Atlantic Way. A tourism trail on the west coast and on parts of the north and south coasts, of Ireland, covering some 2500 km, from the Inishowen Peninsula in Co. Donegal to Kinsale, County Cork.

WSW   West Southwest (see *Points of a Compass* on page 217)

POINTS OF A COMPASS

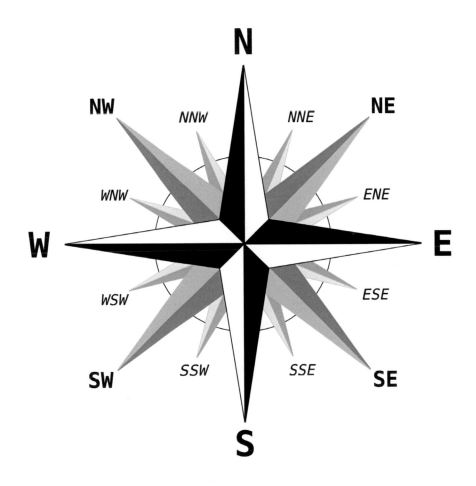

BIBLIOGRAPHY

The Great Lewis and the Siege of Duncannon, 1645 by Kevin Downes

Clyde Built: Blockade Runners, Cruisers and Armoured Rams of the American Civil War by Eric J. Graham, 2006

Reflections on Lough Corrib by Maurice Semple, 1973

Blackbirding: A Brief History of the South Sea Islands Labour Traffic and the Vessels Engaged in It. A paper by E.V. Stevens, read at the meeting of the Historical Society of Queensland, Inc., 23 March 1950

The Role of the Canary Islands in the Atlantic Coal Route from the End of the Nineteenth Century to the Beginning of the Twentieth Century by Miguel Suárez Bosa, 2008

Humble Works for Humble people : A History of the Fishery Piers of Co. Galway and North Clare, 1800-1922 by Noel P Wilkins, 2017

The Streaky Bay compiled by the History Committee of the Streaky Bay District Council, 1988

United States Ship St. Louis, Santa Cruz, Tenerife. New York Times, 18 March 1864

The British Newspaper Library and the multitude of periodicals and newspapers online

The archives of the Board of Public Works, available to the general public at the National Archives, Bishop Street, Dublin

Many thanks to the following for being so helpful

Paul, librarian at the Clifden Library.

Researchers at Madeira.

Streaky Bay National Trust Museum.

Trevor Dowling, William Campbell's great-great-grandson living in South Australia and his patient wife, Marion. I should add that many of the photographs reproduced here were taken by Trevor, who lives hundreds of miles from Streaky Bay and kindly travelled there for this book.

Thanks to all the staff at the following institutions

National Archives, National Library in Dublin.

Archives of Dún Laoghaire Borough at Town Hall, Dún Laoghaire.

Streaky Bay National Trust Museum.

State Library of Australia.

To all those who have contributed anecdotes and photographs that have not been printed here.

Its and endless list but unfortunately, time waits for no man, except to say, many thanks to all of you out there.

INDEX

INFOMAR 59, 215. *See also* Geological
 Survey Ireland; *See also* Marine
 Institute
Inman Line 167
Institute of Civil Engineers 15, 108
Ireland 1, 2, 3, 4, 6, 8, 10, 11, 14, 15,
 18, 19, 20, 22, 23, 24, 25, 26, 27, 28,
 29, 30, 32, 33, 35, 37, 38, 39, 41, 42,
 45, 51, 52, 54, 58, 62, 63, 64, 67, 75,
 77, 78, 79, 80, 83, 84, 85, 90, 94, 98,
 107, 108, 109, 110, 112, 113, 114,
 115, 117, 118, 119, 122, 123, 125,
 126, 127, 129, 130, 132, 133, 136,
 144, 153, 162, 163, 164, 166, 167,
 169, 171, 175, 176, 177, 178, 182,
 183, 185, 189, 197, 199, 202, 215,
 216
The Irish Channel 129, 134, 135, 149,
 156, 171, 175. *See also* St George's
 Channel; *See also* The Irish Sea; *See
 also* The North Channel
Irish coast 62, 87, 91, 124, 148
The Irish Sea 114, 123, 124, 129, 147,
 159. *See also* The Irish Channel
The Irish Times 139, 151
Irish Wasteland Improvement Society
 20, 21, 31
Isle of Man 118
 Douglas 118
Istanbul 77
 Scutari 76
Italy 63, 171
 Naples 152
 Palermo 171
Lord Iveagh 53. *See also* Guinness,
 Edward

J

Jefferson, Thomas 140
Jefferson, Varina 140
Jervis, Deane 64
John Martin & Son 48
John Scally & Company 30
Jones junior, Joshua 140, 141
Jones Quiggin & Company 140
J & R Martin 90

K

Kelleher, Connie (Dr) 59, 71
Captain Kellet 62
Mr Kelly (coal merchant) 139, 140,
 153, 154, 158
Mr Kelly (Kingstown Town
 Commissioner) 139, 140
Kellys of Kingstown 137, 139. *See
 also* Mr Kelly (coal merchant); *See
 also* Mr Kelly (Kingstown Town
 Commissioner)
Kelly & Son (Sackville Street) 139
Mrs Kennedy 34
Kennels Island 208
Kent, Shaun 87, 88
Kidnapping Laws 206
Kilberry, Thomas 169
County Kildare 11, 103
 The Curragh 103
 Maynooth
  Maynooth Seminary 11
  Royal College of Maynooth 58
Kilkenny 50
King George Sound 190, 191
King, John 29
Kingstown Royal Harbour Boat Club
 94. *See also* National Yacht Club
Kingstown Yacht Club 93, 100
Knox, Bessy 77, 142, 143
Knox, M.W. 77, 142, 143, 177

L

Lalor, John 89
Lambert, John (Colonel) 36, 178
 36, 178
Langtry, Edward 139
Langtry, Lillie 139
Larne 14, 80
Lawrence Collection 42, 110, 164. *See
 also* National Library of Ireland
Captain Leamon 175
Leigh, Francis 18
Lennerton, James 98
Lettermullen 26
Liffey (river) 5, 12, 143

Also by Roy Stokes

Between the Tides:
Shipwrecks of the Irish Coast

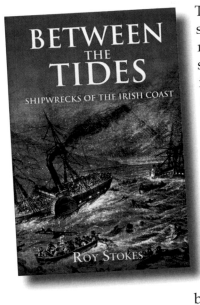

There have been millions of shipwrecks but just a few have been remembered. A ship can disappear suddenly, without a trace or may involve a fascinating web of intrigue and drama – the stuff of story books, great novels and factual accounts. Despite centuries of advancements, ships still wreck for many of the same reasons.

In this volume, Roy Stokes examines some of the historic shipwrecks of the Irish coast. A historic snapshot of the East India trade is provided, with its ability to turn investment into fortune attracting traders, bankers and rogues. Ireland's previously little-understood role in the naval battle with Germany during the First World War is also examined. Many other historic wrecks are also explored, including the paddle steamer, *Queen Victoria*, discovered by the author in 1983 and the first historic shipwreck to be protected under new legislation.

Not only of the shipwrecks themselves but also, the men who crewed them are the subject of this extensive volume of research, suppored by a number of detailed accounts of historic shipwreck events that have occurred around the coast of Ireland.

First published in Great Britain, in 2015, by Amberley Publishing
ISBN: 978-1-4456-5333-4 (print edition)
978-1-4456-5334-1 (e-book edition)

U-Boat Alley:
The U-Boat War in the Irish Channel during World War I

America's declaration of war in 1917 marked a turning point in U-boat tactics, resulting in a dramatic increase in the number of attacks against shipping in the narrow seas that separate Ireland and England. The losses in these new killing zones began to soar and the destruction of vessels soon began to light up the night skies. Mines were laid across the approaches to the ports of Holyhead, Liverpool, The Clyde, Belfast, Dublin and Arklow.

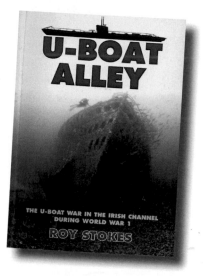

Hundreds of sailors and their vessels were blown to smithereens during the campaign to keep Britain supplied. With only short distances from the shores, on both sides of the channel, many of the victims were seen plunging beneath the waves.

With infrequent exceptions, the importance of the U-boat war in the George's Channel, the Irish Sea and the North Channel, particularly during 1917-18, has not been historically recognised. Preventing food, men and materials reaching Britain had remained the key to a German victory.

The story of the part that Ireland played in preventing Britain from starving during World War I remained untold. Hardly any folklore of the terrible loss of life and brave actions by ordinary sailors in vulnerable vessels has survived. It has often been said that a generation was wiped out by WWI. Perhaps this is why no memory remains of the events that occurred in 'U-boat Alley'.

This book tells that story.

First published in Ireland, in 2004, by Compuwreck
ISBN: 978-0-9549186-0-6

Death in the Irish Sea:
The Sinking of the RMS Leinster

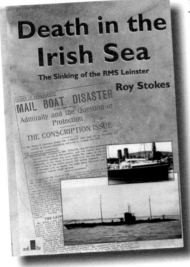

Just one month before the end of the First World War, the mail boat, *RMS Leinster* was sunk by three torpedoes, fired by the German submarine UB123 on 10 October 1918.

Death in the Irish Sea reveals, for the first time, the full circumstances of Ireland's greatest maritime disaster. The sinking occurred in sight of Dublin and claimed the lives of 500 (increased on revision) of the 771 occupants.

The *RMS Leinster* was owned by the oldest steamship company in the world, The City of Dublin Steam Packet Company. This Irish company established offices, in 1823, at Eden Quay, Dublin. The mail boats had become the pride of cross-channel services in the Irish Sea, before and after the turn of the twentieth century but were finally drawn into a military role when the war broke out. The four identical mail boats employed on the route were often requisitioned for troop transport, which included rushing troops and munitions from Liverpool to Ireland to suppress the Easter Rebellion in 1916.

The issues of Home Rule and Conscription were extremely sensitive and demands for a public enquiry into the sinking of the *RMS Leinster* were refused. Very limited investigation followed and its findings were censored.

First published in Ireland, in 1998, by The Collins Press
ISBN: 978-1-898256-52-7